Putting Courts Under Pressure

COMPARATIVE POLITICS

Comparative Politics is a series for researchers, teachers, and students of political science that deals with contemporary government and politics. Global in scope, books in the series are characterized by a stress on comparative analysis and strong methodological rigour. The series is published in association with the European Consortium for Political Research. For more information visit www.ecprnet.eu

The series is edited by Nicole Bolleyer, Chair of Comparative Political Science, Geschwister Scholl Institute, LMU Munich, and Jonathan Slapin, Professor of Political Institutions and European Politics, University of Zurich.

OTHER TITLES IN THE SERIES

The Meaning of Voting for Citizens
A Scientific Challenge, a Portrait, and Implications

Carolina Plescia

How Europeans View and Evaluate Democracy Revisited
Ten Years Later

Edited by Mónica Ferrín and Hanspeter Kriesi

Prime Ministers in Central and Eastern Europe
Careers, Context, and Performance

Florian Grotz, Jan Berz, Corinna Kroeber, and Marko Kukec

The President's Dilemma in Asia

Prof Don S. Lee

Party People
Candidates and Party Evolution

Allan Sikk and Philipp Köker

Centrist Anti-Establishment Parties and Their Struggle for Survival

Sarah Engler

Economics and Politics Revisited
Executive Approval and the New Calculus of Support

Edited by Timothy Hellwig and Matthew Singer

Coalition Agreements as Control Devices
Coalition Governance in Western and Eastern Europe

Heike Klüver, Hanna Bäck, and Svenja Krauss

Putting Courts Under Pressure

When Lawmakers Push Constitutional Boundaries

PHILIPP A. SCHROEDER

ecpr

OXFORD
UNIVERSITY PRESS

OXFORD
UNIVERSITY PRESS

Great Clarendon Street, Oxford, OX2 6DP,
United Kingdom

Oxford University Press is a department of the University of Oxford.
It furthers the University's objective of excellence in research, scholarship,
and education by publishing worldwide. Oxford is a registered trade mark of
Oxford University Press in the UK and in certain other countries

Published in the United States of America by Oxford University Press
198 Madison Avenue, New York, NY 10016, United States of America

British Library Cataloguing in Publication Data

Data available

Library of Congress Control Number: 2025933838

ISBN 9780198953234

DOI: 10.1093/9780198953265.001.0001

Printed and bound by
CPI Group (UK) Ltd, Croydon, CR0 4YY

Preface

We expect courts reviewing the constitutionality of policy to be a passive yet moderating force in politics. Lawmakers in parliament and government anticipate constitutional review and are supposed to shelve policies that are unlikely to survive judicial scrutiny. However, this account of courts' passive political clout misses that lawmakers cannot be counted on to play along. This book shows how lawmakers consciously take constitutional risks in their policy choices and thereby lays bare the limits to courts' control over the boundaries of the constitution. Courts cannot coerce the political branches into faithful compliance with their jurisprudence. Drawing on three decades worth of original empirical evidence from Germany, this book demonstrates that courts' enforcement dilemma is not lost on lawmakers. It uncovers a facet of politics in modern democracies overlooked in existing scholarship: Lawmakers whose policies push the envelope on constitutional boundaries signal credible non-compliance threats to courts and pressure them to ease legal restrictions on their policy-making.

About the author: Philipp A. Schroeder is a postdoctoral researcher at the Geschwister-Scholl-Institute of Political Science at Ludwig-Maximilians-University Munich. He completed his doctoral degree at the Department of Political Science at University College London, supervised by Christine Reh, Lucas Leemann, and Tim Hicks. Prior to arriving in Munich, he was a postdoctoral researcher at the Department of Law at Umeå University, Sweden. His work has been published in journals such as *Comparative Political Studies*, the *Journal of European Public Policy*, and the *Journal of Law and Courts*.

Acknowledgements

Over the course of working on this project, so many of my colleagues, mentors, and friends have generously given their time, offering valuable thoughts on earlier drafts, identifying the project's main story when I could not see the wood for the trees, or simply providing the emotional support I needed to help me going. This book in many parts builds on a doctoral dissertation I wrote during my time at University College London. I cannot thank my supervisors Christine Reh, Lucas Leemann, and Tim Hicks enough for their patience, their excellent and always thoughtful feedback, and the kindness they have shown me. Without them, my doctoral dissertation would have gone off the rails on too many occasions. I would like to thank Chris Hanretty, Lisa Vanhala, and Ben Lauderdale, whose encouraging assessments of earlier versions of this book helped me build the confidence that this is a project worthwhile pursuing. I would also like to thank Sigrid Weber and Lotte Hargrave, two of the brightest minds I have ever met, who made my time at UCL feel so special and helped me keep my sanity.

I am grateful to Daniel Naurin, Johan Lindholm, and Theresa Squatrito, who supported me during challenging times, commuting between London and Northern Sweden during a global pandemic, and convinced me to not abandon this project. To the members of LMU Munich's Comparative Politics Research seminar, who read and commented on several proposals and chapter drafts, thank you so much for your time, with special thanks to Vanessa Boese, Nicole Bolleyer, Jonathan Barry, Lala Laohabut, and Michael Zeller.

I would like to thank my parents, without their support I would have never been able to take a shot at this career. Big thanks to little Miso, who is a constant source of joy, but whose enthusiasm for walks and playtime made sure that it took me a few extra weeks to complete this project. Finally, I cannot say thank you enough to my wife Yesmean, who has been with me from the start to finish of this project. I have no doubt that without her, none of this would have happened. I dedicate this work to her and Edith Pflaum, I wish you were here.

Contents

List of Figures ix
List of Tables xi

1. The Sources and Implications of Constrained Constitutional Review 1
   1.1 Rethinking judicial authority 6
      1.1.1 Sources of judicial authority 7
      1.1.2 Reasons to push boundaries 11
      1.1.3 Strategic mindsets 14
   1.2 A normative quandary 18
   1.3 The universe of cases 19
   1.4 Plan of the book 20

2. When Lawmakers Push Constitutional Limits and Courts Back Down 24
   2.1 Confrontation and judicial self-restraint 26
   2.2 A formal model of constitutional review 30
      2.2.1 Analysis 33
      2.2.2 Interpretation and comparative statics 37
      2.2.3 Empirical implications 44
   2.3 Conclusion 45
   2.4 Technical appendix 46

3. Methodology 48
   3.1 Constitutional review in Germany 49
   3.2 Challenging a trusted court 54
   3.3 A mixed-methods research design 60
   3.4 Conclusion 67

4. When Lawmakers Push Boundaries 69
   4.1 Linking judgments and debates 70
   4.2 Patterns of constitutional risk-taking 73
   4.3 Conclusion 83

5. Judicial Responses: When Constitutional Courts Back Down 84
   5.1 Hypotheses and data 84
      5.1.1 Explanatory variables 85
      5.1.2 Control variables 89

5.2 Estimation and analysis 90
5.2.1 Costly signalling and judicial deference 91
5.2.2 Anticipation of elections 95
5.2.3 Robustness checks 98
5.3 Conclusion 104
5.4 Appendix 105

6. Pushing Boundaries: The Case of State Surveillance in Germany 108
6.1 Persistence amid controversy 110
6.1.1 Debating the 'Lauschangriff' in the Bundestag 111
6.1.2 Partial success for both sides 113
6.2 Pushing for deference 115
6.2.1 Committee proceedings 116
6.2.2 Constitutional controversy at plenary debates 118
6.2.3 Balancing protection by and against the state 121
6.2.4 Linking lawmakers' objections to the court's demands 126
6.3 The costs of provoking confrontation 129
6.4 The response in the Bundestag 132
6.5 Conclusion 136
6.6 Appendix 137

7. Putting Courts under Pressure: Normative Repercussions 139
7.1 Looking forwards, looking backwards 141
7.2 Empirical findings 142
7.3 Links to existing scholarship 143
7.4 Beyond Germany 145
7.5 Normative implications 146

Bibliography 148
Index 158

List of Figures

1.1 Varieties of Democracy aggregated expert ratings for the item 'How often would you say the government complies with important decisions of the high court with which it disagrees?' Response categories range from 'never' (0), 'seldom' (1), 'about half the time' (2), 'usually' (3) to 'always' (4) 12

2.1 Sequence of play and realized outcomes 31

2.2 Equilibrium predictions. The parameter π denotes the probability that the lawmaker controls implementation; p denotes the court's prior beliefs about the lawmaker's type; k denotes court's cost for striking a policy; c denotes the costs the lawmaker pays when the court strikes policy a. The threshold c^* is defined as $c^* \equiv 1 - k$ 38

2.3 Probability $r(c)^*$ of court striking policy a conditional on lawmaker's cost c in a partial-pooling equilibrium with $\pi > 1 - k$ and $p \leq (1 - k)/\pi$ 42

3.1 Annually cumulated proportion of respondents (in %) reporting their vote intention in response to the question 'Which party would you vote for if federal elections were held this Sunday?' Figure reports Politbarometer survey data provided by Forschungsruppe Wahlen (2019) 58

4.1 Legislative provisions reviewed by the GFCC 1977–2017 by their year of adoption. The figure distinguishes between provisions contested as unconstitutional by members of parliament and provisions that passed without contestation of their constitutionality 74

4.2 Contested legislative provisions reviewed by the GFCC 1977–2017 by their year of adoption. The figure distinguishes between provisions contested as unconstitutional by members of the parliamentary opposition parties and the governing coalition 75

5.1 Posterior means, 90% and 95% highest posterior densities for main fixed-effects coefficients of Model 1; posterior distributions are illustrated in grey 92

5.2 First difference in predicted average marginal probabilities for *Constitutional objections by opposition MP(s)* and *Constitutional objections by governing MP(s)* with 5.0th–90th and 2.5th–97.5th percentiles of predictions 94

5.3 Posterior means, 90% and 95% highest posterior densities for main fixed-effects coefficients of Model 2; posterior distributions are illustrated in grey 96

5.4 Predicted average marginal probabilities for *Current government* across range of *Years until election* (solid lines indicate mean values of predicted probabilities, shaded areas indicate 2.5–97.5th percentiles of predictions) 97
5.5 Posterior means, 90% and 95% HPDs for coefficients for main fixed-effects coefficients of Model 3; posterior distributions are illustrated in grey 101
5.6 Posterior means, 90% and 95% HPDs for coefficients for main fixed-effects coefficients of Model 4; posterior distributions are illustrated in grey 103

List of Tables

3.1 Proportion of respondents stating that they trust an institution in response to the question 'I am now going to read you a list of public institutions and organizations. Please tell me for each institution or organization whether you trust it, or whether that is not the case. How about . . .?' Table is based on the work by Vanberg (2005, 98) and reports data from Emnid Institute (1995) 55

3.2 Proportion of respondents reporting values of 5 and above on a 7-point Likert scale in response to the survey item 'I am now going to read out a number of public institutions and organisations. Please tell me for each institution or organisation how much trust you place in it. Please use this scale: 1 means you have absolutely no trust at all – 7 means you have a great deal of trust.' Table reports data from Leibniz Institute for the Social Sciences (2018) 56

4.1 Federal laws objected as unconstitutional by members of the governing coalition caucus and corresponding cases heard by the German Federal Constitutional Court (with year of decision) 80

5.1 Distribution of the variable *Seniority of objecting governing MP(s)* 87

5.2 Posterior means, standard deviations, and 95% HPDs of fixed-effects coefficients of Model 1—GFCC strike of federal laws, 1977–2017 105

5.3 Posterior means, standard deviations, and 95% HPDs of fixed-effects coefficients of Model 2—GFCC strike of federal laws, 1977–2017 106

5.4 Posterior means, standard deviations, and 95% HPDs of fixed-effects coefficients of Model 3—GFCC admission of challenges to federal laws, 1977–2017 106

5.5 Posterior means, standard deviations, and 95% HPDs of fixed-effects coefficients of Model 4—GFCC strike of federal laws, 1977–2017 107

1

The Sources and Implications of Constrained Constitutional Review

Courts reviewing the constitutionality of the actions of the legislative and executive branches of government have become a mainstay of modern democracies. As guardians of constitutions, they are a moderating and when necessary corrective force in politics, ready to censor legislative acts that transgress constitutional boundaries. Prudent lawmakers must anticipate that courts review the constitutionality of their acts, and they are well-advised to shelve plans that are unlikely to survive judicial scrutiny. Such pre-emptive amendments of legislation to avert constitutional review, also known as 'auto-limitation', are an ingenious feature of systems of separation of powers (see Stone, 1992; Rogers and Vanberg, 2007; Brouard and Hönnige, 2017; Engst, 2021). If lawmakers themselves ensure that the most controversial elements of their policy programmes are weeded out *before* legislation is enacted, then constitutional boundaries are never crossed, and both lawmakers and judges spare themselves from potentially bruising confrontations in the courtroom. Put differently, in well-functioning systems of separation of powers courts certainly project but seldom have to prove their political clout.

Except that lawmakers cannot always be counted on to play along. Lawmakers often appear to disregard caution, pushing the limits of constitutional boundaries in their policy decisions. Despite public outcry and legal advisors' warnings, governing majorities persist in advancing policies that are, at best, constitutionally questionable. Below, I discuss two illustrative examples of lawmakers probing and arguably crossing constitutional boundaries, opting for the kinds of policies that invite judicial censure. As we will find out throughout this book, such behaviour is anything but irrational and reveals novel, normatively charged insights into the politics of separation of powers.

Judicial vetoes of their legislative acts are costly for lawmakers. Not only are they a source of political embarrassment for governing majorities, particularly when courts enjoy strong support among the electorate (see Gibson et al., 1998; Vanberg, 1998). Judicial vetoes also consume lawmakers' resources, as they must allocate floor time in parliament to re-legislate after a court

Putting Courts Under Pressure. Philipp A. Schroeder, Oxford University Press. © Philipp A. Schroeder (2025).
DOI: 10.1093/9780198953265.003.0001

invalidated the original legislative text. If lawmakers in the executive and legislative branches were genuinely committed to adhering to constitutional jurisprudence and correcting missteps upon recognition, ignoring expert advice about potential constitutional violations would not be part of their approach. Yet, such policy choices occasionally prevail, which is the central theme of this book. Lawmakers who dismiss warnings from legal counsel and even like-minded colleagues signal their stance towards constitutional constraints on their policymaking authority. Throughout this book, I will make my best effort to convince you that lawmakers' probing of constitutional boundaries has significant implications for the decision-making of the judges who review their policies. I present a formalized theoretical model supported by original quantitative and qualitative evidence, demonstrating that lawmakers who deliberately cross constitutional boundaries have valid reasons to expect judicial deference rather than censure.

In the *Federalist 78*, Alexander Hamilton (1961, 490) cast the judiciary as the 'least dangerous' branch of government, which 'commands neither force nor will, but merely judgment; and must ultimately depend on the aid of the executive arm even for the efficacy of its judgements.' In other words, courts reviewing the constitutionality of the acts of political branches suffer from a *compliance dilemma*—tasked with interpreting and protecting constitutional boundaries but relying 'upon other actors to ensure that their decisions are followed' (Carrubba and Zorn, 2010, 812, see also Vanberg, 2001; Clark, 2010). This book demonstrates that this dilemma is not lost on lawmakers. On the contrary, it fundamentally shapes the dynamics of legislative-judicial interactions in systems of separation of powers. Courts worried about protecting their institutional integrity and maintaining an impression that their decisions are consistently acted upon simply cannot look past signs that lawmakers are prepared to evade compliance. When lawmakers pass ostensibly unconstitutional legislation, dismissing every cautionary voice along the way, they credibly signal resolve to do just that. I argue that courts reviewing such legislative actions face strong incentives to relax their enforcement of constitutional boundaries, ultimately granting lawmakers greater flexibility.

The following examples from the United States and Germany, two consolidated democracies with particularly influential courts at the apex of their judicial hierarchy, the U.S. Supreme Court and the German Federal Constitutional Court (in the following, GFCC), illustrate the puzzle at the centre of this book: Lawmakers pushing the envelope on constitutional boundaries in their policy choices and getting away with it.

On 27 January 2017, just days after taking office, U.S. President Donald Trump signed an executive order titled 'Protection of the Nation from Foreign Terrorist Entry into the United States' into law. The executive order temporarily barred citizens of six predominantly Muslim nations from entering the United States and suspended Syrian refugees' entry indefinitely. The immediate implementation of the order caught travellers on incoming flights from these countries by surprise. Upon arrival, citizens of Iraq, Syria, Iran, Libya, Somalia, Sudan, and Yemen who had held visas to enter and remain in the United States suddenly faced detention by U.S. law enforcement officials and subsequent deportation. Democrat House Representatives labelled the Trump administration's actions 'shameful' and it did not take long before those opposing the executive order pointed out that the White House had delivered on an infamous campaign pledge.[1]

On the campaign trail in 2015, citing polling data allegedly showing that a sizeable proportion of the Muslim population in the United States harboured hatred towards Americans, Trump had called 'for a total and complete shutdown of Muslims entering the United States until our country's representatives can figure out what the hell is going on'.[2] At the time, the constitutionality of an immigration policy based on religious discrimination was widely contested, and senior Republicans had distanced themselves from Trump's campaign.[3] Since the entry ban targeted citizens from predominantly Muslim-majority countries, the executive order was swiftly tied to Trump's campaign promise. Civil rights groups and several state governments filed legal challenges in federal courts, asserting that the policy constituted religious discrimination disguised as a national security measure and was therefore unconstitutional. On 3 February 2017, a U.S. District Court in Seattle, Washington, issued a restraining order in *State of Washington v. Trump*, temporarily blocking the nationwide application of the executive order.

The District Court's judgment was among the first of a series of judicial decisions challenging the Trump administration's immigration policy. Responding to the flurry of legal challenges, the White House replaced the original order with executive order 13780, which itself was superseded by Presidential Proclamation 9645, to include travel restrictions to the United

[1] CNN, 29 January 2017. *Protesters mass at airports to decry Trump's immigration policies*, https://edition.cnn.com/2017/01/28/politics/us-immigration-protests/index.html, accessed 13 February 2019.

[2] Washington Post, 7 December 2015. *Trump calls for 'total and complete shutdown of Muslims entering the United States'*, https://www.washingtonpost.com/news/post-politics/wp/2015/12/07/donald-trump-calls-for-total-and-complete-shutdown-of-muslims/, accessed 13 February 2019.

[3] Politico, 14 June 2016. *Ryan breaks with Trump on Muslim immigrant ban*, https://www.politico.com/story/2016/06/ryan-trump-muslim-ban-224312, accessed 19 February 2019.

States for individuals from North Korea and Venezuela, while removing Iraq from the list. However, constitutional objections to the Trump administration's immigration policy persisted. In early 2018, the U.S. Supreme Court eventually agreed to hear a case brought by the State of Hawaii, which argued that the policy's latest iteration remained motivated by an anti-Muslim animus.

In light of the five-to-four majority of Republican-nominated justices at the U.S. Supreme Court, the Trump administration now faced a 'friendlier' bench than in the lower courts that had censored its immigration policy. However, given the Republican Party's initial opposition to then-candidate Trump's proposed 'Muslim ban' and conservative Justice Anthony Kennedy's history of siding with liberal justices on key ideological issues, a ruling in favour of the Trump administration's Presidential Proclamation appeared far from assured. Further, Justice Sonia Sotomayor warned that allowing the Trump administration's travel ban to go ahead would bear the hallmarks of the U.S. Supreme Court's infamous judgment in *Korematsu v. United States*, which had legitimized the internment of Japanese Americans during World War II.[4] Nonetheless, eventually a five-to-four majority on the bench disagreed with the plaintiff's argument and upheld the Presidential Proclamation. Writing for the majority in *Trump v. Hawaii*, Chief Justice Roberts noted that the proclamation 'is expressly premised on legitimate purposes and says nothing about religion'.[5]

A cavalier attitude towards constitutional boundaries may be a trademark of governing administrations that operate in politically polarized environments, particularly those adopting a political style aimed at energizing their core electoral base. However, such behaviour is not exclusive to administrations that seem to flourish in contentious settings. In 2008, a governing majority in the German Bundestag comprising the Christian-conservative CDU/CSU and the centre-left SPD pushed for controversial changes to the mandate of the Federal Criminal Police Office (in the following, BKA), Germany's federal investigative police agency. With the passage of the so-called Federal Criminal Police Office Act, the BKA took on a new, significant role in countering threats emanating from international terrorism. The BKA's agents would enjoy newfound powers to conduct surveillance in private residences, remotely search information technology systems, and share intelligence with other domestic and international law enforcement agencies.

[4] New York Times, 26 June 2018. *Sonia Sotomayor Delivers Sharp Dissent in Travel Ban Case*, https://www.nytimes.com/2018/06/26/us/sonia-sotomayor-dissent-travel-ban.html, accessed 30 April 2019.

[5] The full text of the U.S. Supreme Court's ruling in *Trump v. Hawaii* is available at https://www.supremecourt.gov/opinions/17pdf/17-965_h315.pdf.

Concerns had been voiced that the act mandated an impermissible encroachment upon the core area of an individual's private life (in German, the 'Kernbereich privater Lebensgestaltung'). Members of the liberal-conservative FDP labelled the act as 'poorly thought out and constitutionally dubious', claiming that it failed to live up to restrictions on state surveillance defined in the GFCC's recent jurisprudence.[6] In a rare turn of events, several members of the governing coalition caucus joined the parliamentary opposition parties in their criticism. Ten members of the SPD, including former Justice Minister Herta Däubler-Gmelin, signed a statement denouncing the act for infringing on citizens' constitutional rights. Despite a number of lawmakers of the SPD breaking party ranks and voting against the government, the controversial legislation eventually passed parliament and entered into force in early 2009.

To little surprise, the act eventually ended up in the GFCC's docket. Plaintiffs including a former federal minister, lawyers, and journalists alleged that the act's provisions infringed upon several constitutional norms enshrined in the German Basic Law. The Court issued its decision in *1 BvR 966/09* on 20 April 2016, stating that '[t]he authorisation of the Federal Criminal Police Office to carry out covert surveillance measures (surveillance of private homes, remote searches of information technology systems, telecommunications surveillance, collection of telecommunications traffic data and surveillance outside of private homes using special means of data collection) is, for the purpose of protecting against threats from international terrorism, in principle compatible with the fundamental rights enshrined in the Basic Law'. The judgment addressed the legal pre-requirements of carrying out covert surveillance measures and data transfers, reining in a number of provisions of the act that judges perceived as too broad and unspecific. Yet, in a highly unusual move, the Court also consolidated and in its own words 'carefully delimited' existing case law. In doing so, the Court eased several restrictions its jurisprudence had previously placed on law enforcement regarding the use of intercepted information for purposes other than those for which it was originally collected.

Lawmakers' pursuit of policies that are ostensibly at odds with constitutional norms, much like the two examples outlined above, presents students of systems of separation of powers with a puzzle. *Why would lawmakers take considerable constitutional risks in their policy choices, well-aware that courts*

[6] Translated from German, excerpt from the second reading of the Act on Prevention by the Federal Criminal Police Office of Threats from International Terrorism, 12 November 2008, 2. Beratung: BT-PlPr 16/186.

may censor their actions? What can such behaviour by lawmakers tell us about courts' influence in the political domain? What are the normative implications for democracy when lawmakers push constitutional boundaries—and succeed? This book offers answers to these questions that lay bare the limits to courts' control over defining the boundaries of the constitution. It uncovers a facet of politics in modern democracies that has been largely overlooked in existing scholarship. *Lawmakers whose policies push the envelope on constitutional boundaries signal credible non-compliance threats to courts and pressure them to ease legal restrictions on their policymaking.*

The theory of legislative-judicial interactions developed in this book shows that, because of courts' non-compliance woes, lawmakers cannot be straitjacketed in their policy choices. Courts' compliance dilemma provides lawmakers with leverage in their interactions with the judiciary. Not every policy is worth the risk of provoking a confrontation with the judiciary, and we would be remiss to expect lawmakers to probe constitutional boundaries at every opportunity. However, on key policy priorities, when the political stakes are high, lawmakers can exploit courts' compliance dilemma and box themselves out of the constraints that constitutional jurisprudence usually imposes on them. This argument questions several of the existing scholarship's expectations for courts' influence over the legislative and executive branches. A prominent strand of literature has centred on the—arguably unduly—powerful role of courts in the political domain (Vallinder, 1995; Stone Sweet, 2000b; Hirschl, 2009). Citing courts' authority to invalidate legislative acts and issue more or less precise instructions for lawmakers on how a constitutionally sound policy would look like, scholars have diagnosed and cautioned against a 'government of judges' (Stone Sweet, 2000b, 2007). There are certainly good reasons for these concerns. Courts' jurisprudence and constitutional interpretations often influence legislative decision-making. However, just as policies are sometimes effectively crafted by judges rather than lawmakers, constitutional limits on policy are not always established in courtrooms. Occasionally, these boundaries are redefined within parliaments and government cabinets.

1.1 Rethinking judicial authority

In the following section, I outline how the insights from this book engage with what we know about legislative-judicial interactions in systems of separation of powers and push us to rethink our perspective on courts' authority in modern democracies. I begin by discussing the sources of judicial authority identified in the existing literature, noting that lawmakers draw benefits from courts' exercise of constitutional review and face costs for undermining or even abolishing these review regimes. I then turn to lawmakers' motives to evade compliance with constitutional jurisprudence, nonetheless. Finally, I engage with prominent game-theoretic accounts of legislative-judicial interactions and spell out what they have taught us about the strategic calculus of courts and lawmakers in systems of separation of powers.

The excellent scholarship referenced throughout this section provides the building blocks for the theoretical argument discussed in detail in Chapter 2 of this book. However, where applicable, this section also spells out how the argument laid out in the next chapter contrasts with or expands on the existing literature's expectations for the behaviour of lawmakers and courts in modern systems of separation of powers.

1.1.1 Sources of judicial authority

Courts exercising constitutional review of the acts of the elected branches occupy a peculiar role in systems of separation of powers. Despite lacking the power of the proverbial 'purse and sword', courts have proven themselves as remarkably consequential and resilient players in modern democracies (see Kapiszewski et al., 2013). Existing literature has identified two sources of courts' authority in the political arena, one revolving around lawmakers' endogenous incentives to tolerate judicial constraints on their actions and another involving the political branches' exogenous costs of undermining the independence of the judiciary (see Vanberg, 2008, 2015).

Endogenous incentives

Prominent existing literature claims that independent courts allow the political branches of government to secure benefits they could otherwise not obtain. Douglass North and Barry Weingast trace the origins of independent judiciaries in charge of controlling the actions of government to seventeenth-century Great Britain. The British Crown was accustomed to raising money through forced loans from its wealthy constituents, unilaterally renewing loans and paying less interest than originally agreed (North and Weingast, 1989, 820). Faced with a Crown that controlled both policy and the courts, lenders had little choice but to grudgingly agree to the monarchy's terms. However, affluent strata of society eventually demanded institutional change to limit the monarchy's arbitrary power and threatened to overthrow the Crown (see Ervin, 1970). With parliament's passage of the Act of Settlement in 1701, the British Crown relinquished control over the judiciary to make a credible commitment to respect the property rights of its constituents and ensure it could continue borrowing to serve its fiscal needs (for similar arguments see Laffont and Meleu, 2001; Feld and Voigt, 2003; Moustafa, 2007; Voigt et al., 2007).

The concept of independent courts enabling the elected branches of government to 'lock in' commitments and rules of engagement has been a prominent theme in political science scholarship, particularly through the framework of the so-called insurance theory (see Ramseyer, 1994; Stephenson, 2003). By committing to respect the decisions of an independent judiciary, governing majorities agree to accept limitations on their own actions. Simultaneously, by promoting judicial independence, current incumbents ensure that their political opponents will be bound by the same constraints when they assume power in the future (see Ferejohn and Weingast, 1992; Ramseyer and Rasmusen, 2001; Chavez et al., 2011). As long as lawmakers anticipate rotating in and out of government office, an independent judiciary empowered to invalidate policies that conflict with the constitution offers them 'the indirect benefit of the promise of enjoying judicial protection when in opposition' (Vanberg, 2015, 173).

Independent courts provide another, more tangible benefit for governing majorities. Developing policies that effectively address the societal issues they are designed to resolve is unsurprisingly difficult. Until policies meet a typically complex reality, lawmakers cannot be sure whether they produce their desired effect (Callander, 2011). Rogers (2001) offers a formal theoretical model, which shows that independent courts' review of policy provides an informational benefit to lawmakers (see also Fox and Vanberg, 2014). In reviewing policy and its effects on society, 'courts can draw upon not only the information that the legislature had available when enacting a statute, but also have access to additional information acquired from actual experience with the implemented law' (Rogers, 2001, 86). Hence, courts' review provides a 'sober second thought' on policy, while '[i]t is often easier for the Court to strike down an enacted law when it is revealed to be inappropriate than it is for the legislature to repeal the law' (Rogers, 2001, 87).

The accounts summarized in the preceding paragraphs stress that lawmakers have convincing, endogenous incentives to tolerate judicial authority in the political domain. Unquestionably, lawmakers accrue a range of benefits from committing to a set of constitutional rules that constrain legislative and executive power, and placing independent arbiters, namely the judiciary, in charge of interpreting these rules. Changing the rules of the game through constitutional amendments may remain a possibility for lawmakers, yet doing so requires legislative super-majorities that governing majorities usually cannot muster.

Still, the theoretical argument and empirical evidence in this book demonstrate that lawmakers have not entirely relinquished control to courts when it comes to defining constitutional limits on policy. They do not need to amend constitutions to reshape these boundaries, nor do they have to threaten to curb courts' authority to extort favourable judgments. While courts remain in charge of providing interpretations of the constitution and its implications for policy, lawmakers have a hand in where constitutional boundaries to policy are drawn. Even after committing to constitutional rules and respecting judicial independence, lawmakers continue to enjoy the discretion to probe these boundaries when they consider it necessary (see Staton et al., 2022). Because courts are caught in a compliance dilemma, lawmakers thereby leave a lasting impact on courts' jurisprudence. Pushing constitutional boundaries in their policy choices, lawmakers can credibly signal non-compliance threats and put pressure on courts to come up with interpretations that ease legal constraints on their policymaking.

Exogenous constraints

A separate strand of explanations of courts' influence in the political domain stresses that the costs lawmakers would have to bear for challenging judicial authority render this option unattractive. Decades of scholarship have shown that most courts sitting at the top of their judicial hierarchies enjoy comfortable reservoirs of public support (see Caldeira and Gibson, 1992; Mondak, 1992; Gibson and Caldeira, 1995; Gibson et al., 1998; Gibson and Caldeira, 2003; Gibson and Nelson, 2016). Members of the public may occasionally disagree with the direction of individual judgments. However, as long as courts avoid consistently issuing decisions out of touch with dominant public opinion, the public's faith in courts' institutional legitimacy is unlikely to waver (see for example Easton, 1965; Durr et al., 2000; Gibson et al., 2005; Ura, 2014, but see Bartels and Johnston, 2013 for a different perspective).

The public's support for the judiciary has consequences for the relationship among courts and the elected branches. Vanberg (2001) highlights that lawmakers frustrated by the constraints courts place on their actions risk the public's ire at the ballot box and spoil their electoral prospects should they decide to move against the courts, including by flouting judicial orders (see also Mayhew, 1974; Weingast, 1997; Engst, 2021). Public support and institutional legitimacy thus play a critical role in ensuring that the elected branches respect the constraints courts place on their actions (Carrubba and Zorn, 2010; Clark, 2010). Once courts can rely on the public's backing, their decisions become 'institutionally based exogenous constraints' on the actions of the political branches (Carrubba, 2009, 68).

In light of the judiciary's legitimacy and its eminent status in modern democracies, well-established literature has argued that courts' mandate to review and where necessary strike legislative acts has fostered 'the infusion of judicial decision-making and of courtlike procedures into the political arena' (Vallinder, 1995, 13). Put simply, politics has become 'judicialized' (see Tate and Vallinder, 1995; Stone Sweet, 1999; Hirschl, 2008). Lawmakers must act with foresight and ensure that their policies stand the test of judicial scrutiny. Legal rather than political considerations are shaping the tenor of policy, and otherwise feasible policy options are effectively removed from lawmakers' agenda (Schmidt, 2018, 246, see also Grimm, 2016). Stone Sweet (1999, 175) argues that governing majorities become susceptible to 'constitutional blackmail' as the mere threat of taking government to court over the alleged unconstitutionality of policy becomes a powerful tool for the political opposition to elicit compromises from government. Governing lawmakers' pre-emptive amendment of legislation to avoid constitutional review thus become the norm (see Stone, 1992).

This book challenges these accounts. When considering policy decisions, lawmakers undoubtedly weigh the likelihood of constitutional review and the potential consequences of clashes with the judiciary. However, they cannot always be 'blackmailed' into abandoning their policy objectives merely to avoid judicial scrutiny. Lawmakers understand that courts ultimately lack the means to enforce compliance with rulings that challenge their policies. While defying judicial authority and ignoring court orders may alienate voters and incur political costs, pursuing controversial policies—particularly those of critical importance to the political leadership—may still represent the most viable option, even if it involves evading compliance with judicial objections. There is a somewhat counter-intuitive, not immediately obvious logic to lawmakers' signalling of resolve to challenge judicial authority despite the costs that a confrontation with the judiciary would entail. Courts must recognize lawmakers' signals of resolve as credible precisely when sending them involves high risks for lawmakers—*costly* signals make for *credible* signals (see Fearon, 1997; Humphreys, 2016; Staton et al., 2022). After all, only lawmakers firmly committed to implementing a constitutionally questionable policy—even if it requires evading compliance with an unfavourable judgment—would choose to pursue it. Lawmakers whose support for a controversial policy would waver in the face of a judicial veto would likely have abandoned their plans from the outset.

To summarize, the existing literature referenced here has identified plenty of good reasons for lawmakers to respect courts' jurisprudence and to comply even with judgments that are unfavourable to their interests. Yet, the argument that I develop in this book asserts that lawmakers cannot always be counted on to do so, and lawmakers' motivations for flouting court orders are the subjects of the following section.

1.1.2 Reasons to push boundaries

Compliance with court orders, understood as the 'full execution of the action (or complete avoidance of the action) called for (or prohibited) in one or more court rulings' (Kapiszewski and Taylor, 2013, 806), is a cornerstone of the rule of law in democracies. But even in well-established democracies, such compliance is not guaranteed. Data provided by the Varieties of Democracy (V-Dem) project offers cross-country, time series evidence of just how prepared state governments are to comply with unfavourable judgments.[7] V-Dem annually surveys country experts inter alia asking 'How often would you say the government complies with important decisions of the high court with which it disagrees?', with the response categories ranging from 'never' (0), 'seldom' (1), 'about half the time' (2), 'usually' (3) to 'always' (4). Figure 1.1 plots the average expert ratings for compliance with unfavourable high court rulings since 1990 for OECD Member States and globally.

Unsurprisingly, country experts generally considered compliance with high court rulings to be more prevalent in OECD Member States than the average country, with OECD scores consistently falling between 3 (usually) and 4 (always). However, we can also see that these expert ratings have dipped slightly albeit consistently since the late 2000s, for both OECD countries and globally. The picture painted here is that even courts in well-established democracies cannot always count on compliance with their judgments. Hence, there must be reasons for lawmakers to occasionally probe judicial authority and flout the faithful implementation of court rulings.

[7] V-Dem's dataset along with the accompaniying documentation is publicly available at https://v-dem.net/data/the-v-dem-dataset/.

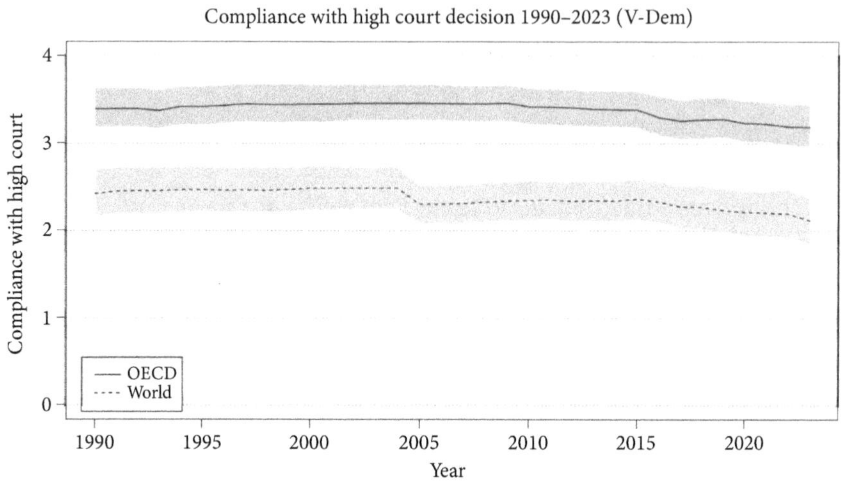

Figure 1.1 Varieties of Democracy aggregated expert ratings for the item 'How often would you say the government complies with important decisions of the high court with which it disagrees?' Response categories range from 'never' (0), 'seldom' (1), 'about half the time' (2), 'usually' (3) to 'always' (4)

A likely motivator for lawmakers is the value of a particular policy, which must be high enough to warrant the risk of flouting courts' extant jurisprudence and breaking with a fundamental principle of constitutional democracy. The value of policy to lawmakers has featured prominently in existing theoretical models of legislative-judicial interactions, with higher values tipping the scale in favour of lawmakers pursuing 'riskier' policy options (see Clark, 2009). For instance, Vanberg's (2001) seminal model of legislative-judicial relations includes a parameter that captures lawmakers' opportunity costs of not passing their preferred legislation to pre-empt judicial review. 'Auto-limiting' their policy choices comes with costs for lawmakers, and these costs increase with the value the policy holds for them.

Additionally, work by Fox and Stephenson (2011) suggests that lawmakers opt for controversial policies inviting judicial censure when they expect short-term electoral pay-offs from doing so (see also Ward and Gabel, 2019). Lawmakers have incentives to take 'bold but unwarranted action in response to a perceived emergency in order to appear competent to the voters' (Fox and Stephenson, 2011, 397). Assuming that voters find it difficult to evaluate whether a particular policy choice is appropriate to address an acute crisis, for example an economic recession or a terrorist threat to national security, lawmakers' irresponsible policy choices can initially resonate with voters despite their eventual detrimental effects on voters' welfare. A similar argument is made by Staton et al. (2022), who argue that '[p]ublic health or economic crisis, natural disasters, domestic disturbances, and war all typically require a leader to pursue extraordinary actions, which might not be ordinarily tolerated' (Staton et al., 2022, 21). They point out that non-compliance with a court order that censures an extraordinary action provides political leaders with an opportunity to credibly signal to the electorate their willingness to take necessary—albeit controversial—steps to address exceptional challenges. Because non-compliance may prompt backlash from the public and is hence costly, it is a 'visible way of credibly signaling a sincere rationale for engaging in behavior that might be interpreted as violations of fundamental limits on authority' (Staton et al., 2022, 29).

Literature exploring how a growing electoral success of populist, radical-right challenger parties (PRRPs) in several European democracies has affected party competition suggests that lawmakers may not only opt for constitutionally dubious policy choices in response to what they themselves perceive as an emergency or crisis (see van Spanje, 2010; Gessler and Hunger, 2022). Strong electoral performances of parties such as the *Alternative für Deutschland* in Germany, the *Rassemblement National* in France or the *Partij voor de Vrijheid* in the Netherlands put pressure on mainstream parties to accommodate the positions of these challengers (see for example Spoon and Klüver, 2020; Hjorth and Larsen, 2022; Williams and Hunger, 2022; Krause et al., 2023). PRRPs typically focus on immigration as their core issue and advocate restrictive immigration policies, in particular with respect to immigrants' access to national social security systems (De Vries and Hobolt, 2020). As Hackenesch et al. (2022, 1394) highlight, '[w]hen PRRPs gain electoral support or parliamentary seats, mainstream parties have indeed been found to adjust their policy positions or even to co-opt PRRPs' policy positions in order to "recapture voters lost to the challenger parties"' (see also Schain, 2006).

Governing parties switching positions to match PRRP's proposals and prevent voter transitions, however, risk violating constitutional rights in the process. To illustrate, in the wake of a strong electoral performance of the *Alternative für Deutschland* in the 2017 federal parliamentary elections, a German governing coalition of the CDU/CSU and SPD amended the Asylum Seekers Benefits Act, inter alia introducing a reduced 'special rate' of benefits for adult, single asylum seekers living in shared public accommodation. During the German parliament's plenary debate on the government's proposal, a member of the opposition party *Die Linke* remarked:

> Gökay Akbulut (Die Linke): It is cynical that you cite the Federal Constitutional Court's ruling of 18 August 2012 in your proposal. You clearly misunderstood what the highest court of our country wanted to express in this ruling. The human dignity guaranteed by Article 1 of our constitution cannot be qualified in the context of immigration policy. This also means that further reductions for these welfare beneficiaries are unacceptable. Yet, that is exactly what you propose.[8]

The act's amendment was later challenged at the GFCC, which indeed agreed that it conflicted with its 2012 judgment. The reduction of the welfare benefits was subsequently ruled as incompatible with the fundamental right to an existential minimum in the GFCC's decision *1 BvL 3/21* on 19 October 2022.

To summarize, this section has shown that non-compliance with court judgments is a feature common enough even in well-established democracies to register on judges' radars. Lawmakers are incentivized to risk non-compliance for policies that are by themselves particularly valuable to them or policies that promise an electoral edge over competitors. Coupled with the insights on endogenous and exogenous reasons to respect judicial authority discussed in the previous section, existing literature paints a picture of legislative-judicial interactions characterized by actors' careful balancing of competing incentives. Game theory is especially well-suited to explain behaviour in these types of scenarios, and it is therefore unsurprising that many of the most impactful studies of legislative-judicial interactions have employed formal theoretical models. The following section discusses a selection of these formal models that are particularly important for my own model developed in Chapter 2.

1.1.3 Strategic mindsets

Epstein and Knight (1998, 10) argue that 'justices are strategic actors who realize that their ability to achieve their goals depends on a consideration of the preferences of other actors, the choices they expect others to make, and the institutional context in which they act', a notion that equally applies to lawmakers. Strategic calculus in the decision-making of both courts and lawmakers has thus featured prominently in existing work analysing legislative-judicial interactions (see Gely and Spiller, 1990; Bergara et al., 2003; Whittington, 2007;

[8] Translated from German, excerpt from the second reading of the Third Act on the Amendment of the Asylum Seekers Benefits Act in the German Bundestag, 7 June 2019, 2. Beratung: BT-PlPr 19/105.

Harvey and Friedman, 2009; Bailey and Maltzman, 2011; Segal et al., 2011; Hall and Ura, 2015).

In this section, I engage with seminal studies that rely on game-theoretic models to predict the behaviour of lawmakers and courts in their interactions. Consider first a recent study by Engst (2021), who develops a game-theoretic model in which a legislative majority selects a policy knowing that it may subsequently be reviewed by a constitutional court. Whenever the court considers a policy as incompatible with the constitution, the legislative majority then either responds by implementing a policy that is consistent with the court's instructions, or opts for a policy that deviates from what the court had asked for. Engst (2021, 32) highlights that the 'government will have to invest resources to mobilize legislators to respond to a court decisions', that its 'reaction to a court decision can cause public backlash', and that a government may discount any of these costs if the policy in question is of major importance. Each of these considerations already factors into the legislative majority's policy choice at the outset of the game, and Engst is able to show that the legislative majority only opts for policies at the first stage of the game which avoid judicial reactions that would eventually leave government worse off than if it had decided not to legislate at all. Although lawmakers cannot know with certainty which of their policy choices fail to survive judicial scrutiny, 'former court decisions become legal signals', revealing 'information that allow the government to make an educated guess' which policies the court would accept (Engst, 2021, 67).

The formal model developed in Chapter 2 mirrors this account in many respects. However, I highlight that it is not just lawmakers who look to the past to infer information about the future. *Both* courts and lawmakers look to each others' previous choices to learn something about their counterpart's true preferences. This argument builds on excellent work by Clark (2010, 2009), who developed a series of formal models capturing interactions between the U.S. Supreme Court and Congress. Informed by interviews with justices and clerks at the U.S. Supreme Court, Clark (2010, 90) argues that the Court exercises self-restraint in its decisions when 'the political environment is too treacherous', i.e. when the Court believes that a sufficiently large share of the public has lost faith in its institutional legitimacy. The Court updates its beliefs about the public support it enjoys based on the positions that members of Congress adopt in their sponsored bills. When members of Congress introduce bills including measures to curb the Court's authority, the Court has reason to believe that its support among the public is suffering and should therefore tread carefully. Here, the signals sent by lawmakers reveal—and possibly, misrepresent—information about the political environment that the Court is navigating. This book illustrates a similar mechanism but emphasizes that lawmakers do not need to use court-curbing bills to influence a court's decisions. Simply defying the court's established jurisprudence can signal a potential threat of future non-compliance, prompting the court to exercise deference when reviewing policies that test constitutional limits.

Scholars of judicial politics have understandably focused much of their work on courts' responses to these threats. Prominent work by Vanberg (2001, 2005) has highlighted that courts have strong incentives to avoid non-compliance with their jurisprudence to protect their institutional integrity. Vanberg's interviews with German Constitutional Court justices reveal that even a well-established constitutional court such as the GFCC is treading carefully to avoid non-compliance. To illustrate, consider the following admission by one of the GFCC's justices:

> You know, the court has issued many decisions that were never complied with, for example about the treatment of civil servant pensions. And there really isn't anything the court can do about that. If no one else takes an interest in it, that's just the way it is going to be. And of course the court has to be worried about that, that a tradition of ignoring the court isn't established (Justice of the GFCC, quoted in Vanberg, 2005, 122).

A court—or any other institution, for that matter—that regularly issues inconsequential decisions ultimately becomes obsolete. This fear of irrelevance, demonstrated by regular non-compliance with their decisions, is what pushes courts to strategically pre-empt non-compliance by avoiding judgments that are at risk of the latter. There is robust evidence indicating that domestic and international courts indeed factor the detrimental effects of future non-compliance into their decision-making (see Vanberg, 2005; Carrubba and Zorn, 2010; Hall, 2011; Carrubba and Gabel, 2015). At the same time, although courts certainly prefer to see their decisions implemented, their concern for institutional integrity does not equate to avoidance of non-compliance at all costs. As touched upon in Section 1.1.2, Staton et al. (2022, 80) argue that 'noncompliance with judicial orders can be part of a robust political system', and 'part of a process by which leaders communicate about their resolve and the seriousness of the policy problems they confront'. For such a system to work, judges need to accept that some of their decisions will simply not be implemented. We will find elements of this argument in my theoretical model as well. Non-compliance comes with a price tag for courts, but this will not always deter them from issuing decisions that are likely to be ignored. Instead, courts carefully balance the costs of allowing an unconstitutional policy to remain in effect against the risks that a ruling invalidating the policy might be disregarded, as well as the potential backlash from supporters of the policy.

The final feature of the strategic calculus in legislative-judicial interactions that plays an important role in my theoretical model draws on excellent studies by Helmke (2002, 2005) and Krehbiel (2021). Their work picks up on an often overlooked but critical factor in courts' constitutional review of policy—timing. Analysing the behaviour of high courts in authoritarian political systems, lacking high levels of judicial independence, Helmke (2002) points out that judges have incentives to engage in so-called 'strategic defection'. Judges gauge the staying power of incumbents, and Helmke (2002, 291) asserts that 'once the government in office begins to lose power, judges who lack institutional security begin facing incentives to increase their antigovernment rulings to distance themselves from a weakening government'. Krehbiel (2021) identifies a somewhat similar rationale for constitutional courts in electoral democracies. His formal model accounts for the possibility that the implementation of a court's judgment might occur after an election. In such cases, if a legislative majority's policy is struck down by the court and they subsequently lose the election, they no longer have the opportunity to respond to the court's ruling. Hence, a constitutional court can 'leverage the political and electoral circumstances surrounding its decisions' (Krehbiel, 2021, 832), as an incumbent's non-compliance threats lose their bite if it is likely that they would have left office once the court issues its decision.

The studies referenced in this section highlight that just as lawmakers draw on existing jurisprudence to anticipate the outcomes of future constitutional review cases, courts infer information about the current political environment based on lawmakers' previous policy choices. Further, costs of non-compliance are an important but not all-determining factor in courts' decision-making calculus, and the electoral (mis)fortunes of lawmakers can alleviate justices' non-compliance concerns. Each of these features of legislative-judicial interactions plays an important part in my own theoretical argument developed in Chapter 2. Before I get there, I close this chapter out by briefly discussing the normative implications of my argument and the universe of cases that my argument applies to, concluding with an outline of the book's structure.

1.2 A normative quandary

The argument and evidence presented throughout the next chapters have significant normative implications. They tie in with a longstanding debate on the countermajoritarian, even undemocratic nature of courts' constitutional jurisprudence in modern democracies (Bickel, 1986; Mishler and Sheehan, 1993; Friedman, 1998; Casillas et al., 2011; Hall and Ura, 2015). Courts' exercise of constitutional review invokes a 'countermajoritarian difficulty'. After all, allowing unelected judges to review and, where they deem necessary, strike down elected lawmakers' policies sits somewhat uneasy with the ideals of representative democracy.

Against this backdrop, maybe it is not all that bad if we find lawmakers who are willing to take on constitutional risks in their policy choices and show resolve to reclaim decision-making authority from courts in the legislative domain. Where exactly constitutional norms draw the line for unlawful political action is hardly ever clear cut, which is why we need independent courts stacked with learned judges to resolve these questions in the first place. But if elected lawmakers, notably without overturning the fundamental pillars of systems of separation of powers, can push courts to ease judicial constraints on their actions and themselves have some say in where the constitutional boundaries to policy are drawn, then the countermajoritarian nature of constitutional review may be dialled down just a notch.

This admittedly benign reading of the implications of this book's argument would appear to mitigate concerns that legal scholars and political scientists had voiced about the piling on of judicial constraints on lawmakers' creative spirit (see Stone Sweet, 2000b; Schmidt, 2018). Courts' constitutional jurisprudence surely leaves its mark on policy choices of parliaments and governments, but ultimately it cannot subjugate lawmakers. Both in its theoretical analysis and empirical findings, the book shows that lawmakers find ways to disentangle the web of constraints spun through courts' constitutional jurisprudence.

What sounds like an assurance against concerns about a 'government of judges', however, has a normatively charged flip side. The limits of courts' influence in the political arena shine through on highly salient, high-stakes issues. Examples from Germany discussed in subsequent chapters include controversial restrictions to the right of asylum in the early 1990s in response to a rapid increase of applicants seeking asylum in Germany, as well as the centre-right governing coalition's proposals in the late 1990s to expand law enforcement's use of intrusive surveillance instruments to combat organized crime. These competences were further extended by a 'grand' governing coalition of the CDU/CSU and SPD following the terrorist bombings in Madrid in March 2004 and London in July 2005.

When governments encroach on core constitutional norms in their policy choices, often riding a momentary wave of support among some of their key electoral constituencies, courts are expected to provide an effective line of defence against constitutional transgressions of the political branches, offering the valued 'sober second thought' on policy (see Stone, 1936; Rogers, 2001; Staton and Vanberg, 2008). Yet, precisely when the political stakes are high, when governing majorities take considerable political risks in their effort to probe core constitutional norms, courts' authority over the demarcation of constitutional boundaries is hamstrung. Courts may be a countermajoritarian force in the grind of everyday politics, yet they cede a sizeable part of their political clout on the high-stakes policy issues that spark constitutional controversy but are ultimately pushed through by lawmakers. After all, averting the lamented 'government of judges' has its price.

1.3 The universe of cases

The evidence presented in this book in support of my argument centres on Germany and the GFCC's exercise of constitutional review. The GFCC has been listed among if not as *the* most influential constitutional court in modern democracies (see Landfried, 1992; Kommers, 1994; Vanberg, 2005; Hönnige and Gschwend, 2010; Engst, 2021). Considering the GFCC's political clout and prestige among the German public, Germany presents a hard case for the book's argument. Enjoying comfortable reservoirs of public support (see for example Vanberg, 2005; Engst, 2021), a powerful constitutional court like the GFCC should be unlikely to back down in confrontations with the political branches. Consequently, we would also expect German lawmakers to rarely muster the courage to provoke such confrontations in the first place. At the same time, there is promise in focusing attention on the German case. The German system of constitutional review is a textbook example of centralized constitutional review that characterizes Western, Central, and Eastern European democracies since World War II. If the GFCC cannot deter lawmakers from pushing constitutional boundaries and eases constraints on policymaking in response, courts enjoying similar powers elsewhere are unlikely to be in a better position to protect constitutional norms against transgressions of the political branches.

The core of my argument—that lawmakers signal credible non-compliance threats by consciously opting for constitutionally dubious policies—extends beyond Germany. I anticipate observing this dynamic in any political system with constitutional review, as long as the court enjoys sufficient public support. In these contexts, courts typically expect compliance with their rulings, and lawmakers' actions suggesting otherwise are more likely to be noticed by judges. More importantly, as long as the public trusts the court's judgments and holds lawmakers accountable for disregarding constitutional boundaries despite expert advice to the contrary, lawmakers can send costly and therefore credible signals of non-compliance. As a result, I expect this dynamic to occur in well-established democracies with strong public support for the judiciary, such as the United States, France, and Italy.

The argument, though framed differently, also applies to the exercise of judicial review by international courts. Unlike domestic courts, international courts may not benefit from a vigilant public that holds governments accountable for non-compliance. However, other mechanisms exist through which costs are imposed on non-compliant governments. Take, for example, the Court of Justice of the European Union (CJEU) and its review of Member States' policies to ensure conformity with EU law, for instance through infringement proceedings initiated by the European Commission or another Member State (see Craig and de Búrca, 2020). Similar to the domestic context, national governments must anticipate that their policies could violate European rules and, if so, may be instructed by the CJEU to cease their infringement. Because non-compliance with CJEU rulings carries substantial financial penalties, Member States are incentivized to heed legal experts' advice and avoid breaching EU law from the outset. However, when a Member State is willing to bear these penalties, the CJEU depends on other national governments to exert political pressure on the recalcitrant state to enforce the ruling (see Carrubba and Gabel, 2015;Larsson and Naurin, 2016). In this scenario, a Member State's pursuit of a national policy that clearly contradicts European law—despite expert legal advice—signals a costly and, for the Member State, credible threat of non-compliance.

1.4 Plan of the book

The book is organized into seven chapters. The next chapter expands on the theoretical argument outlined above and develops a formal model of legislative-judicial interactions, generating several expectations that will be tested in the following chapters. While my focus is on explaining courts' decisions in constitutional review cases, the argument I present in this book emphasizes the *process* leading up to these decisions. The primary goal is to demonstrate how lawmakers' choices during the process, which ultimately results in courts exercising constitutional review, influence judicial decision-making. A formal model is an ideal analytical tool for telling this story, as it allows—and indeed requires—me to clearly outline the various options available to lawmakers and courts at each stage of their interaction. Importantly, the formalization of my argument helps to reveal how and under what conditions lawmakers' decisions to pursue constitutionally questionable policies, rather than sound alternatives, send signals to courts and can compel them to show deference in their constitutional review. To make the exposition of my formal model accessible to readers who may be unfamiliar with formal theory, I avoid technical jargon throughout the chapter as much as possible when discussing the model's key assumptions, and walk the reader step by step through the model's sequence of play and equilibrium solutions, concluding with visualizations of its empirical implications.

The formal model's focus on the process preceding courts' exercise of constitutional review sets the tone for empirical analyses in the subsequent chapters. Chapter 3 introduces the reader to the research design that is employed to test the empirical implications of the theoretical model. The book offers original quantitative and qualitative evidence supporting its theoretical expectations, revolving around the constitutional jurisprudence of the GFCC developed between the late 1970s and 2017. The chapter lays out how original quantitative data capturing the advice German lawmakers had received during legislative proceedings on the constitutionality of their policy drafts and data on the cases subsequently heard at the GFCC allows for a statistical analysis testing the model's predictions across a large set of observations. I then explain how a qualitative analysis of case study evidence—drawing on sources such as archival records of committee hearings in the German Bundestag, media coverage, and expert legal analyses of the GFCC's judgments—helps uncover the motivations of lawmakers and courts that underlie the patterns identified in the statistical analyses.

Chapter 4 provides the reader with a comprehensive overview over the original data that was collected for the subsequent statistical analysis. The chapter discusses the various episodes of constitutional controversy Germany witnessed since the late 1970s, illustrated with excerpts from parliamentary debates and the cases heard at the GFCC. The chapter allows readers to familiarize themselves with the empirical material at the heart of the book, understand and retrace coding decisions, and link the effects observed in the subsequent statistical analyses to concrete events.

Chapter 5 then puts the hypothesis derived from the theoretical model to the test. Relying on Bayesian regression analyses, the chapter studies the effects of lawmakers ignoring constitutional concerns that arose during legislative proceedings on subsequent decisions of the GFCC. The statistical analyses show that policies raising constitutional concerns among lawmakers from various political factions—including both opposition members and those in the governing coalition—are less likely to be struck down by the GFCC, rather than more likely, compared to less controversial policies. The theoretical model introduced in Chapter 2 explains this seemingly counter-intuitive pattern: When governing majorities disregard well-founded constitutional concerns, they send a credible signal to the GFCC that they are unwilling to let constitutional jurisprudence limit their policy choices, thereby pressuring the court to back down. The chapter offers easily accessible illustrations of this finding and provides several robustness checks. It concludes by discussing the limitations to the inferences we can draw from the statistical analyses and explains how a qualitative analysis can overcome them.

Chapter 6 complements the quantitative evidence with a qualitative case study and analytic narrative of the game-theoretic model's argument. The statistical analyses of the previous chapter establish a robust link between lawmakers ignoring constitutional concerns and the GFCC's show of deference. However, this type of analysis necessarily cannot capture every facet of the court's justification and reasoning behind its judgments. Judicial reasoning explaining how the court arrived at a particular judgment is equally if not more important for lawmakers' future decisions than the court's conclusions whether a particular policy is constitutional or not. This nuance, which is often lost in purely quantitative analyses, is captured in the book's qualitative case study. The case study of Chapter 6 analyses several episodes of confrontation between German lawmakers and the GFCC over policies linked to law enforcement's use of intrusive surveillance measures to obtain evidence for prosecutors in the fight against organized crime and terrorism. The episodes of confrontation over the constitutionality of law enforcement's surveillance powers between the late 1990s and mid-2010s allow me to investigate whether the formal theoretical model can explain the choices of German lawmakers in the face of stringent rules on privacy rights and the GFCC's responses, when lawmakers had ostensibly dismissed these rules.

The final chapter then summarizes the book's key message for the reader. Not all lawmakers self-censor their policy choices in anticipation of constitutional review. Those who intentionally pursue constitutionally questionable policies, despite widespread warnings, send a credible signal to courts about their readiness to evade compliance with unfavourable judgments. The book presents evidence that this message is clearly received by courts. It demonstrates that German lawmakers were repeatedly able to pressure the GFCC, one of the most powerful constitutional courts in modern democracies, to relax legal constraints on their policy choices by deliberately crossing constitutional boundaries.

The chapter concludes with a discussion of the normative importance of the book's findings. Constitutional courts are intended to serve as a safeguard against constitutional violations by the political branches. However, the book demonstrates that this safeguard is not without its weaknesses. When lawmakers are willing to evade compliance with court rulings and endure any electoral consequences, courts ultimately lack the power to stop them. The normative implications of this finding are complex and challenging. It cannot be encouraging for democracies that value the rule of law if determined lawmakers can bypass constitutional limits. On the other hand, if unaccountable judges continue to impose constitutional jurisprudence that restricts the decision-making of elected lawmakers, they too undermine the principles of representative democracy. Ultimately, the book argues against the notion that modern democracies are effectively governed by courts. However, this assurance against 'juristocracy'—or rule by courts—comes with a cost: constitutional norms and rights may not always be enforced on the issues most important to lawmakers and their core constituents.

2
When Lawmakers Push Constitutional Limits and Courts Back Down

In most modern constitutional democracies, courts can invalidate executive and legislative acts for their constitutional incompatibility and play a critical role in ensuring that the elected branches respect constitutional norms (see Ginsburg and Versteeg, 2014). Prominent scholars have provided extensive evidence of how courts exercising constitutional review *passively* shape the actions of lawmakers. Stone (1989) shows that analysts of the legislative process in the French parliament must consider both the direct and indirect influence of the French Constitutional Council. The French parliament operates in the shadow of the Constitutional Council and 'there is some basis for the view that the institution does function as a kind of third legislative chamber within parliamentary space', an umpire in the political game (Stone, 1989, 30). Similar arguments have been made regarding the indirect influence the German Federal Constitutional Court (GFCC) exerts on the legislative process in the German parliament, compelling lawmakers to 'self-censor' their policy-making (see for example Landfried, 1992; Vanberg, 2005; Hönnige and Gschwend, 2010; Engst, 2021), and the Court of Justice of the European Union, which sees lawmakers in EU Member States draft their policies 'with Luxembourg in mind' (Blauberger, 2012, see also Wasserfallen 2010).[1]

However, as I argued in the introductory chapter to this book, the prospects of courts' exercise of constitutional review cannot always deter lawmakers from probing the constitutional boundaries to policy. Not every case of constitutional review actually merits a judicial veto, and not every act that is eventually invalidated by a court represents an instance of lawmakers willingly flouting constitutional limits on their policy-making. Yet, there is evidence that some policies end up in court because lawmakers in government persisted in their pursuit of controversial plans despite tangible risks of breaching constitutional limits. Hönnige and Gschwend (2010, 510) show that between

[1] Luxembourg is the seat of the Court of Justice of the European Union.

Putting Courts Under Pressure. Philipp A. Schroeder, Oxford University Press. © Philipp A. Schroeder (2025).
DOI: 10.1093/9780198953265.003.0002

1997 and 2007, members of the German Bundestag and state governments in the German Länder referred approximately five federal laws to the GFCC for review each year, with about half ultimately being declared unconstitutional by the Court. In subsequent chapters of this book, I provide ample evidence from debates in the German Bundestag, which suggests that its members tend not to wait until a policy's adoption to voice their constitutional concerns. Instead, lawmakers are not afraid to make their voices heard throughout the legislative process, in committee hearings and parliamentary debates. The following excerpt from a Member of Parliament's statement during the German Bundestag's debate on the 2008 *Act Reforming Inheritance and Valuation Taxation* is illustrative:

> Christine Scheel (Greens): For today's vote, you submitted a highly complex body of legislation, envisioning preferential treatment for some citizens and disadvantages for others. I'm predicting that owing to its unconstitutionality—this has been widely discussed—this legislation will end up in Karlsruhe.[2] It doesn't bode well for parliamentary democracy if legislation is passed, despite knowing it fails to conform with our constitutional guidelines.[3]

Put simply, judicial vetoes of governing majorities' policies rarely come out of the blue, and the writings often had been on the walls of parliamentary chambers. What seems puzzling is that the evidence laid out in subsequent chapters of this book shows that lawmakers in government not only disregard constitutional concerns coming from the opposition benches, which may be motivated by political opportunism rather than genuine constitutional concerns. Every once in a while, warnings from independent experts heard during the committee stages and governing majorities' own political allies also fall on deaf ears. Why would lawmakers pursue policies that provoke confrontation with a court capable of censoring them?

This chapter's focus is to present a theoretical model that can explain this behaviour and identify its implications for the decision-making of courts in systems of limited government. The model I present in this chapter draws on a formal, game-theoretic analysis. I have laid out the general gist of my argument in the introductory chapter and here I provide a detailed but accessible

[2] Karlsruhe is the seat of the GFCC.

[3] Translated from German, excerpt from the second reading of the 2008 Act Reforming Inheritance and Valuation Taxation, German Bundestag, 27 November 2008, 2. Beratung: BT-PlPr 16/190.

discussion of the more intricate elements of the model and its empirical implications, while leaving the mathematical proofs of my argument to an appendix at the end of this chapter.

2.1 Confrontation and judicial self-restraint

At the heart of the theoretical model is a dilemma for courts tasked with reviewing the acts of the legislative and executive branches. Judges know that their decisions censoring the policies of governing majorities are unlikely to be viewed favourably by the latter and increase the chance of backlash. Not every instance of criticism of courts amounts to serious court-curbing or threatens to undermine courts' institutional integrity. However, it is unlikely that a court challenging the elected branches will ever escape some form of resentment and complaints that unaccountable judges unduly constrain the will of the democratically elected institutions (Carrubba et al., 2015, but see Fox and Stephenson 2011; Ward and Gabel 2019 for a discussion of reasons why lawmakers themselves may welcome judicial vetoes).

At the same time, even if courts are prepared to face the music and challenge policies favoured by a political majority, they know that lawmakers may attempt to evade compliance with their judgments and find ways to continue to apply the policies objected by the court (see Vanberg, 2005; Staton and Vanberg, 2008; Carrubba and Zorn, 2010). Hence, courts challenging the constitutionality of policy not only risk backlash, they do so knowing that they may walk away from confrontation with the elected branches without achieving their preferred outcome, the correction of policy in line with their constitutional jurisprudence.

The dilemma for courts is then to assess whether challenging lawmakers over policy is worth the risk. In the following, I model this dilemma as courts' uncertainty about the *type* of lawmakers they are facing. Given that lawmakers themselves risk to spoil their electoral prospects if they choose to evade compliance with the demands of courts (see Vanberg, 2001; Clark, 2010), some, but certainly not all, lawmakers may be willing to defend their policy choices against a judicial veto and accept the electoral risks that come with it.

Section 1.1.2 of Chapter 1 outlined several plausible reasons from the existing literature that explain why and when certain lawmakers might be more likely than others to risk evading compliance. First and foremost, lawmakers may simply value some policies more than others and be more willing to evade compliance with judicial vetoes on policies they consider as a key priority and highly salient (Dahl, 1957, 286). Responding to a judicial veto by abandoning a policy central to a governing majority's political agenda may be more painful than backing down on a policy of lesser importance, prompting the former to risk non-compliance. Further, some lawmakers may hope to increase their (short-term) support from a particular electoral constituency by pursuing a controversial policy (see for example Fox and Stephenson, 2011; Ward and Gabel, 2019). Finally, existing literature shows that the transparency of the political environment affects the costs of non-compliance (Vanberg, 2005; Staton, 2006; Krehbiel, 2016), and it may be easier for lawmakers than judges to assess whether a political issue is likely to gain traction in the media and create the necessary transparency and public attention that would render non-compliance too risky (but see Blauberger et al., 2018, highlighting that judges 'read the newspapers, too').

Regardless of which combination of these expectations is at work in reality, the critical assumption at the heart of my theoretical model is that courts lack *perfect information* of whether or not lawmakers would evade compliance with their judgments. Note that a lack of perfect information does not imply that courts are entirely clueless about the type of lawmakers they are facing. The model developed below incorporates courts' prior beliefs about lawmakers' types, meaning that courts can form reasonable expectations of what type of lawmakers they are facing. For example, courts are likely to acknowledge that they operate in a political environment where lawmakers face pressure to pursue a constitutionally controversial policy—potentially defying the court's ruling—to address intense political competition or meet the demands of a specific electoral constituency. The key to the model is simply the absence of courts' *certainty* about the lawmakers' type.

I expect courts to prefer challenging the actions of lawmakers who will eventually comply with their judgments over walking away bruised and empty-handed from run-ins with non-compliant lawmakers. Crucially, the solution to courts' dilemma over figuring out which of these two scenarios they are navigating lies in the costs that lawmakers themselves risk from confrontation with the courts. Being censored by a court comes with political costs for those who had openly supported the objected policies. These costs bite in situations in which the target of a judicial veto is not the correction of an unintended consequence of policy (see Rogers, 2001), but when lawmakers had received clear and unequivocal advice during the policy-making stages that their choices infringe on constitutional norms. When lawmakers ignore credible warning signs that their favoured policies are unconstitutional and choose to push these policies through parliament regardless, censure by a court offers ammunition to lawmakers' political opponents, including critics within their own party, to discredit their political acumen among the electorate. After all, upon taking up their mandate in the legislature or executive office, lawmakers are sworn to respect and protect the constitution. Ignoring concerns of breaching constitutional norms voiced by representatives of all political colours, followed by censorship through a court, allows members of the opposition parties and critics to publicly question lawmakers' commitment to 'play by the rules' (see Vanberg, 1998).

Notably, these costs are distinct from the costs lawmakers risk paying should they evade compliance and get caught (Mayhew, 1974; Vanberg, 2001). Should a court strike constitutionally controversial policies, lawmakers who had pushed these policies through the legislature pay the price for provoking confrontation regardless of whether or not they actually choose to evade compliance with the court's judgment. In other words, lawmakers who willingly risk confrontation with a court create political costs they suffer *ex post* should a court veto their policies.

Lawmakers' demonstrated willingness to bear these costs weighs on courts' decision to challenge and strike down their policy choice. Lawmakers are aware that they risk paying a political price for provoking confrontation with courts over the constitutionality of their policies. Accordingly, compliant lawmakers, who are ultimately willing to faithfully implement a judgment that struck their policy should be less likely to take this route. They would have to pedal back, re-draft their policies in light of the court's jurisprudence, while still suffering the political fallout from the judicial veto. For these types of lawmakers, 'auto-limiting' their policy choices and accommodating any constitutional concerns to avoid a court's scrutiny in the first place appears to be the more attractive option. On the flip side, this implies that the lawmakers who do *not* avoid confrontation with the court and are undeterred in their pursuit of constitutionally controversial policy are more likely to be the types of lawmakers prepared to evade compliance. Before I formalize the argument in the next section and show how lawmakers' choices at the policy-making stage affect courts' decision-making, I discuss the final building block of my theoretical model.

The model rests on an assumption that lawmakers can actually identify the constitutional limits to their policies at the policy-making stage and are thus able to evaluate whether a court would be likely to strike their policy choices. This assumption effectively requires that lawmakers can form reasonable expectations about the direction of future constitutional review judgments. The legal reasoning that courts provide in existing case law plays a critical role here. Such reasoning embedded in courts' decisions 'is helping to structure the outcomes of future disputes' (Hansford and Spriggs, 2006, 6, see also Bueno de Mesquita and Stephenson 2002; Clark 2016). In other words, the legal precedent courts set in a particular judgment provides clues for lawmakers how the former will decide similar cases in the future.

Resolving constitutional review cases, courts create rules, which define what kind of policies would qualify as compatible with the constitution and guide the resolution of future cases (see Lax and Cameron, 2007; Carrubba and Clark, 2012; Clark and Lauderdale, 2012; Callander and Clark, 2017). Several recent studies draw on a doctrinal-politics approach, the so-called 'case-space model', which seeks to bring the theoretical arguments of scholars of judicial politics closer to what judges are actually doing in their day to day work. Making the case for the usefulness of a doctrinal-politics approach, Jeffrey Lax writes:

> This model highlights legal cases as the vehicles for policymaking, but of course judicial policymaking is more than simply case disposition after case disposition. When appellate courts address judicial policy more generally, they typically do so in opinions that establish (new or modified) legal rules for deciding current and future cases. The possible set of cases is the 'case space.' A rule is a partition of the case space into winners and losers (Lax, 2011, 133).

It is these legal rules contained in courts' jurisprudence, which separate constitutional from unconstitutional policies and serve as the constitutional guardrails for lawmakers' policy-making. In reality, these existing legal rules and jurisprudence are unlikely to always provide lawmakers a definite answer of whether a particular policy is unconstitutional or not, not least because some of the rules courts create in their judgments stick closely to the facts of a particular case and are unsuitable to be applied beyond the latter (see Fox and Vanberg, 2014). Here, the model presented in this chapter, like most game-theoretic models (Clarke and Primo, 2012), abstracts from reality and assumes that lawmakers can perfectly distinguish between policies in line and at odds with a court's jurisprudence. While this assumption benefits theoretical parsimony at the costs of simplifying reality, the model still provides a useful insight into how lawmakers' choice to adopt a policy despite expecting that it conflicts with existing jurisprudence affects a court's decision-making.

2.2 A formal model of constitutional review

In the following, I develop a game-theoretic model that captures an interaction between a lawmaker L mulling over a policy choice, and a court C which subsequently reviews the lawmaker's policy for its constitutional compatibility. To keep things simple, let the lawmaker choose from two policy options, $\rho \in \{a, b\}$. Policy a is a high-risk, high-reward policy choice for the lawmaker. For instance, the policy could entail a sweeping reform to social welfare payments (see illustration below), the introduction of a highly intrusive government surveillance programme (see Fox and Stephenson, 2011), or any other policy that engineers a significant albeit controversial change in a particular sector. The issue with policy a is that it conflicts with constitutional provisions and the court's existing constitutional jurisprudence.

To illustrate this set-up with an example, consider the sweeping labour market reforms initiated by Germany's centre-left government of the SPD and Greens in the early 2000s, with its centrepiece commonly known as the 'Hartz IV legislation'. The governing majority pushed for a reform of existing unemployment and social welfare assistance, effectively creating a uniform, means-tested provision of benefits to employable individuals and their dependents. The governing parliamentary groups of the SPD and Greens, the driving forces behind the reform, sought to respond to worsening unemployment trends in Germany and to overhaul a social welfare system perceived as largely 'inefficient and intransparent'.[4] In the course of the reform, the governing majority inter alia had to decide on standard benefits payments for employable yet jobless individuals and their dependents, i.e. their partners living in the same household and their children. Clearly, deciding on relatively low payment rates promised to relieve pressure on the public purse. Yet, in their deliberations lawmakers also had to respect the German constitution's requirement that public social assistance must guarantee a subsistence minimum that is in line with human dignity. As it turned out, in this instance lawmakers fell short of the mark. A case questioning the constitutionality of the payment rates eventually reached the GFCC, which ruled in February 2010 that benefit payments envisioned by the Hartz IV legislation failed to meet the constitution's requirement of guaranteeing an acceptable subsistence minimum for those who received the assistance.

[4] See draft legislation for the Fourth Act on Modern Services in the Labour Market, 5 September 2003, BT-Drucksache 15/1516.

The German lawmakers of the SPD and Greens could have opted for a different, less ambitious reform, albeit one that also promised lower expected pay-offs (e.g. a policy that made only minor changes to existing rules on social assistance or one that envisioned higher benefit payments to avoid falling foul of constitution provisions). In the model presented here, these lower-risk, lower-reward policies are captured by the policy b. These types of policies allow lawmakers to pre-empt judicial scrutiny, but the reward from implementing the policy is ultimately lower than what the more ambitious plans for policy a promised. In other words, policy b captures lawmakers' 'auto-limitation' option in the face of judicial scrutiny (see Stone, 1992; Vanberg, 2005; Engst, 2021).

With this distinction in hand, let us consider the sequence of play of the theoretical model. I develop an extensive form game of incomplete information involving three players, Nature N, the lawmaker L and the court C. Adding a third player, Nature, is a tool commonly used in formal models to allow one player, here the lawmaker, to be better informed about a certain aspect of the game than the other player, here the court. The model's sequence of play is shown in Figure 2.1.

At the start of the game, Nature randomly selects the lawmaker's type, $\theta \in \{0, 1\}$. If $\theta = 1$, the lawmaker is non-compliant and evades compliance with a judicial veto that censors her policy choice. If $\theta = 0$, the lawmaker is compliant and corrects any policy struck by the court in line with the spirit of the latter's

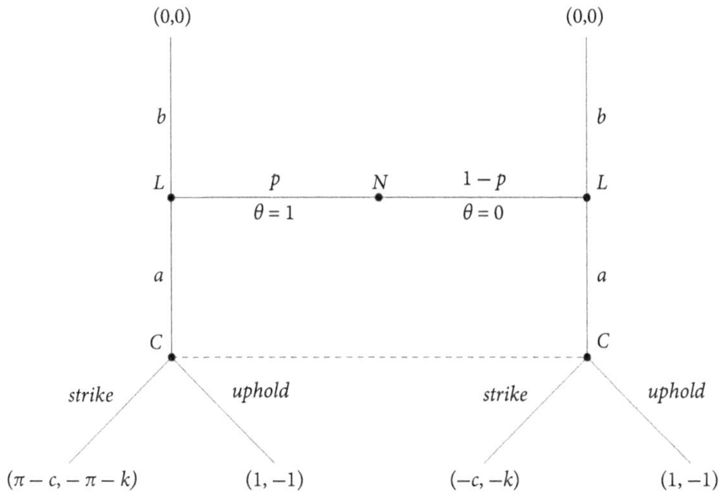

Figure 2.1 Sequence of play and realized outcomes

decision. Nature's draw is only revealed to the lawmaker, hence the court is uncertain about the lawmaker's type. The court's prior beliefs that it is facing a non-compliant lawmaker are characterized by the probability $Pr(\theta = 1) = p$. As indicated above, the court is not clueless but ultimately unsure about what type of lawmaker it is dealing with. Following Nature's draw, the lawmaker then chooses from her two policy options, $\rho \in \{a, b\}$. Given policy *a* conflicts with constitutional norms, if the lawmaker chooses option *a*, the court is called upon to exercise constitutional review and decides whether to strike or uphold policy *a*, $d \in \{strike, uphold\}$. After the court's choice, the lawmaker's type is revealed and the respective pay-offs are allocated to the lawmaker and court.

The lawmaker prefers policy *a* over *b*, and ceteris paribus would like to see policy *a* being implemented at the end of the game. The court, on the other hand, would suffer a cost whenever the unconstitutional policy *a* continues to be applied at the end of the game, either because the court decided to uphold the policy or because the lawmaker evaded compliance with a ruling striking the policy. When policy *a* remains on the books after the court's decision, the lawmaker receives a pay-off of 1, while the court suffers costs of –1. For simplicity, let both the lawmaker and the court receive a pay-off of 0 when policy *b*, the 'auto-limitation' option, is on the books at the end of the game. Note that these pay-offs' values are essentially arbitrary, yet not their relation. What is important is that the lawmaker strictly prefers policy *a* over *b*, while the opposite is the case for the court.

The lawmaker and the court both anticipate costs should the court decide to strike policy *a* as unconstitutional. The court knows that the lawmaker may discipline it for striking her preferred policy. Hence, let the court anticipate costs $k \in \mathbb{R}_+$ (i.e. any positive, real number) for striking policy *a*. Lawmakers' backlash in response to an unfavourable judgment can come in many forms, including statements seeking to undermine the public's faith in courts' institutional legitimacy, cuts to courts' budgets or even amendments to their jurisdiction (see for example Whittington, 2003; Llanos et al., 2015). Given the severity of threats to courts' authority varies across these different responses, the model allows the court's anticipated costs *k* to vary as well. The lawmaker, on the other hand, knows that a judicial veto of policy *a* comes with costs $c \in \mathbb{R}_+$, the political fallout from being censored by the court. The model allows the lawmaker's costs to vary as not every judicial veto of a policy will throw the political future of those who authored the policy in jeopardy. Yet, as discussed in the previous section, a court's veto can provide lawmakers' political opponents the necessary tailwind to successfully undermine the electorate's belief in lawmakers' commitment to 'play by the rules' (see Vanberg, 1998).

Finally, the court knows that it may rely on the lawmaker responsible for passing policy *a* to give effect to its decision to strike policy *a*. Typically, lawmakers' response to a court's constitutional veto of their policy does not immediately follow the court's decision. Floor time in the legislature has to be re-allocated and the policy addressing (or at least pretending to address) the court's judgment needs to be shuttled through the legislative process, which requires time. Accordingly, the lawmaker's ability to evade compliance with a judicial veto is conditional on her retaining office long enough to actually be in charge of implementing the court's decision. Let $\pi \in (0, 1)$ denote the probability that the same lawmaker responsible for policy *a* will still be in office to take charge of implementing the court's decision.

Summarizing the model's primitives yields the following Bernoulli utility functions for the lawmaker and the court:

$$U_L = I_L(I_C(\theta\pi - c) + (1 - I_C))$$
$$U_C = I_L(I_C(-\theta\pi - k) - (1 - I_C))$$

Here, I_L identifies the lawmaker's choice of policy ($I_L = 1$ if the lawmaker chooses policy *a*; $I_L = 0$ if she chooses policy *b*) and I_C identifies the direction of the court's decision ($I_C = 1$ if the court chooses to strike policy *a*; $I_C = 0$ if the court chooses to uphold policy *a*). To illustrate, assume the lawmaker's type is non-compliant, $\theta = 1$. If she chooses policy *a* ($I_L = 1$) and the court chooses to uphold ($I_C = 0$), the lawmaker's utility is simply $U_L = 1$, whereas the court's utility is $U_C = -1$. However, should the court instead decide to strike ($I_C = 1$), the lawmaker's utility is determined by $U_L = \pi - c$, while the court's utility is determined by $U_C = -\pi - k$. In this game, a strategy for the lawmaker is a mapping from her type into a policy choice, $\rho : \theta \rightarrow \{a, b\}$. A strategy for the court is a mapping from its prior beliefs about the lawmaker's type into a constitutional review decision, $d : p \in (0, 1) \rightarrow \{strike, uphold\}$.

2.2.1 Analysis

In the following, I derive predictions about both the lawmaker's policy choice and the court's response should the lawmaker choose policy *a*. The type of game described above is commonly known as a *signalling game*. Here, the actions of one player, typically the one who gets to choose an action first, reveal or *signal* information about a particular aspect of the game, in our case the lawmaker's type. Equilibrium solutions to signalling games are known as perfect

Bayesian equilibria (PBE). In these equilibria, every player forms beliefs about where exactly they are along the game tree, and then selects their best possible response given these beliefs (McCarty and Meirowitz, 2007, 209). In our case, it is the court which has to figure out whether it is making its choice to strike or uphold the policy on the left or right branch of the game tree shown in Figure 2.1, i.e. whether it is facing a non-compliant or compliant lawmaker.

Three types of PBE can be supported in this signalling game. First, in a so-called *separating equilibrium* the lawmaker chooses different strategies contingent on her type and the court can subsequently perfectly update its prior beliefs about the lawmaker's type. Put simply, after the lawmaker has made her policy choice, the court is no longer uncertain about her type but knows exactly whether it faces a compliant or non-compliant lawmaker. Second, the game supports several *pooling equilibria*. In these kinds of equilibria, the lawmaker chooses the same strategy regardless of her type and the court is unable to update its prior beliefs. Whatever beliefs the court had about which type of lawmaker it is dealing with, the lawmaker's policy choice provided no further clues that would allow the court to reduce its uncertainty about the lawmaker's type. Finally, the game supports a so-called *partial-pooling equilibrium*. In these scenarios, a particular type of lawmaker may mix (or randomize) among her strategies, and while the court can glean some information from the lawmaker's choice, it is ultimately unable to perfectly update its prior beliefs about the lawmaker's type.[5] In the following paragraphs, I first identify the various equilibria that are supported by the game, and in the subsequent section then discuss their empirical implications. All formal proofs for these equilibria are gathered in the technical appendix to this chapter.

I begin the formal analysis with scenarios in which the court never defers to the lawmaker should the latter opt for policy a. Whenever the probability that the lawmaker responsible for policy a would also take control of the implementation of the court's judgment is low enough relative to the court's costs of striking policy a, the court has no incentive to defer to the lawmaker. Specifically, when $\pi \leq 1 - k$, two types of PBE can be supported. A separating equilibrium exists, in which the non-compliant lawmaker ($\theta = 1$) opts for policy a and the compliant lawmaker ($\theta = 0$) for policy b. As long as the lawmaker's costs satisfy the condition $c < \pi$, the non-compliant lawmaker's preferred choice is to opt for policy a, despite knowing that the court would strike it. In addition, given $\pi \leq 1 - k$, two (similar) pooling equilibria exist, in

[5] Note that the formal proofs in the technical appendix to this chapter show that the court remains uncertain whether or not it faces a non-compliant lawmaker should the lawmaker choose policy a, yet knows that it faces a compliant lawmaker should the latter choose policy b.

which both types of lawmakers self-censor their policy-making in anticipation of the court's veto and never opt for policy *a*.

Proposition 1. *Provided* $\pi \leq 1 - k$, *the court strikes whenever the lawmaker chooses policy a. Given* $c < \pi \leq 1 - k$, *a* separating *PBE exists in which the lawmaker chooses policy a if* $\theta = 1$ *and policy b if* $\theta = 0$, *and the court chooses to strike policy a. Given* $\pi \leq 1 - k \leq c$, *a* pooling *PBE exists in which the lawmaker always chooses policy b, and the court would have struck policy a off the equilibrium path. Finally, given* $\pi \leq c < 1 - k$, *a* pooling *PBE exists in which the lawmaker always chooses policy b and the court chooses to strike off the equilibrium path.*[6]

The separating equilibrium exemplifies an interesting dynamic. It shows that despite the court's best response to strike down any policy conflicting with its jurisprudence, the non-compliant lawmaker will still opt for policy *a* whenever the probability π that she gets a shot at evading implementation of the court's ruling is sufficiently high relative to the costs *c* she suffers from a veto. This finding suggests that as long as the lawmaker's anticipated political fallout from a judicial veto is negligible, the mere possibility of revisiting and redrafting the policy in the future undermines the deterrent effect that constitutional review is expected to impose on lawmakers. I further discuss this finding in my interpretation of the formal results below and return to it in subsequent chapters that discuss the quantitative and qualitative empirical evidence from Germany. The two pooling equilibria identified in Proposition 1 show that otherwise, the lawmaker's expected costs from suffering a judicial veto induce her to pass policies respecting the court's jurisprudence and pre-empt the court's exercise of constitutional review altogether.

Next, I analyse equilibrium behaviour for the remaining parameter space of π, i.e. $\pi > 1 - k$. In these scenarios, two types of PBE can be supported. I first consider a pooling equilibrium, in which the lawmaker always picks policy *a* over policy *b*, irrespective of her type. If the court's prior beliefs of facing a non-compliant lawmaker are sufficiently high relative to its own costs *k* and the probability of relying on the lawmaker for faithful implementation π, the court' best response is to show deference in its exercise of constitutional review and uphold policy *a*.

6 Referring to the choice(s) of the court 'off the equilibrium path' here simply says how the court would react if the lawmaker chose policy *a*. Given that in equilibrium the lawmaker never chooses policy *a* in these scenarios, the node where the court can actually make a decision in the game tree in Figure 2.1 is never actually reached.

Proposition 2. *Provided $\pi > 1 - k$ and $p > (1 - k)/\pi$, a* pooling *PBE exists in which the lawmaker always chooses policy* a *and the court always upholds policy* a.

The pooling equilibrium defined in Proposition 2 shows that the court defers to the lawmaker when it expects to suffer high costs from striking the lawmaker's preferred policy, i.e. high values on k, and faces a lawmaker with a lasting grip on political power, i.e. high values on π.[7] This finding resonates with existing scholarship showing that the prospects of turnover in government office—or lack thereof—are systematically related to the deference courts show towards the elected branches in their jurisprudence (see Ramseyer and Rasmusen, 2001; Ishiyama Smithey and Ishiyama, 2002; Stephenson, 2003). For instance, analysing more than 7,500 decisions issued by justices on the Argentine Supreme Court between 1976 and 1995, Helmke (2002) provides evidence that justices increasingly issue judgments challenging government towards the end of both weak dictatorships and weak democratic governments, yet act more deferentially as long as the incumbent demonstrates a firm grip on political power.

The model's final equilibrium shows that under certain conditions, the court has an incentive to self-restrain even when it occupies a generally powerful position, that is when the prospects of being disciplined by lawmakers for striking policy are low (i.e. low values on k) and when the court can generally expect that its rulings are subsequently implemented (i.e. low values on p). Provided the probability that the lawmaker responsible for policy a would also take charge of implementing the court's decision is sufficiently high, the court makes a probabilistic decision of whether or not to strike policy a, which is conditional on the lawmaker's costs c.

Proposition 3. *Given $\pi > 1 - k$ and $p \leq (1 - k)/\pi$, a* partial-pooling *PBE exists in which the lawmaker always chooses policy a if $\theta = 1$ and policy a with probability $q(\pi)^* = \frac{p(\pi + k - 1)}{(1-k)(1-p)}$ if $\theta = 0$, and the court chooses to strike policy a with probability $r(c)^* = 1/(1 + c)$.*

Notably, in situations described by this partial-pooling equilibrium, the probability $r(c)^*$—the likelihood that the court strikes down policy

[7] Note, the threshold $(1-k)/\pi$ decreases in both k and π, hence an increase in both k and π means that the parameter space for the court's prior beliefs p supporting the pooling equilibrium of Proposition 2 increases as well.

a—decreases as c, the cost the lawmaker would incur from a judicial veto, increases. Similarly, the probability $q(\pi)$, i.e. the probability that the compliant lawmaker opts for policy a increases with the costs of the backlash the court expects from striking policy a. Evidently, in the context of the partial-pooling equilibrium their counterpart's costs play an important role in the court and compliant lawmaker's optimal strategies. I explore the logic behind this finding in my interpretation and discussion of the comparative statics in the next section.

2.2.2 Interpretation and comparative statics

The equilibrium behaviour of the court and lawmaker for the full space of the parameter π (i.e. the probability that the same lawmaker who passed policy a would also control the implementation of a judicial veto of policy a), and the parameter p (i.e. the court's prior belief that it is facing a non-compliant lawmaker) is illustrated in Figure 2.2. The five equilibria discussed above and displayed in Figure 2.2 can be ranked according to the court's ability to ensure that only policies respecting the boundaries it defines in its constitutional jurisprudence eventually find their way into the statute books. I discuss them in the order of this ranking in the following.

The two pooling equilibria *Pooling (1)* and *Pooling (2)* in Figure 2.2 suggest that the court is most successful in preventing the application of policies conflicting with its constitutional jurisprudence when lawmakers' expected costs from being censored by a court are sufficiently high and when it is unlikely that lawmakers can hold on to political power long enough to be in a position to evade compliance with the court's judgment.[8] This observation fits neatly with the expectations of scholars arguing that courts do not necessarily have to play an active role in order to ensure that policies stay within the boundaries of the constitution (see Landfried, 1992; Stone, 1992; Rogers and Vanberg, 2007).

Provided that it is sufficiently costly for lawmaker to be at the receiving end of a court's veto, opting for a high-reward albeit constitutionally controversial policy is simply not worth it for any lawmaker lacking the prospects of having a shot at evading compliance with the court's judgment. As long as the court

[8] This latter expectation is captured by the threshold $1 - k$ for the parameter π. In every equilibrium that falls to the left of the threshold $1 - k$ in Figure 2.2, the court censors any policy conflicting with its jurisprudence (but note that this does not necessarily prevent that such policies are eventually applied, which is further illustrated in the discussion of the separating equilibrium).

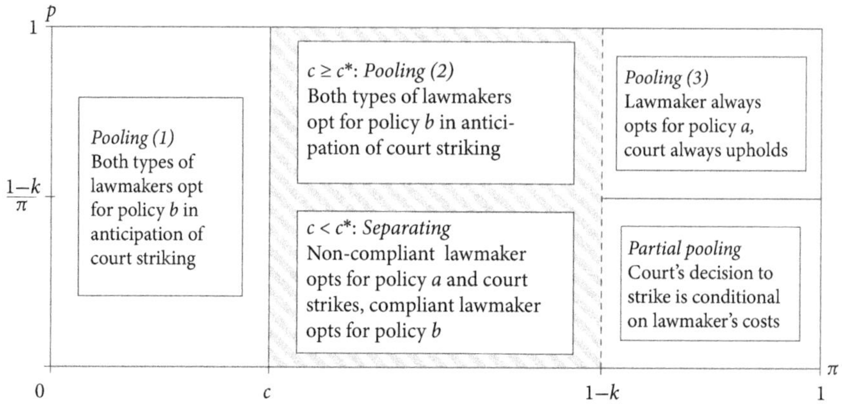

Figure 2.2 Equilibrium predictions. The parameter π denotes the probability that the lawmaker controls implementation; p denotes the court's prior beliefs about the lawmaker's type; k denotes court's cost for striking a policy; c denotes the costs the lawmaker pays when the court strikes policy a. The threshold c^* is defined as $c^* \equiv 1 - k$

has little to fear in the way of both backlash in the immediate aftermath of a judicial veto and non-compliance once lawmakers re-legislate, it can essentially act unconstrained and would censor any policy that conflicts with its interpretation of the constitution. Knowing that, the lawmaker 'auto-limits' her policy-making and addresses any constitutional concerns that come up during the policy-making stages to ensure that the policies she adopts align with the court's constitutional jurisprudence (for a similar argument, see Stone Sweet, 2007). The drivers of such 'auto-limitation' are the costs the lawmaker expects to pay should the court censor her policies. Unless there are costs to ignoring constitutional boundaries, the lawmaker has no incentive *not* to opt for its preferred policy, even if an application of such policy would violate constitutional norms. This dynamic is evident again in the model's separating equilibrium. It is important to note that in this equilibrium the court still chooses to strike any policy that conflicts with its interpretation of the constitution. If we think of the court's judgments in constitutional review cases in terms of legal rules separating constitutional from unconstitutional policies (see Lax, 2007; Landa and Lax, 2009), then the legal rules the court establishes in scenarios captured by the separating equilibrium reflect its sincere interpretation of the constitution.

However, the separating equilibrium also shows that the non-compliant lawmaker will still opt for its preferred policy, despite knowing that the court will strike it. While this behaviour may initially seem counter-intuitive, the separating equilibrium provides the first indication that a lawmaker's choice to provoke confrontation with a court capable of striking her policies can be entirely rational. Provided the expected costs of a judicial veto, c, are outweighed by the pay-offs the lawmaker receives from her chosen policy and as long as the lawmaker has a realistic shot at controlling government office in the aftermath of the court's veto, adopting the high-risk high-reward, constitutionally controversial policy option is preferable over 'auto-limiting' and working out an alternative, lower-reward policy that respects the court's constitutional jurisprudence. In other words, there is a space for scenarios in which neither a determined lawmaker nor a court would be willing to back down from confrontation. Notably, this separating equilibrium indicates that the court's ability to ensure that applied policies fall within the limits of its constitutional jurisprudence can be compromised without the court ever deferring to the elected branches. Under the conditions stated above, the prospects of the court's exercise of constitutional review fail to be an effective deterrent for some lawmakers. While the court *formally* defines legal rules that match its sincere interpretation of the constitution, it cannot prevent at least some lawmakers from—at least temporarily—implementing policies with effects that stray beyond constitutional boundaries *in practice*.

Lawmakers' costs from confrontation with the court operate in an intuitive way in scenarios captured by the separating equilibrium. The lesser the costs from a judicial veto weigh against the pay-offs from policy, the fewer the inhibitions among lawmakers against pursuing policies that conflict with courts' constitutional jurisprudence. Moving on to the partial-pooling equilibrium illustrated in the bottom-right corner of Figure 2.2, the formal model shows that lawmakers' costs from confrontation with a court can play another, distinct role in the strategic interactions among courts and lawmakers in systems of limited government.

Compared to the conditions captured by the equilibria discussed in the previous paragraphs, the political environment captured by the partial-pooling equilibrium differs in one respect. While the court still has little to fear from court-curbing (i.e. low values on the parameter k), lawmakers now stand a good chance of staying in office long enough to be in charge of implementing and possibly evading a court's judgment that challenges their policies (i.e. high values on the parameter π).[9] Technically, for the partial-pooling equilibrium to take centre stage, the relationship between these two parameters could also

[9] Note that high values on π and low values on k (or vice versa) also mean that the court's prior beliefs are more likely to satisfy the partial-pooling equilibrium's condition $p \leq (1 - k)/\pi$ than if both π and k have high values.

be inverted (i.e. high values on k and low values on π). However, I believe that in reality we are more likely to encounter the former kind of political environment, where courts enjoying comfortable levels of diffuse public support that shield them from serious assaults on their institutional integrity face lawmakers able to count on getting a shot at responding to the court's decision during their time in government office.

The model's partial-pooling equilibrium shows that under these conditions, both the non-compliant and compliant lawmaker are prepared to pursue policies that conflict with the court's constitutional jurisprudence. Notably, the latter type of lawmaker makes a probabilistic choice of whether or not pursue such a policy. The probability with which the compliant lawmaker opts for a policy that provokes conflict with the court increases with the likelihood that she stays in office to take charge of implementation (i.e. the parameter π), the costs the court expects to pay should it strike the policy (i.e. the parameter k), and the court's prior beliefs of facing a non-compliant lawmaker (i.e. the parameter p).[10] This seems intuitive: As higher values on these parameters make striking policy riskier and costlier for a court hoping to avoid non-compliance with its judgments, the tide turns in favour of the (compliant) lawmaker, who in turn becomes less inhibited in her pursuit of policy conflicting with the court's jurisprudence.

Like the compliant lawmaker, the court plays mixed strategy and makes a probabilistic choice whether to strike down an unconstitutional policy. In Section 2.2.1, we saw that the probability of the court striking an unconstitutional policy *decreases* in the lawmaker's costs c. This finding appears somewhat odd. Why would the court reduce the rate at which it strikes policy a as lawmakers' costs from a judicial veto increase? Put differently, why would the court decide whether to strike a controversial policy based on the costs that lawmakers—not the court itself—would suffer as a consequence? The proofs for the partial-pooling equilibrium in the appendix show that the court is *less* likely to believe that it is facing a non-compliant lawmaker when it assumes that the compliant lawmaker in equilibrium *frequently* opts for policy a.[11] Vice versa, if compliant lawmakers rarely opt for policy a, the court has reason to believe that it is most likely dealing with a non-compliant lawmaker whenever it reviews policy a. From the court's viewpoint, a compliant lawmaker should

[10] Recall that the partial-pooling equilibrium shows that the compliant lawmaker chooses policy a with probability $q(\pi)^* = \frac{p(\pi+k-1)}{(1-k)(1-p)}$.

[11] Note that the court's posterior beliefs of facing a non-compliant lawmaker given by $Pr(\theta = 1 \mid a) = \frac{p}{p+q(1-p)}$ decrease in q, the probability with which the compliant lawmaker opts for policy a.

generally be more cautious about opting for the unconstitutional policy *a* if the costs of a judicial veto are high. After all, the compliant lawmaker would not challenge the court's decision to strike policy *a* and implement the less-attractive policy *b* in response while still suffering the costs from the judicial veto's fallout. In such scenarios, opting for policy *a* despite looming high costs *c* allows the lawmaker to send a potentially painful but therefore credible signal of a non-compliant type (see Humphreys, 2016, 60).

This logic also bears out in the compliant lawmaker's decision-making in the partial-pooling equilibrium, albeit not in immediately obvious ways. On the one hand, for the compliant lawmaker to stick with her mixed strategy (i.e. probabilistically choosing policy *a* over policy *b*) and to prefer it over always defaulting to policy *b*, she must be indifferent between the average pay-offs she receives from either of the two policies. High costs *c* for the lawmaker following a judicial veto simply make it less likely that this condition holds.[12] On the other hand, my discussion of the compliant lawmaker's strategy suggests that the likelihood of choosing an unconstitutional policy is entirely independent of the costs the lawmaker expects to incur in the event of a judicial veto. This implies that the lawmaker's costs do not directly influence the court's updating of its beliefs about the lawmaker's type. However, the compliant lawmaker is aware of the court's strategy. The lawmaker understands that, in equilibrium, the court will reduce the frequency with which it strikes down policy *a* as the lawmaker's costs *c* from a judicial veto increase, following the logic described earlier. In other words, while the lawmaker's costs seem to affect only the court's strategy, they are crucial for the lawmaker as well. This is because the lawmaker's expectations about the court's strategy influence her own decisions, which in turn affect the court's beliefs about the lawmaker's type.

In essence, in scenarios captured by the partial-pooling equilibrium, the court 'listens to the pain' that lawmakers appear prepared to bear (see Humphreys, 2016, 60, see also Fearon 1997), and factors the lawmaker's costs of a judicial veto into its decision-making. Figure 2.3 provides a simple illustration of how the variation in the lawmaker's costs translates into the decision-making of the court. The horizontal axis displays the lawmaker's (increasing) costs, while the vertical axis displays the probability of the court striking a policy that conflicts with its constitutional jurisprudence. It is easy to see that the probability of the court striking policy decreases as the lawmaker's

[12] In fact, the proofs for the partial-pooling equilibrium show for that for this condition to hold, the court needs to lower the rate at which it strikes policy *a* sufficiently to offset the costs the compliant lawmaker suffers in the event of a judicial veto.

expected costs from being censored by the court increase (including scenarios where the lawmaker's costs c actually exceed the pay-off she receives from implementing her preferred policy). The court becomes more likely to defer to the lawmaker as the costs the lawmaker appears willing to bear from confrontation with the court increase.

Note that in scenarios captured by the partial-pooling equilibrium the court never becomes entirely deferential to the lawmaker. The negative marginal effect of the lawmaker's costs shown in Figure 2.3 gradually decreases as these costs increase and the court always strikes policy with some positive probability.[13] Consequently, it is these environments, with a powerful lawmaker facing a powerful court, in which we should be able to observe lawmakers and courts repeatedly clashing over the constitutionality of policy, as neither faces sufficient incentives to consistently shy away from confrontation. Yet, it is also these kinds of environments in which we should expect courts to defer to lawmakers over the constitutionality of policy from time to time. The model predicts that courts will grant lawmakers more leeway in their constitutional jurisprudence than they would ideally prefer—and that the likelihood of courts deferring increases with the costs lawmakers risk from confrontation.

The model's final equilibrium, *Pooling (3)* in Figure 2.2, captures scenarios in which the cards are stacked against the court. In these political environments it is highly likely that lawmakers will stay in office long enough to be in a position to evade compliance with a judicial veto (i.e. high values on the parameter π) while the court also expects to pay high costs for striking lawmakers' policies (i.e. high values on the parameter k).[14] Put simply, it is

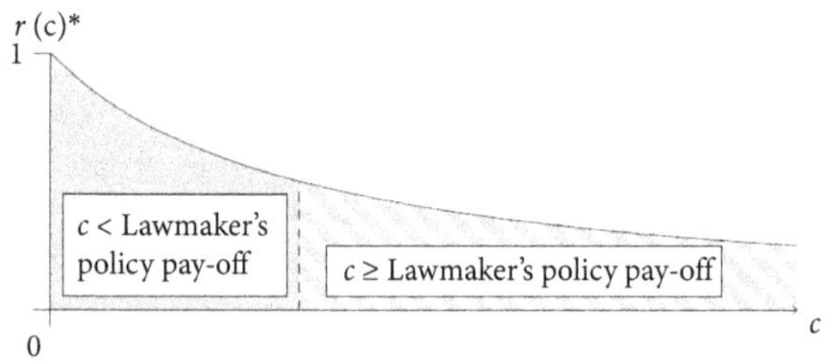

Figure 2.3 Probability $r(c)^*$ of court striking policy a conditional on lawmaker's cost c in a partial-pooling equilibrium with $\pi > 1 - k$ and $p \leq (1 - k)/\pi$

[13] Technically, the probability $r(c)^* = 1/(1 + c)$ can take on the value zero in its limit as $c \to \infty$.

[14] Note that high values on the parameters π and k also lower the threshold $(1 - k)/\pi$ for the parameter p, which means that the court finds itself subject to the incentives characterized by the pooling equilibrium *Pooling (3)* even if its prior beliefs of facing a non-compliant lawmaker are relatively low.

these scenarios in which a court is most likely to walk away empty-handed from a bruising confrontation with lawmakers.

The model then predicts that the court will choose to defer to lawmakers whenever the latter pursue policies that conflict with the court's jurisprudence. Knowing that, neither type of lawmaker is deterred from pursuing such policies. In other words, in these scenarios courts are in the least favourable position to ensure that policies stay within the limits of its constitutional jurisprudence: The court deliberately crafts legal rules to classify lawmakers' policies as constitutional.

In reality, we may find such environments in (semi-)authoritarian polities, which at least formally grant courts the power of constitutional review (see for example Gandhi, 2008; Moustafa and Ginsburg, 2008). In these environments, the electoral connection between those controlling the levers of political power and their constituents may be compromised, which allows the former to stay in office long enough to respond to any court judgment concerning their policies. An underdeveloped electoral connection also diminishes the potential inhibitions lawmakers may have against curbing courts.

This does not necessarily mean, however, that courts facing such an environment are indefinitely trapped in the pooling equilibrium. While the model developed in this chapter stays silent on this issue, others have shown that even courts facing initially adverse political environments can gradually develop their institutional authority and become an effective constraint on political power (see Ginsburg, 2003; Carrubba, 2009). Moustafa (2003), for instance, shows how the Egyptian constitutional court developed from an institutional guarantee signalling the Egyptian regime's commitment to property rights into an authority capable of providing activists and human rights groups an avenue to challenge the state (see also Ginsburg, 2003; Moustafa, 2007).

Before I summarize the observations I have made based on my formal analysis of the model and translate them into empirically testable hypotheses in the final section of this chapter, I briefly discuss what I believe should not be concluded from my formal analysis. Arguably the two most interesting and novel findings of my analysis are that under certain conditions, pursuing policies that will be struck by a court is a rational choice for lawmakers, while at times courts will choose to defer to lawmakers when the latter risk provoking a potentially costly confrontation for themselves. One may gain the impression upon reading this chapter that we should expect lawmakers to frequently and willingly pursue policies that conflict with courts' existing constitutional jurisprudence. However, it is worth recalling that the model is built on the premise that a lawmaker prefers a policy that conflicts with a court's jurisprudence over any other possible alternative.

In reality, this may actually be the case from time to time, and the evidence laid out in the next chapter in fact shows that incidentally German lawmakers pursue evidently unconstitutional policies. At the same time, there appears to be little reason to believe that lawmakers *generally* favour policies a court would object to. In other words, lawmakers' choice to provoke confrontation with courts over policy is a rare yet nonetheless important event for understanding and explaining courts' decision-making in systems of limited government.

2.2.3 Empirical implications

The formal model developed in this chapter has several implications, which can be empirically evaluated. In the remainder of this book, I will provide empirical tests for some of these implications, and where this is not possible I will nonetheless make an effort to provide quantitative and qualitative evidence to illustrate the plausibility of these claims. The first empirical implication I consider draws on the observation derived from the formal model's separating equilibrium. The model predicts that some lawmakers pursue policies despite knowing that the court will strike them. Provided the political costs from being at the receiving end of the court's veto are negligible, these lawmakers also know that they may get a chance at evading compliance with the court's decision in the future, making confrontation with the court worth the risk. Hence, under these conditions, lawmakers opt for their preferred albeit constitutionally controversial policies instead of settling for any less attractive alternatives that would be in line with the court's constitutional jurisprudence:

Hypothesis 1. *Ceteris paribus, lawmakers should be more likely to risk confrontation with a court when the costs from such confrontation are low.*

The second empirical implication I consider in the remainder of the book concerns the probability that the authors of a policy reviewed by a court would also be in charge of implementing the latter's decision on that policy. As we move through the theoretical model's equilibria, the formal analysis suggests that, ceteris paribus, as it becomes more likely that lawmakers will cling onto power long enough to take charge of implementing a judgment on their policy choices, the risks of non-compliance increase for a court. Assuming courts lacking the 'power of the purse or sword' face incentives to avoid issuing decisions that are ultimately not enforced by the legislative and executive branches then leads to the following hypothesis:

Hypothesis 2. *Ceteris paribus, a court should be less likely to strike a policy when the probability that the policy's author controls implementation of the court's decision is high.*

The probability that a policy's authors would take charge of implementing the court's corresponding constitutional review decision also plays an implicit role in the model's final empirical implication I consider here. The model predicts that a court should be more likely to deal with constitutionally controversial policies when lawmakers can expect to hang onto power long enough to respond to the court's decisions. In these scenarios, the shadow of constitutional review fails to deter non-compliant *and* compliant lawmakers in government from pursuing policies at odds with a court's jurisprudence.

A key implication of the model is that courts should be more likely to show self-restraint in their decision-making when lawmakers had ignored advice on the constitutionality of their policies and thus face prospects of suffering high political costs *ex post* a judicial veto. Ignoring warning signs of constitutional violations during the policy-making stages can come back to bite lawmakers should a court actually censor their policies. It lends the political opposition and critics (including those in lawmakers' own party), who had identified constitutional issues later addressed by the court, an opportunity to score political points by publicly questioning their political acumen and commitment to upholding the constitution. The model suggests that lawmakers showing their willingness to bear these costs are signalling a credible non-compliance threat to the court, leading to the following hypothesis:

Hypothesis 3. *Ceteris paribus, a court should be less likely to strike a policy when lawmakers had risked suffering high political costs for provoking confrontation with a court.*

2.3 Conclusion

In this chapter, I presented a formal theoretical model, which explains why lawmakers at times adopt policies that conflict with courts' constitutional jurisprudence and predicts how courts respond when lawmakers provoke confrontation with them by pursuing such policies. The model explicitly addresses a dilemma for courts lacking immediate control over the implementation of their constitutional review rulings: How can courts avoid issuing judgments that are subsequently not implemented by lawmakers? The model provides a simple answer to this question. Lawmakers credibly signal a non-compliance threat if their actions provoking confrontation with courts are tied to high political costs.

The theoretical model predicts that when facing a credible non-compliance threat, courts become less likely to strike policy as unconstitutional and establish legal rules in their jurisprudence that grant lawmakers more leeway for their policy-making. Accordingly, by provoking confrontation with courts over the constitutionality of their policies, lawmakers can indirectly shift the constitutional limits to policy in their favour. In the remainder of this book, I bring original evidence from the GFCC's exercise of constitutional review and the German Bundestag's policy-making to bear on this and other claims made in this chapter. The next chapter discusses the rationale behind selecting Germany as the case for this study and shows how a combination of quantitative and qualitative research designs allows me to test the theoretical model's empirical implications.

2.4 Technical appendix

This appendix provides formal proofs of the propositions defined in this chapter. Without loss of generality, consider the following tie-breaking assumptions:

- If indifferent between policy *a* and *b*, the lawmaker will choose policy *b*.
- If indifferent between striking and upholding policy *a*, the court will choose to strike.

Proof of Proposition 1 (Separating equilibrium): *Suppose the lawmaker chooses policy a if* $\theta = 1$ *and policy b if* $\theta = 0$. *The court's posterior beliefs are given by* $Pr(\theta = 1 \mid a) = 1$ *and* $Pr(\theta = 0 \mid a) = 0$. *The court chooses to strike policy a if* $-\pi - k \geq -1$. *Solving for* π *yields* $\pi \leq 1 - k$. *Given* $\pi \leq 1 - k$ *and* $\theta = 1$, *the lawmaker has no incentive to deviate from choosing policy a if* $\pi - c > 0$. *Solving for* π *yields* $\pi > c$. *Given* $\pi \leq 1 - k$ *and* $\theta = 0$, *the lawmaker has no incentive to deviate from choosing policy b if* $-c \leq 0$ *or* $c \geq 0$. *A separating equilibrium exists if* $c < \pi \leq 1 - k$.

Proof of Proposition 1 (Pooling equilibria): *Suppose the lawmaker chooses policy b if* $\theta = 1$ *and policy b if* $\theta = 0$. *Off the equilibrium path, arbitrary* *values can be assigned to the court's posterior beliefs, i.e.* $Pr(\theta = 1 \mid a) = \lambda$ *and* $Pr(\theta = 0 \mid a) = 1 - \lambda$. *Off the equilibrium path, the court chooses to strike policy a if* $\lambda(-\pi - k) + (1 - \lambda)(-k) \geq -1$. *Solving for* λ *yields* $\lambda \leq (1 - k)/\pi$. *Given* $\lambda \leq (1 - k)/\pi$ *and* $\theta = 1$, *the lawmaker has no incentive to deviate from its prescribed strategy if* $0 \geq \pi - c$. *Solving for* π *yields* $\pi \leq c$. *Given* $\lambda \leq (1 - k)/\pi$ *and* $\theta = 0$, *the lawmaker has no incentive to deviate from its prescribed strategy if* $0 \geq -c$ *or* $c \geq 0$. *If* $c < 1 - k$ *and* $\pi \leq c$, *then the condition* $\lambda \leq (1 - k)/\pi$ *is always satisfied and a pooling equilibrium exists if* $\pi \leq c < 1 - k$. *If* $c \geq 1 - k$ *then the condition* $\lambda \leq (1 - k)/\pi$ *is always satisfied if* $\pi \leq 1 - k$ *and a pooling equilibrium exists if* $\pi \leq 1 - k \leq c$.

Proof of Proposition 2: *Suppose the lawmaker chooses policy a if* $\theta = 1$ *and policy a if* $\theta = 0$. *The court's posterior beliefs are given by* $Pr(\theta = 1 \mid a) = p$ *and* $Pr(\theta = 0 \mid a) = 1 - p$. *If the lawmaker chooses policy a, the court chooses to uphold policy a if* $p(-\pi - k) + (1 - p)(-k) < -1$. *Solving for p yields* $p > (1 - k)/\pi$. *Given* $p \in (0, 1)$, *this condition is satisfied if* $\pi > 1 - k$. *Given the court always chooses to uphold policy a, the lawmaker has no incentive to deviate from its prescribed strategy. A pooling equilibrium exists if* $\pi > 1 - k$ *and* $p > (1 - k)/\pi$.

Proof of Proposition 3: *Suppose the lawmaker chooses policy a if* $\theta = 1$ *and policy a with probability* $q(\pi)^*$ *if* $\theta = 0$. *Suppose the court strikes policy a with probability* $r(c)^*$. *The court's posterior beliefs are given by* $Pr(\theta = 1 \mid a) = \frac{p}{p+q(1-p)}$ *and* $Pr(\theta = 0 \mid a) = \frac{q(1-p)}{p+q(1-p)}$. *Playing a mixed strategy, the court is indifferent between striking and upholding if* $\frac{p}{p+q(1-p)}(-\pi - k) + \frac{q(1-p)}{p+q(1-p)}(-k) = -1$. *Solving for q yields* $q(\pi)^* = \frac{p(\pi+k-1)}{(1-k)(1-p)}$. $q \in [0, 1]$ *requires that* $\frac{p(\pi+k-1)}{(1-k)(1-p)} \leq 1$. *Solving for p yields* $p \leq (1 - k)/\pi$. *Given* $p \in (0, 1)$, *this condition is satisfied if* $\pi > 1 - k$. *If* $\theta = 0$, *the lawmaker has no incentive to deviate from her mixed strategy if* $r(-c) + 1 - r = 0$. *Solving for r yields* $r(c)^* = 1/(1 + c)$. *If* $\theta = 1$, *the lawmaker has no incentive to deviate from choosing policy a if* $r(\pi - c) + 1 - r > 0$. *Solving for r yields* $r < 1/(1 + c - \pi)$. *Plugging in* $r(c)^*$ *and solving for* π *yields* $\pi > 0$, *which is always satisfied given* $\pi \in (0, 1)$. *A partial pooling equilibrium exists if* $\pi > 1 - k$ *and* $p \leq (1 - k)/\pi$.

3
Methodology

The previous chapter has spelled out my expectations for how courts' compliance dilemma shapes legislative-judicial interactions in modern systems of separation of powers. Throughout the remainder of this book, I bring quantitative and qualitative evidence to bear on the hypotheses derived from the theoretical model of Chapter 2. Yet, before I dive into the details of how I collected this data and my analyses thereof, this chapter discusses the rationale behind the mixed-methods research design employed in this book and the choice of Germany as the focus of my study.

I begin by familiarizing the reader with the role the German Federal Constitutional Court (GFCC) plays in Germany's political system, and note the similarities Germany's system of constitutional review shares with courts' exercise of constitutional review in other domestic and supranational contexts. I then highlight why Germany, and specifically the GFCC's review of federal legislation, presents a suitable environment to test the key empirical implications of my game-theoretical model. More importantly, I discuss why Germany is a 'hard case' for my argument, making it likely that the dynamics found here are relevant to other democratic settings as well. I outline how the model's empirical implications map onto Germany's political environment, and discuss which of the model's equilibrium predictions we should find at play in the GFCC's interactions with the governing coalitions controlling the levers of political power in the federal government and the Bundestag.

In the next section, I then zero in on the choice of a mixed-methods research design to test the game-theoretical model's empirical implications. I show how a statistical analysis of the GFCC's constitutional review decisions of federal legislation coupled with evidence from the legislative proceedings that had produced the reviewed legislation allows me to evaluate key claims of my theoretical model. Here, I also discuss the types of insights a statistical analysis of my data cannot deliver, and outline how a focused, qualitative case study of a string of connected cases heard at the GFCC and the political branches' responses offers an insight into the motivations of both the Court and lawmakers that drive the patterns observed in the quantitative analysis. The chapter

Putting Courts Under Pressure. Philipp A. Schroeder, Oxford University Press. © Philipp A. Schroeder (2025).
DOI: 10.1093/9780198953265.003.0003

then closes out by summarizing what types of patterns we should see in the behaviour of German lawmakers and the GFCC, and how a combined look at quantitative and qualitative evidence allows me to gauge whether the game-theoretical model of the previous chapter can explain why lawmakers take ostensibly ill-advised constitutional risks in their policy choices—and why they can have reasonable hopes of getting away with it.

3.1 Constitutional review in Germany

In many ways, the GFCC is an archetypical example of a constitutional court at the heart of a *centralized* system of constitutional review, a system envisioned by the Austrian legal scholar and philosopher Hans Kelsen, popularized throughout much of Western Europe in the aftermath of World War II (see Capelletti, 1989; Vanberg, 2005). Unlike in the judicial system of the United States in which 'any judge of any court, in any case, at any time, at the behest of any litigating party, has the power to declare a law unconstitutional' (Shapiro and Stone Sweet, 1994, 400), the GFCC is the only court in Germany that can resolve legal questions that involve Germany's constitution, the Basic Law (see Vanberg, 2005, 79). Every institution in Germany that exercises public authority is obliged to observe the provisions of the Basic Law, ranging from Germany's public agencies administering unemployment benefits to regional fiscal courts adjudicating taxation claims and, of course, Germany's federal parliament and government. The German Basic Law provides a comprehensive portfolio of fundamental rights and constitutional protections, including not just personal rights along with a general guarantee of the right to equality but also state duties such as ensuring the provision of an educational system affording young people adequate educational opportunities (see Stone Sweet, 2000a).

The GFCC consists of two so-called Senates, each of which comprises eight judges, with at least formally distinct jurisdictions. The First Senate predominantly hears cases involving an alleged incompatibility of legal provisions with fundamental rights, and is hence designated as the GFCC's 'Grundrechtssenat' (i.e. fundamental rights senate). Aside from any proceedings not expressly assigned to the First Senate, the Second Senate inter alia adjudicates disputes concerning the distribution of legislative competences between the federal state organs and the German Länder, and is thus often referred to as the 'Staatsrechtssenat'. Decisions by the two Senates are reached via simple majorities. Notably, in the event of a tied vote in a case concerning the constitutional compatibility of legislation, the GFCC cannot declare the legislation as unconstitutional. Further, unless individual judges disagreeing with the majority opinion write a published dissenting opinion, there is no way of knowing how judges voted in a particular case as voting records are not made public.

The German system of constitutional review offers several avenues for how the rights, freedoms, and duties guaranteed by the Basic Law can be invoked at the GFCC. First, *constitutional complaints*, by far the most common type of proceeding heard at the GFCC with roughly 6,000 complaints landing in the Court's docket annually, can be lodged by any natural or legal person to assert their fundamental rights vis-à-vis the state. Constitutional complaints afford private actors an important role in constitutional adjudication and the development of constitutional jurisprudence in Germany, offering a direct route for individuals and private interests to the GFCC provided certain preconditions regarding their claims are met.[1]

Second, any ordinary court in Germany's judicial system can refer an act of public authority for review to the GFCC. Courts make use of this proceeding known as *concrete norm control* whenever they believe that the act resulted in a breach of a constitutional right of a party to a particular case they need to adjudicate. Lower federal and state courts often hear cases involving disputes between individuals and public authorities. Generally, authorities' decisions are made pursuant to federal or state laws, and in deciding their cases courts may find that the application of a particular law results in infringements of individuals' constitutional rights. Given that ordinary courts in Germany cannot invalidate laws for their constitutional incompatibility themselves, they then refer these cases to the GFCC.

Finally, the federal government itself, state governments, or one-quarter of the members of the German Bundestag can refer a statutory act for review to the GFCC via a proceeding known as *abstract norm control*. Contrasting concrete norm control proceedings, the GFCC exercises abstract norm control in the absence of a particular legal dispute in an ordinary court and *a posteriori*, i.e. after the promulgation of a statutory act. Typically, abstract norm control proceedings are initiated by members of the opposition parties in the Bundestag or one of Germany's 16 state governments, providing another—last ditch—avenue to challenge government policy outside of the legislative arena (see Stone Sweet, 1999; Hönnige and Gschwend, 2010; Brouard and Hönnige, 2017).

[1] Natural and legal persons lodging a constitutional complaint with the GFCC against a sovereign act of the state, including legislation, must show that they are individually, presently, and directly affected by the challenged act, and they must have exhausted all other legal remedies before ordinary courts prior to lodging their complaint with the GFCC.

While the GFCC's decisions in response to constitutional complaints and referrals from lower courts can have significant implications for the work of lawmakers in parliament and government, abstract norm control proceedings are arguably the clearest sign that the GFCC assumes an important political role in Germany's polity. At least formally, the GFCC's decisions are the final word on constitutional questions and binding on all other institutions exercising public authority, albeit with the caveat highlighted in the previous chapters that the GFCC effectively lacks the power to enforce its rulings (see Vanberg, 2005). In accordance with the Federal Constitutional Court Act (FCCA), the GFCC's decisions concerning the constitutionality of legislation themselves have the force of law, although legislation struck by the GFCC for its unconstitutionality may not always immediately cease to have effect. To avoid the detrimental effects of voiding a legislative provision without an adequate replacement at hand, the Court may determine a date until when the law can continue to be applied, while urging lawmakers to find an alternative, constitutionally compatible arrangement within that timeframe (see Krehbiel, 2021).

Importantly, we find many of the features of Germany's decentralized system of constitutional review in other national contexts as well. Specialized constitutional courts with an exclusive mandate to interpret constitutional provisions and their implications for state acts, including the authority to strike legislation as unconstitutional, are a centrepiece of the judicial systems in several Western European countries, such as France, Italy, Portugal, and Spain (see Stone Sweet, 2000b; Volcansek, 2000; Hanretty, 2012). Kelsen's favoured system of centralized review via a specialized court guarding the constitution also served as the blueprint for the judicial systems instituted in Central and Eastern Europe in the aftermath of the fall of the Soviet Union (Schwartz, 2000; Epstein et al., 2001b; Vanberg, 2005, for a more recent discussion of constitutional politics in Central and Eastern Europe, see Pócza, 2018). Of course, there are also differences between the German system and the systems of constitutional review found in other European countries. Not every system offers a direct route for citizens to a constitutional court to invoke their rights via a complaint proceeding, and in some countries abstract review may only be exercised *a priori*, before legislation is enacted (see for example the French Conseil constitutionnel's review powers discussed in Stone, 1989, 1992; Brouard and Hönnige, 2017). Further, the catalogue of constitutional rights and norms that can be invoked varies across polities (Stone Sweet, 2000a). Yet, the core feature of a constitutional court that can review the actions of lawmakers, scrutinize legislation against constitutional provisions, and where it deems necessary strike policy to send lawmakers back to the drawing board, is present throughout these systems, a feature that throws these constitutional courts into the fray of legislative politics.

Germany's system of constitutional review not only has close cousins in other nation states, some of its key characteristics can also be found at the European Union's supranational level. Not unlike the GFCC, with its exclusive competence to interpret Germany's constitution and spelling out its implications for the actions of institutions exercising state authority, the Court of Justice of the European Union (CJEU) fulfils a very similar role in the European Union's political system. Among the CJEU's main tasks is the interpretation of European Union law, clarifying how Union primary (i.e. the treaties of the European Union) and secondary law shape what the EU's Member States can and cannot do in their policies at the national and supranational level (see Alter, 2014; Carrubba and Gabel, 2015; Larsson and Naurin, 2016; Ovádek, 2021). The CJEU has thus arguably assumed the role of the 'Master of the Treaty', asserting Union law even when it compromises EU Member States' national sovereignty (Alter, 1998, but see for example Garrett et al., 1998; Carrubba et al., 2008; Larsson and Naurin, 2016 highlighting that the CJEU is not immune to influences from Member States).

A key pillar of the CJEU's ability to foster the uniform application of Union law throughout the EU, even against the interest of at least some national governments, has been the so-called preliminary reference procedure (see Alter, 2001, 2014; Conant, 2001; Craig and de Búrca, 2020). The preliminary reference procedure allows any national court adjudicating a dispute involving Union law to refer a question regarding its interpretation to the CJEU, including questions concerning the compatibility of national and Union law (Craig and de Búrca, 2020). Coupled with the principles of Union law's direct effect and its supremacy over national law (Burley and Mattli, 1993), the preliminary reference proceeding opens the door to domestic actors in EU Member States challenging national policies that ostensibly conflict with the provisions of primary and secondary Union law (for an example of how domestic interest groups were able to influence the United Kingdom's gender equality policy via the preliminary reference proceeding, see Alter and Vargas, 2000). Hence, similar to concrete review proceedings in the German system, lower (here, national) courts play an important role in providing a steady stream of cases for the CJEU to develop its jurisprudence, while private actors have access to an indirect route to challenge national policies in court (see Kelemen, 2006, 2011; Pavone, 2019).

Several scholars have highlighted the CJEU's political impact and shown how the CJEU's jurisprudence shapes political decision-making at both the national and European levels (see Wasserfallen, 2010; Blauberger, 2012; Martinsen, 2015, 2011; Blauberger and Schmidt, 2017). The CJEU's political impact is not only felt when it rules that a national measure contravenes Union law, lawmakers in European capitals are also urged to ensure that their policies comply with the CJEU's past and, crucially, its *future* jurisprudence (Wasserfallen, 2010; Martinsen, 2015). As Blauberger (2012) aptly puts it, national governments craft their policies 'with Luxembourg in mind' and are keenly aware in the drafting stages that their legislation may eventually be reviewed by the CJEU.

To summarize, the GFCC is one out of a universe of cases of courts exercising constitutional review of executive and legislative acts, scrutinizing policies for their compatibility with constitutional law, and striking those policies where constitutional boundaries are crossed. These types of courts inevitably assume a political role in their respective polities, not just by striking policies off the statute books but also by incentivizing lawmakers in governments and parliaments to consider courts' constitutional jurisprudence when drafting their policies. In other words, constitutional courts project a 'second face of power' (Engst, 2021, see also Vanberg, 2001, 2005; Blauberger, 2012). Put simply, the GFCC, like other well-established constitutional courts in modern systems of separation of powers, is acting as a veto player in the Germany political system, an institution that the political branches must reckon with in their legislative decision-making (Hönnige and Gschwend, 2010; Brouard and Hönnige, 2017). However, as highlighted in the introductory chapter to this book, courts like the GFCC are far from exercising constitutional review in a political vacuum and must consider other, in particular political, actors' responses to their jurisprudence when writing their judgments (Epstein and Knight, 1998; Epstein et al., 2001a; Epstein and Jacobi, 2010). None of these courts, whether at the national or the supranational level, can fully escape the compliance dilemma and the implications of their inability to enforce their own decisions discussed in the previous chapters and existing scholarship (see Vanberg, 2005; Carrubba et al., 2008; Carrubba and Zorn, 2010; Clark, 2010).

With such a plethora of constitutional courts reviewing the acts of lawmakers for their constitutional compatibility to choose from for this study, why pick the GFCC as the case for this book? In the following section, I discuss why the GFCC's interplay with lawmakers in the Bundestag and federal government provides an insightful albeit challenging environment for an empirical analysis of the game-theoretic model's empirical implications set out in Chapter 2.

3.2 Challenging a trusted court

While the GFCC is not operating in a political vacuum and its judges are well-aware of the political implications of their decisions, mechanisms are in place to foster the Court's independence from the political branches and its political impartiality. Pursuant to the FCCA, judges at the GFCC are appointed for 12-year terms and cannot be reappointed to the Court after their term expires.[2] Eliminating the possibility of reappointment reduces judges' incentives to prioritize political expediency in their decisions, as they no longer need to seek favour with the governing coalition to secure another term (see Vanberg, 2005, 85). Further, following the appointment procedure spelled out in the FCCA, half of the GFCC's judges are elected by the Bundestag upon a proposal of a selection committee, comprising 12 members of the Bundestag, while the other half is elected by the representatives of the 16 state governments in Germany's upper parliamentary chamber, the Bundesrat. Two-thirds majorities are required in these chambers, respectively, hence effectively granting the main opposition parties veto power in the appointment process and somewhat defusing the often highly politicized nature of such proceedings that we can observe elsewhere, especially in the United States (Moraski and Shipan, 1999; Shipan, 2000). Notwithstanding these supermajority requirements, Germany's major political parties maintain an informal agreement that half of the seats in each of the GFCC's Senates are filled with candidates favoured by the centre-right CDU/CSU and the other half with candidates favoured by the centre-left SPD, while their likely junior coalition partners, the liberal, business-friendly FDP and the ecologist Green party, generally get to propose a favoured candidate of their own while in government (Vanberg, 2005, 83).

Political considerations are certainly not absent from appointment proceedings to the GFCC,[3] yet they are far less politicized than appointments

[2] In addition, judges cannot serve on the GFCC beyond their retirement age, currently 68 years in Germany, and cannot serve in any other professional occupation other than professor of law in German higher education during their term.

[3] A case in point is the political drama that unfolded in determining the successor of Justice Ernst Gottfried Mahrenholz, a SPD-appointee, in the early 1990s, as the CDU/CSU blocked the appointment of Herta Däubler-Gmeling, then a member of the SPD's federal board, to the GFCC. Der Spiegel, 28 March 1993. *Diskretes Dutzend: Die Union will Herta Däubler-Gmelin nicht zur Verfassungsrichterin wählen*, accessed 10 August 2023.

to the U.S. Supreme Court (see for example Krehbiel, 2007; Bartels and Johnston, 2013). Generally, despite its undeniable political influence, the GFCC has managed to develop its profile as an independent, impartial, and thus well-respected institution among the German public since its establishment in 1951. Data covering the mid-1980s up until the early 1990s collected by the Emnid Institute and reported by Vanberg (2005, 98) provides evidence of the German public's trust in and support for the GFCC. Table 3.1 shows that the public's trust in the GFCC as an institution not only seems to be high, consistently outranking trust in the Bundestag or the federal government, it also appears to be fairly stable over the years (the general drop in trust in institutions shown for 1993 in Table 3.1 captures the inclusion of respondents from East Germany, a pattern also reflected in the data provided by Gibson et al., 1998). Further, there is no indication that the German public's high trust in the GFCC abated in more recent years. Table 3.2 reports data from the German General Social Survey, again capturing the German public's trust in the GFCC, the Bundestag, and federal government between 2008 and 2018, which reinforces the impression that the GFCC's standing among the German public by far outweighs that of the executive and legislative branches.

The German public's trust in the GFCC plays a critical role in my case selection in several ways. The observed high level of trust strongly implies that challenging the court's authority and failing to faithfully comply with its jurisprudence comes with high political costs for lawmakers, most likely in the form of electoral backlash (see Mayhew, 1974; Vanberg, 2001, 2005; Clark, 2009). Accordingly, the GFCC is in a relatively comfortable position vis-à-vis the political branches and can reasonably expect that its decisions are generally complied with by the latter. In the language of the game-theoretic model of Chapter 2, the GFCC's prior beliefs that is facing a non-compliant lawmaker

Table 3.1 Proportion of respondents stating that they trust an institution in response to the question 'I am now going to read you a list of public institutions and organizations. Please tell me for each institution or organization whether you trust it, or whether that is not the case. How about . . .?' Table is based on the work by Vanberg (2005, 98) and reports data from Emnid Institute (1995)

Institution	1982	1986	1990	1993
GFCC	82%	85%	84%	73%
Bundestag	61%	74%	65%	44%
Federal government	59%	66%	61%	43%

Table 3.2 Proportion of respondents reporting values of 5 and above on a 7-point Likert scale in response to the survey item 'I am now going to read out a number of public institutions and organisations. Please tell me for each institution or organisation how much trust you place in it. Please use this scale: 1 means you have absolutely no trust at all – 7 means you have a great deal of trust.' Table reports data from Leibniz Institute for the Social Sciences (2018)

Institution	2008	2012	2018
GFCC	62%	67%	70%
Bundestag	27%	36%	42%
Federal government	29%	37%	40%

(i.e. the model's parameter p) are generally very low. Lawmakers should rarely value a policy so highly or have the resolve to risk challenging the authority of Germany's most trusted state institution over it.

Further, should the GFCC actually strike government policy, the backlash from the governing coalition and its supporters is likely to keep within limits. The GFCC is certainly not immune to criticism and German lawmakers are not afraid to occasionally vent their frustration with the judges in Karlsruhe. For instance, in response to a series of GFCC decisions invalidating federal laws, one of the most senior members of the Christian-conservative CDU and then-President of the Bundestag, Norbert Lammert, penned a rather thinly veiled threat in one of Germany's most prominent newspapers, the *Frankfurter Allgemeine Zeitung*. Lammert wrote that a parliament left overly restricted by the GFCC's jurisprudence may 'choose to defend itself' and amend the constitution 'in order to avoid unwelcome jurisprudence in the future'.[4] Publicly characterizing the GFCC's impact on politics as out of place certainly has its effects and may shake some citizens' confidence in the Court. Yet, against the backdrop of the GFCC's comfortable reservoir of public support, the likelihood that such threats translate into more serious action against the Court, for instance in the form of restrictions to its jurisdiction, budget cuts or even the abolition of the institution altogether, is minimal in Germany.

Where does that leave us when it comes to studying the game-theoretic model's expected effects of the judiciary's compliance dilemma on the

[4] Original in German, Frankfurter Allgemeine Zeitung, 10 May 2017. *Lammert fordert Zurückhaltung*, https://www.faz.net/aktuell/politik/inland/bundesverfassungsgericht-lammert-fordert- zurueckhaltung-15009324.html, accessed 2 April 2019.

decision-making of lawmakers and courts? First, recall that the model solves for a pooling equilibrium in which a court never challenges unconstitutional policy given it fears the costs of lawmakers' backlash, which outweigh the benefits of keeping unconstitutional policy off the statute books. In the German context, this equilibrium is effectively off the table. Given the strong public support that the GFCC can count on, the GFCC is highly unlikely to *always* capitulate in the face of lawmakers pushing constitutional boundaries in their policy choices. As far as the model's pooling equilibria are concerned, we are instead much more likely to find instances of German lawmakers 'auto-limiting' their policies as constitutional issues in their drafts become apparent, fixing controversial provisions and opting for alternative options instead (see Figure 2.2 in Chapter 2, see also Stone Sweet, 2000a; Engst, 2021). We can reasonably expect that a policy's value for lawmakers is typically not worth the hit their electoral stock would take from defying the GFCC's instructions. Notably, that doesn't mean that lawmakers' non-compliance with GFCC jurisprudence is entirely absent from Germany, as the case study evidence provided by Georg Vanberg shows, along with insights from interviews with GFCC judges who are aware that not all of their judgments are complied with (see Chapters 5 and 6 in Vanberg, 2005). Yet, even if German lawmakers take the plunge and opt for a policy that pushes constitutional boundaries, the GFCC's standing among the German public suggests that judges would most likely respond with censure rather than deference, the scenario captured by the model's separating equilibrium. In simple terms, Germany is hardly the place where we would expect to see lawmakers pushing policies that cross constitutional boundaries *and* the GFCC retreating from challenging them to avoid non-compliance or backlash from lawmakers.

In line with this reasoning, the German political environment presents itself as a hard case to test the implications of the game-theoretic model's partial-pooling equilibrium, arguably the model's most interesting equilibrium state. Recall that in this equilibrium, the Court refers to the costs that lawmakers appear willing to pay when risking a confrontation with the Court to inform its decision to strike down an unconstitutional policy, a classic signalling dynamic (see Figure 2.3 in Chapter 2). The higher the costs for lawmakers the stronger the signal and the lower the likelihood that the Court strikes the policy, expecting that doing so would ultimately be in vain. A key precondition for this partial-pooling equilibrium to hold is that lawmakers have reasonable expectations to cling to political power long enough to get a shot at responding to the Court's decision that struck their policy. At least with respect to this condition, over the past few decades the German political context resembles a relatively favourable case for the model's partial-pooling equilibrium. German governing coalitions have been relatively stable, and at least the major coalition party of the day consistently had reasonable hopes of holding the reins of power beyond a single term.

Figure 3.1 provides an overview of every German government cabinet in office between 1983 and 2017, along with survey data from the German Politbarometer (Forschungsruppe Wahlen, 2019), which has documented political parties' popularity among the German electorate since 1977. Figure 3.1 shows that a conservative-liberal coalition under Chancellor Helmut Kohl consistently controlled government office between 1983 and 1998. For Chancellor Kohl's first three full terms in office, Politbarometer data suggests that the governing coalition's electoral popularity dipped each mid-term, yet recovered in time for federal elections to the Bundestag in 1987, 1990, and 1994.[5]

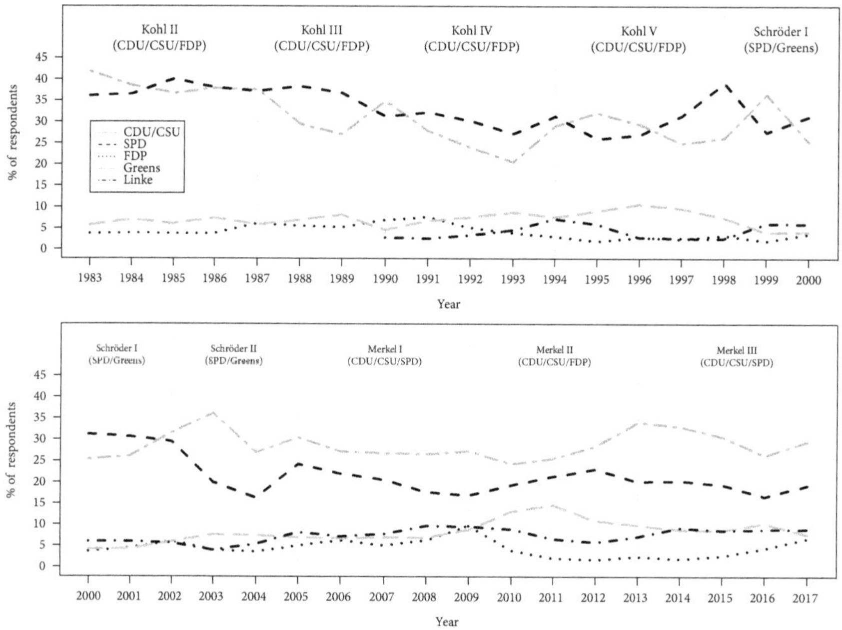

Figure 3.1 Annually cumulated proportion of respondents (in %) reporting their vote intention in response to the question 'Which party would you vote for if federal elections were held this Sunday?' Figure reports Politbarometer survey data provided by Forschungsruppe Wahlen (2019)

[5] Helmut Kohl was first elected chancellor in October 1982 when his predecessor Helmut Schmidt of the SPD lost a so-called 'constructive vote of no-confidence' in the Bundestag. Following the change in government office from a SPD/FDP-led cabinet to a CDU/CSU/FDP governing coalition, early elections were then called for March 1983.

Towards the end of Kohl's last term in office, the governing coalition of the CDU, CSU, and FDP saw its electoral support waver and lost its parliamentary majority in the 1998 elections to the SPD and the Green party. During its two terms in office, Chancellor Gerhard Schröder's cabinet pursued a sweeping reform of social welfare policy, alienating some of the SPD's traditional electoral constituencies.[6] The loss of electoral support for the SPD and Green party's governing coalition was exemplified by the SPD's performance in state parliamentary elections. Most notably, the SPD experienced dramatic losses in elections to the state parliament of North Rhine-Westphalia, one of the party's traditional strongholds, in May 2005, which prompted the Chancellor to seek early federal elections to 'find clarity whether the German public will continue to support the government's agenda'.[7] The SPD and Green party subsequently lost their governing mandate in the 2005 federal elections. From 2005 until 2021, government office had then been controlled by the CDU/CSU and Chancellor Angela Merkel, albeit with different junior coalition partners, including several so-called 'grand-coalitions' with the SPD.

This illustrative overview of public opinion and electoral shifts in Germany between the early 1980s and late 2010s supports the rationale behind my case selection: Over the past few decades, most lawmakers in government enjoyed the kind of electoral fortunes that—according to the model—would provide lawmakers with enough incentives to pursue constitutionally controversial policies provoking confrontation with the GFCC, given that they could reasonably expect to be in office to respond to judicial vetoes of their policies. From the early 1980s until the mid-1990s, the GFCC faced a relatively popular conservative-liberal coalition that managed to hold on to government office for 16 consecutive years,[8] while the political (sister) parties, the Christian-conservative CDU and CSU, consistently defined the government's agenda between 2005 and 2021 under the leadership of Chancellor Merkel.

Provided the theoretical model adequately reflects the behaviour of lawmakers and courts in systems of limited government, periods of consistency

[6] Coined as the 'Agenda 2010', Chancellor Schröder's cabinet responded to a trend of stagnating economic growth with policies reforming the labour market, social security, taxation, and public budgets. Particularly the so-called 'Hartz' legislative reform package caused controversy, as it inter alia provided incentives to individuals experiencing long-term unemployment to take up work by cutting welfare payments by up to 30% should they refuse to take a 'reasonable' job (effectively any form of legal employment), see Bundeszentrale für politische Bildung, 31 June 2007, *Die Agenda 2010*, accessed 4 April 2019.

[7] Original in German, Spiegel Online, 22 May 2005. *Politisches Beben: Schröder will Neuwahlen*, https://www.spiegel.de/politik/deutschland/politisches-beben-schroeder-will-neuwahlen-a-357076.html, accessed 4 April 2019.

[8] Effectively, Chancellor Kohl's first term in office began in October 1982 with then-Chancellor Schmidt's defeat in the Bundstag's 'constructive vote of no confidence'.

in government office should coincide with lawmakers being prepared to take high political risks when pursuing policies that provoke confrontation with the GFCC (e.g. the Conservative-led coalitions between 1983 and 1998 as well as 2005 and 2017). Yet, we should be less likely to observe lawmakers' high-risk taking when governing coalitions struggle for electoral support (e.g. the SPD-led coalitions between 1998 and 2005). I'll revisit this expectation in the next chapter, where I provide a descriptive overview of the original quantitative data I collected for this study, which substantiates my line of argument. Before doing so, I close out this chapter by outlining the benefits of a mixed-methods research design to test key empirical implications of the game-theoretic model.

3.3 A mixed-methods research design

Before I offer a deep-dive into my data collection in the next chapter, I discuss the benefits of a mixed-methods research design to test the key, and in my view most interesting, empirical implication of my game-theoretic model: Ceteris paribus, the GFCC court should moderate the rate at which it strikes policy when German lawmakers had risked suffering high political costs for provoking confrontation with the Court (see Hypothesis 3 in Chapter 2). Given the frequency with which the GFCC reviews federal legislation adopted by Germany's governing coalitions, a statistical analysis designed to test this expectation is possible. Between 1977 and 2017, the GFCC's two Senates reviewed the constitutionality of 417 legislative provisions contained in 275 federal laws, roughly ten provisions per year. A statistical analysis of these cases allows me to identify general patterns in the GFCC's review of federal legislation, and provides insights that a closer, more qualitatively minded look at a relatively small subset of cases would not be able to deliver.

Identifying whether or not the GFCC struck a reviewed provision as unconstitutional, the outcome variable of my statistical analysis, across a large set of cases is in principle relatively straightforward. After all, the GFCC explicitly states whether it found that a provision is incompatible with the Basic Law in its judgments.[9] For my analysis, I was able to draw on data provided by the *Constitutional Court Database* (CCDB, Engst et al., 2019), which provides this information for GFCC judgments published between 1972 and

[9] Although it should be noted that in the context of the GFCC's constitutional review, identifying which exact provision of which exact law was reviewed is not as trivial as one might think, an issue I will discuss in more detail in Chapter 4.

2010, and replication data provided by Krehbiel (2016), which covered GFCC decisions until 2015. I then extended this data for GFCC judgments until 2017 myself, relying on the Court's own published records. Without going into too much detail here, it is worth noting that the GFCC struck 213 out of 417 reviewed legislative provisions as unconstitutional, about half of the provisions that landed in its docket. This pattern already hints that lawmakers' auto-limitation may not reign supreme in Germany. If German lawmakers were extremely cautious not to adopt policies that are at risk of being censored by the Court, we should expect to see a much lower strike rate. It remains to be seen, however, whether there is any evidence suggesting that there are legislative provisions which the GFCC would have wanted to strike but ultimately decided to uphold.

In contrast to identifying which provisions were or were not struck by the Court, the challenge for the quantitative analysis is the development of a measure that adequately captures the political costs lawmakers risk paying when adopting ostensibly unconstitutional policies. When presenting the theoretical model in the previous chapter, I linked these costs to lawmakers' choice to ignore advice received at the policy making stages, highlighting that their plans would violate constitutional norms. When a court strikes down a policy that was already criticized for violating constitutional norms before its adoption, it gives lawmakers' critics and political opponents an opportunity to undermine their credibility with the electorate and question their commitment to upholding constitutional principles (see Vanberg, 1998). Hence, ignoring the constitutional concerns voiced during legislative proceedings can turn out to be politically costly for lawmakers should the GFCC in fact strike their policy. Crucially, lawmakers' choice to ignore objections raised publicly in parliament is also a signal easily observed by the GFCC. Each judge at the GFCC is supported by a team of four law clerks, who prepare extensive documentation on the federal laws that are reviewed, and judges are thus typically well-informed about the legislative proceedings which produced the policies they review (see also McCubbins et al., 1992).

To assess the political costs lawmakers risk when advocating for constitutionally controversial policies, I analysed the parliamentary debates surrounding all federal laws that were eventually reviewed by the GFCC between 1977—when the Bundestag's Parliamentary Documentation Division began publicly releasing debate transcripts—and 2017. I then identified whether lawmakers in the Bundestag had considered legislative provisions of the reviewed federal laws as unconstitutional prior to their adoption. Note that different provisions of the same law can be challenged in different cases heard by the

Court. For instance, separate provisions of the 2007 *Act Implementing the Residency and Asylum Directives of the European Union* were challenged in two different cases heard by the GFCC, *2 BvL 16/09* and *1 BvL 4/12*.[10] In the former, the Higher Administrative Court of Baden-Württemberg referred a case to the GFCC to consider the constitutionality of legislation allowing government to refuse residence permits for immigrants, whose next of kin had been convicted of particular crimes. The latter case involved a challenge of the constitutionality of legislation excluding immigrants with particular types of residence permits from access to public parental allowances. The fact that different parts of federal laws can be challenged in separate cases adds complexity to the statistical models I estimate, a point I revisit in Chapter 5.

Once I identified the challenged federal laws for each GFCC case, I referred to the Bundestag's Documentation and Information System for Parliamentary Material (DIP) to access the texts of the final parliamentary debates for each challenged law. Specifically, in order to avoid including lawmakers' constitutional concerns which had been addressed through a subsequent amendment, I only considered statements delivered by members of the Bundestag at debates which took place right before final votes on the law were cast.[11] I then read each of these debates and identified whether members of the Bundestag had considered the legislative provision later reviewed by the GFCC as unconstitutional. I reserve a more in-depth discussion of the coding scheme I used for my data collection for the subsequent chapter. However, to illustrate the types of statements I identified as constitutional objections, consider the following examples from several different parliamentary debates:

> Horst Gobrecht (SPD): After hearing from so many experts, I find it difficult to understand how a majority here can, I may say with open eyes, adopt a

[10] The GFCC uses a simple system to label its cases. The first number identifies the Senate hearing the case. The following code then identifies the type of proceeding: *BvL* marks concrete norm control proceedings, *BvR* marks constitutional complaints, and *BvF* marks abstract norm control proceedings. Finally, the first number of the last block identifies the annual running case file, while the second number identifies the year the respective application was filed with the court.

[11] For ordinary legislative procedures, the Bundestag schedules three readings. The third reading generally does not include a substantive debate of the law, concludes with Members of Parliaments voting on the law and usually follows straight after the second reading. Unless the Bundestag substantively debated the law at the third and final reading, I accessed the text of lawmakers' statements delivered during substantive debates at the second reading. When a federal law was passed following the meeting of a conciliation committee comprising selected representatives of the Bundestag and the Bundesrat, I considered statements delivered by members of the Bundestag after the conciliation had met.

provision that goes against the constitution and thus must end negatively, quite frankly negatively for everyone who sat here today.[12]

Rainer Funke (FDP): Federal officials employed at the Federal Post Office should not be treated differently than federal officials, for instance, working for the Federal Ministry of Finances. The FDP and myself remain committed to this principle. And that is why we will not consent to this unconstitutional law.[13]

Horst Seehofer (CSU): You simply pretend that the entire population invests four percent of its income into a private pension provision. I predict: Your approach will eventually fail at the Federal Constitutional Court. It amounts to a socio-political injustice to ask pensioners to make additional sacrifices based on an unfounded assumption that everyone in Germany invests into some form of private provision.[14]

We can reasonably expect that members of the parliamentary opposition feel far fewer inhibitions to launch such attacks on policy than lawmakers of the governing coalition caucus. Further, we would be remiss to conclude that every instance of governing majorities ignoring constitutional concerns voiced from the opposition benches is an example of lawmakers willingly disregarding constitutional norms in their policy choices. To be sure, a federal law that was objected to by the opposition parties for its supposed constitutional incompatibility is probably more likely to be eventually struck by the GFCC than a law that did not raise such concerns at all in the Bundestag. Further, ignoring well-founded concerns voiced by the parliamentary opposition, only to see their policy choices struck down by the GFCC, comes with political costs for the governing majority. However, we need to recognize that publicly discrediting policy for its alleged unconstitutionality may very well be an attempt by the opposition to score political points and reflect political opportunism rather than genuine legal concerns.

[12] Translated from German, excerpt from the second reading of the Act on the Recovery of the Economy and Employment and Unburdening of the Federal Budget in the German Bundestag, 15 December 1982, 2. Beratung: BT-PlPr 09/139.

[13] Translated from German, excerpt from the second reading of the First Act on the Amendment of the Federal Post Office Employee Act in the German Bundestag, 24 September 2004, 2. Beratung: BT-PlPr 15/127.

[14] Translated from German, excerpt from the second reading of the Act to Secure the Sustainable Financing of Public Pensions in the German Bundestag, 11 March 2004, 2. Beratung: BT-PlPr 15/97.

On the other hand, taking the step to publicly describing their political allies' policy choices as unconstitutional is a far more consequential step for members of the governing coalition caucus. While we cannot confidently rule out that these statements are also instances of political virtue-signalling, defying party discipline and publicly accusing their colleagues of failing to uphold constitutional norms is not something a member of parliament would do on a whim. Accordingly, we can expect that members of the governing coalition caucus should generally be more likely to voice constitutional concerns only if they genuinely believed that the government's plans infringe on constitutional norms.[15] Ignoring the concerns voiced by members of their own political caucus then sends a much louder, clearer signal to the GFCC, not least because doing so comes with higher political risks for lawmakers in government, relative to ignoring constitutional concerns voiced solely by the parliamentary opposition.

To summarize, I expect to find variation in the political costs lawmakers appear willing to pay when risking confrontations with the GFCC based on the sincerity of constitutional concerns members of parliament had voiced during legislative proceedings. Regressing the GFCC's decision whether or not to strike a legislative provision on the kinds of constitutional concerns the reviewed provision had evoked is the centrepiece of my empirical strategy in the quantitative analysis. Working with such observational data prevents me from making strong *causal* inferences with respect to the observed relationship between these two variables. Nonetheless, while controlling for a variety of other characteristics of the reviewed legislative provisions (further discussed in Chapter 5), the statistical analysis allows me to identify whether the GFCC increased or moderated its rate of striking legislation when lawmakers of the governing majority had joined the chorus of constitutional concerns, relative to legislation that was objected solely by members of the opposition and legislation that was not objected at all.

Albeit useful, there are insights that the statistical analysis cannot offer. First, to make the analysis of the GFCC's more than 400 constitutional review decisions feasible, I rely on an outcome variable that captures whether the reviewed legislative provision was struck down by the Court. This choice appears plausible, after all what arguably matters most is whether a legislative provision remains on the statutory books or not. However, there is more

[15] Consider for example the decision of Justice Minister Sabine Leutheusser-Schnarrenberger to resign from office in protest against government's plans for a so-called 'big eavesdropping operation' eventually implemented through the 1998 *Act on Improving Measures to Combat Organised Crime*.

nuance to the judgments of the GFCC and other courts exercising constitutional review. Prominent scholars of law and judicial politics have highlighted that the legal reasoning found in the text of courts' judgments is at least as consequential as the decisions that follow from such reasoning. Hansford and Spriggs (2006, 3) note that 'Court opinions create precedents that are relevant for future disputes and thus shape the behavior of forward-thinking actors', including lawmakers, while Clark and Lauderdale (2010, 871) argue that 'decisions are often most important because of the qualitative changes in law that they effect, rather than because of the decision they provide on the case facing the Court'. While courts' legal reasoning plays a prominent role in much of the theoretical and formal work on judicial decision-making (see for example Bueno de Mesquita and Stephenson, 2002; Lax and Cameron, 2007; Carrubba, 2012; Lax, 2012; Clark and Clark, 2016; Callander and Clark, 2017), quantitative empirical studies in the domain of political science and more specifically judicial politics have generally disregarded its significance (see Tiller and Cross, 2006). This is not surprising, considering that developing and implementing a coding scheme to operationalize the political implications of a court's legal reasoning is both highly complex and labour-intensive.

Second, although the game-theoretical model of Chapter 2 is for the sake of its simplicity drawn up as a single-shot interaction between a court and a lawmaker, it in effect captures a *repeated* game. While the game-theoretical model ends after the court issued its decision, striking or upholding the challenged policy, lawmakers responding with non-compliance will likely trigger another round of the game. In essence, the act of non-compliance is simply lawmakers adopting a new policy that conflicts with constitutional jurisprudence, the lawmaker's choice at the start of the game described in Chapter 2. With the available data, the statistical analysis cannot take account of such, often complex, connections that span across multiple cases heard at the GFCC and legislation adopted by the Bundestag. Although the statistical models I estimate in Chapter 5 take account of the fact that different legislative provisions reviewed by the Court may stem from the same law, it is incredibly difficult to establish and represent the chain of events of lawmakers adopting policy, courts reviewing them, and lawmakers' subsequent responses to jurisprudence in quantitative data. Clark and Lauderdale (2012) liken the development of a court's jurisprudence to a tree that grows over time, that branches out over different cases, and may wind into different directions with each additional case. A focused, qualitative case study, on the other, hand is perfectly suited to cover precisely such kinds of complex, interconnected events. The qualitative element of my research design allows me to track the development of a particular line of jurisprudence by the GFCC across several years and proceedings heard at the Court, and offers insight into how—if at all—German lawmakers' policy choices contributed to changes in this jurisprudence.

Finally, even though the quantitative data that I collected for this study itself stems from what is effectively a 'qualitative' text analysis of the parliamentary debate transcripts for every law challenged at the GFCC between the late 1970s and 2010s, it cannot match the rich evidence that a qualitative case study can provide. As explained above, I restricted my attention in my data collection to debate transcripts that immediately preceded the adoption of a policy to capture constitutional concerns that were ultimately left unaddressed. However, by restricting my attention to this particular set of documents, I necessarily miss out on insightful contextual evidence, including relevant press coverage, lawmakers' own commentary in the media, trends in public opinion on a particular policy issue, and—wherever publicly available—constitutional law experts' statements heard in earlier committee hearings. Approaching the empirical test of my theoretical argument through a mixed-methods design allows me to not only draw on the strengths but also complement the weaknesses of quantitative and qualitative techniques, respectively, 'techniques that are appropriate for different research tasks and are designed to achieve different research goals' (Goertz and Mahoney, 2012, 3). A qualitative case study allows me to capture relevant contextual evidence and complements the breadth of my statistical inferences with the depth of an intensive study of a single, bounded phenomenon (see Gerring, 2004). In other words, it provides a voice to the relevant actors in the legislative-judicial interactions that I am interested in and allows me to take a closer look at the process of interactions between the GFCC and German lawmakers.

In my case study, I focus on the back and forth between German lawmakers and the GFCC over surveillance powers granted to German law enforcement agents in their fights against organized crime as well as domestic and international terrorism between the late 1990s and mid-2010s. Several reasons inform this choice. First, within this timeframe we find several episodes of lawmakers taking high constitutional risks in their policy choices, notably against the advice of members of parliament from both sides of the aisle. Arguably the most prominent example of governing lawmakers denouncing government policy as unconstitutional is the former Federal Justice Minister Sabine Leutheusser-Schnarrenberger of the FDP. Leutheusser-Schnarrenberger first resigned from her ministerial post in 1995 in protest over the CDU/CSU/FDP governing coalition's plans to radically extend law enforcement's surveillance competences, and then challenged the corresponding legislation at the GFCC herself in 1999.[16]

Second, aside from its overall political salience of the issue, the Bundestag and GFCC's back and forth over policy designed to combat organized crime and terrorism represents precisely the kind of chain of events that the statistical analysis struggles to capture. Setting my focus on this particular policy issue over nearly two decades allows me to trace how the GFCC's jurisprudence and interpretation of the Basic Law shaped deliberations in the Bundestag, whether or not lawmakers 'auto-limited' their policy choices on several occasions, and how—if at all—the Court adapted its decisions on the constitutionality of challenged legislative provisions and the legal reasoning behind these decisions in response to lawmakers pushing the boundaries of the constitution.

3.4 Conclusion

In this chapter, I laid out my plans for testing the empirical implications of the game-theoretical model developed in Chapter 2. I focus on Germany and the GFCC's review of the constitutionality of federal legislation. With its strong support among the German public, the GFCC is not a court that seems prone to quickly back down from challenging unconstitutional policies pushed by lawmakers. Hence, the GFCC's comfortable position in Germany's system of separation of powers stacks the cards against finding evidence for my theoretical expectation that courts are less likely to strike policy when lawmakers credibly signalled their resolve to implement a policy, if necessary by flouting a court's jurisprudence. Yet, in light of its political stability and longevity of its governing coalitions, Germany provides the kind of political environment where lawmakers are incentivized to push the envelope in their policy choices knowing that they are likely to get a shot at responding to a GFCC judgment that strikes their policy. Thus, I expect to find that German lawmakers are less likely to cautiously self-limit their policy choices than existing literature suggests (see Stone Sweet, 2000a; Engst, 2021), and anticipate that the GFCC does moderate the rate at which it strikes down challenged policies when lawmakers have pushed constitutional boundaries in their legislative initiatives.

[16] See Deutschlandfunk, 16 January 2018. *Vor 20 Jahren: Der Bundestag beschloss den großen Lauschangriff*, https://www.deutschlandfunk.de/vor-20-jahren-der-bundestag-beschloss-den-grossen-100.html, accessed 16 August 2023.

I presented a mixed-methods research design to test the model's empirical implications. To capitalize on the strengths of both types of methodologies, I combine a statistical analysis drawing on original data of every federal law reviewed by the GFCC between 1977 and 2017 with a qualitative case study spanning two decades of the Bundestag and GFCC's tug-of-war over German law enforcement agents' surveillance competences. While the quantitative analysis promises generalizable findings of how constitutional courts like the GFCC respond when lawmakers' signal credible non-compliance threats, the qualitative case study offers a much deeper, richer insight into how the decisions of German lawmakers and the GFCC shape their behaviour, respectively. Combining these two strands of my research design allows me to provide comprehensive evidence that lawmakers who take high risks in their policy choices, crossing constitutional boundaries, can successfully put pressure on even powerful courts to shift these boundaries in lawmakers' favour.

4

When Lawmakers Push Boundaries

To study how judges at the German Federal Constitutional Court (GFCC) respond to lawmakers taking constitutional risks in a statistical analysis, I needed access to data that would enable me to identify the policies pursued by lawmakers despite warnings about their unconstitutionality. To construct a dataset for testing my theoretical argument, I relied on the detailed documentation of legislative proceedings that led to the policies later reviewed by the GFCC, which is published by the German Bundestag's Parliamentary Documentation Division (DIP).

In this chapter, I explain how I linked information from the judgment texts published by the GFCC to DIP records to reconstruct key parts of the Bundestag's legislative proceedings of the policies, which were eventually reviewed by the Court for their constitutionality. I discuss how I identified whether—and if so, which—members of parliament had voiced which types of constitutional concerns. This chapter provides important background information for the analyses that follow in subsequent chapters. It points out key descriptive patterns in the behaviour of German lawmakers, documenting prominent, illustrative episodes of constitutional controversy in the Bundestag over four decades between 1977 and 2017.

The chapter proceeds as follows: I first explain how I established which provisions in federal laws were reviewed by the GFCC within the timeframe of this study, and how I linked this information to the DIP's records. I then detail my coding process for parliamentary debate transcripts, with the goal of establishing instances of governing coalitions ignoring constitutional concerns—including the concerns of their own political allies. Following a discussion and visualization of key descriptive patterns in the data, I produce a list of policies that governing coalitions pushed through the Bundestag against the advice of lawmakers from both sides of the aisle. Finally, I discuss what these descriptive patterns can tell us about lawmakers' behaviour in the face of constitutional review, and how these observed patterns map onto the expectations laid out by the game-theoretical model of Chapter 2.

Putting Courts Under Pressure. Philipp A. Schroeder, Oxford University Press. © Philipp A. Schroeder (2025).
DOI: 10.1093/9780198953265.003.0004

4.1 Linking judgments and debates

The GFCC is diligent in defining in its judgments which legislative provisions it reviewed and announcing its final decision whether the challenged provisions are consistent with the Basic Law. What makes establishing a link between the Court's exercise of constitutional review and parliamentary debates of the eventually challenged provisions a tricky endeavour, however, is the convoluted nature of German federal laws. Most federal laws adopted over the past decades are so-called 'amendment laws' (in German, Änderungsgesetze), legislation that amends existing laws often replacing the wording of individual provisions while leaving the rest of the law intact. To illustrate, consider the GFCC's decision in case *1 BvL 4/12* that I briefly touched upon in the preceding chapter. Here, the Court was asked to review whether Paragraph 1, Section 7, Number 2, Letter D of the 2006 *Act on Parental Allowance and Parental Leave* was consistent with the German constitution.[1] However, while formally this is the challenged legislative provision, its relevant text for the case stems from the 2007 *Act Implementing the Residency and Asylum Directives of the European Union*, which amended the aforementioned provision.

As the first step of my data collection, I identified every decision by one of the GFCC's two Senates between 1977 and 2017 that ruled on the constitutionality of one or more legislative provisions contained in federal laws. For GFCC decisions published between 2015 and 2017, I referred to the GFCC's own records to identify the relevant judgments. For GFCC decisions published prior to 2015, I was able to draw on data provided by the *Constitutional Court Database* collated by Engst et al. (2019) as well as replication data provided by Krehbiel (2016). However, while these latter data sources list the challenged federal law, I am specifically interested in the exact challenged provision(s). This distinction is important for my analysis. For instance, two separate provisions of the same federal law may have been challenged at the GFCC, and it is possible that German lawmakers had voiced concerns over the constitutionality of one of these provisions but not the other.

To avoid losing this nuance, I devised a coding protocol that was admittedly tedious but ultimately yielded a dataset that linked constitutional review decisions at the GFCC on specific legislative provisions to—where applicable—the moments these provisions had previously come up in parliamentary debates

[1] The challenged provision excluded immigrants holding particular types of residence permits from receiving public parental allowances, a provision that the Federal Social Court of Germany believed to violate Art. 3 of the Basic Law, the constitutional guarantee for a right to equality.

in the Bundestag. First, I identified the exact challenged legislative provision, relying on judgments' operative parts as well as the GFCC's case description, typically found in the first few paragraphs of the judgment text. These descriptions summarize the background to the case, including which provisions of the law were challenged, by whom they were challenged and why. With this information in hand, I then searched up the challenged federal law via the Bundestag's online records system, DIP, to access the relevant parliamentary debate transcripts. Here, I focused my attention on the transcripts of the final debates held in parliament, just prior to the federal law's adoption, given that at this stage in the legislative proceedings, lawmakers no longer make amendments to the debated law.

Formally, federal laws adopted by the Bundestag pass through three consultations (in German, 'Beratungen') held in plenary sessions, which are public and allow members of parliament to debate the legislation. In practice, however, almost all federal laws are only debated twice, as laws are adopted at the third consultation, which typically follows immediately after the second consultation without debate. Hence, I generally referred to transcripts of parliamentary debates at the second consultation in the Bundestag. Notable exceptions were, on the one hand, federal laws that were passed only after a conciliation committee involving lawmakers of both the Bundestag and representatives of the 16 state governments had hammered out a compromise that ultimately found a majority in both the Bundestag and Bundesrat.[2] On the other hand, federal laws that included Germany's annual fiscal budget typically saw parliament's final debate continue into the Bundestag's third consultation. In the former scenario, I referred to the Bundestag's debate of the compromise submitted by the conciliation committee. In the latter scenario, I referred to the final debate spanning both the second and third consultation.

Once I identified the relevant debate transcript, I searched the statements issued by members of parliament for a set of keywords that all revolved around the terms 'constitutional' and 'basic law'. Specifically, I stemmed these terms, or rather their German equivalents, to capture the entire range of linguistic forms in which they could occur in statements that even remotely touched upon the constitutionality of a provision. For instance, by searching for the term 'verfass', I would capture any mentioning of terms like 'Verfassung' (i.e. 'constitution'), 'verfassungsrechtlich' (i.e. 'concerning constitutional law'), 'verfassungskonform' (i.e. 'conforming with the constitution'), and so on. For every hit of

[2] The Bundesrat is Germany's second parliamentary chamber comprising representatives of state governments in the German Länder, which has a veto right on federal laws that affect exclusive or shared competences of the Länder.

these search terms in a debate transcript, I first established whether the member of parliament in fact referred to the legislative provision which was later challenged at the GFCC, and if so whether they actually warned against the provision's unconstitutionality.

To illustrate the importance of this step for the integrity of my data, consider the following example. In a high-profile case, *2 BvF 1/05*, the GFCC heard a challenge against the 2005 *Aviation Security Act*, in particular against provisions concerning the use of military force in the event of a terrorist attack involving an aircraft. Key provisions of the challenged law envisioned that the call to send military jets to respond to a terrorist threat, and if necessary shoot down a hijacked aircraft, would ultimately be made by the federal government rather than state governments where the incident is occurring. The state governments of Bavaria and Hesse questioned the constitutionality of these provisions, inter alia challenging the federal government's powers to deploy the armed forces within German territory. At the time of the Court's review, some of the provisions in question had last been amended via the 2009 *Act on Establishing a Federal Air Traffic Controlling Office*. Notably, lawmakers of the Green party and the leftist party Die Linke had voiced constitutional concerns in the final parliamentary debate concerning this act. Yet, none of their concerns related to the substance of the GFCC's case in *2 BvF 1/05*. Instead, lawmakers of the Greens and Die Linke admonished that provisions of the 2009 *Act on Establishing a Federal Air Traffic Controlling Office* would open the door to a privatization of aviation security, a step that would undermine constitutionally guaranteed core state competences.[3] Clearly, it would be inaccurate to conclude that these concerns are evidence that the government had ignored constitutional warnings by the parliamentary opposition parties when it devised its anti-terrorism policy in the event of an airborne terrorist attack.

To further complicate matters, some of the challenged provisions in case *2 BvF 1/05* had been left untouched by the amending act of 2009. As it turns out, these provisions in fact had raised constitutional concerns among lawmakers of the CDU/CSU that specifically speak to the distribution of competences between states and the federal government in the event of an airborne terrorist attack. Consider the following statement by Clemens Binninger, then serving as the CDU/CSU's parliamentary group rapporteur in the Bundestag's committee for internal security:

[3] See parliamentary debate transcript of the second reading of the Act on Establishing a Federal Air Traffic Controlling Office, 28 May 2009, 2. Beratung: BT-PlPr 16/224.

> Clemens Binninger (CDU): In the event of terrorists hijacking an airplane, obviously every minute counts, and we need short chains of command. But your plans require that the concerned state government has to first request the use of armed forces at the federal ministry, which then has to review and approve the request, before any military aircraft can even take off. At this point, your law is not only unconstitutional but also entirely impracticable.[4]

Whenever a search hit revealed a statement like the one above that was linked to the actual substance of the later case at the GFCC, I assessed whether the statement criticized the provision(s) for their unconstitutionality (rather than defending its constitutionality). If so, I recorded whether the statement was given during the oral debate section of the parliamentary debate or whether it was submitted as a written statement, which is subsequently attached to the published transcripts.[5] Further, I noted the political party of the member(s) of parliament submitting the statement. Hence, for every legislative provision challenged at the GFCC, I ended up with the counts of members of parliament voicing their constitutional concerns over the provision, separated by political party and the type of their statement, oral or written. In the following, I take a closer look at this data and illustrative patterns in German lawmakers' willingness to take constitutional risks in their policy choices.

4.2 Patterns of constitutional risk-taking

Figure 4.1 plots the number of legislative provisions reviewed by the GFCC between 1997 and 2017 by the year they were adopted, and shows how many of these legislative provisions had been contested as unconstitutional by members of parliament at their respective final plenary debates. For instance, Figure 4.1 shows that 20 of the 417 reviewed provisions were adopted in 1994, and two of these provision had been labelled as unconstitutional by members of parliament prior to their adoption. In contrast, ten of the 15 reviewed provisions

[4] Translated from German, excerpt from the second reading of the Aviation Security Act in the German Bundestag, 18 June 2004, 2. Beratung: BT-PlPr 15/115.

[5] Debate time for most federal laws in the Bundestag is limited and typically oral statements are made by ministers, shadow ministers, party rapporteurs, and spokespersons with specific policy expertise relating to the debated law. However, other members of parliament can make use of written statements appended to debate transcripts if they want to go on record with their disapproval of a law. Commonly, several members of parliament go on record with the same written statement, see for example the written statement signed collectively by the parliamentary group of Die Linke, noting the unconstitutionality of the 2011 *Act on Determining Standard Needs and Amending the Second and Twelfth Book of the Code of Social Law*, 11 February 2011, Abstimmung über Vermittlungsvorschlag, BT-PIPr 17/91.

that were adopted in 1992 had previously been contested as unconstitutional by lawmakers. Note that the relatively small number of provisions plotted for the latter years on the right of Figure 4.1 does not necessarily suggest that the number of challenges of federal legislation at the GFCC decreased in recent years. Rather, it is likely that several federal laws adopted in the early to mid-2010s had only made their way to the GFCC after 2017, and therefore do not show up in my data.

Notwithstanding spikes in contested provisions for some of the years included in my data, Figure 4.1 shows that most of the challenged provisions, roughly 72%, had made their way through the legislative proceedings without causing constitutional concerns among lawmakers. Subsetting for the type of proceeding at the GFCC, I find that roughly 21% of provisions challenged via concrete norm control proceedings and 31% of provisions challenged via constitutional complaints had seen their constitutionality contested by lawmakers. This percentage increases substantially to 44% for abstract norm control proceedings, i.e. challenges initiated by members of parliament or state governments, which seems unsurprising given that it is likely that lawmakers

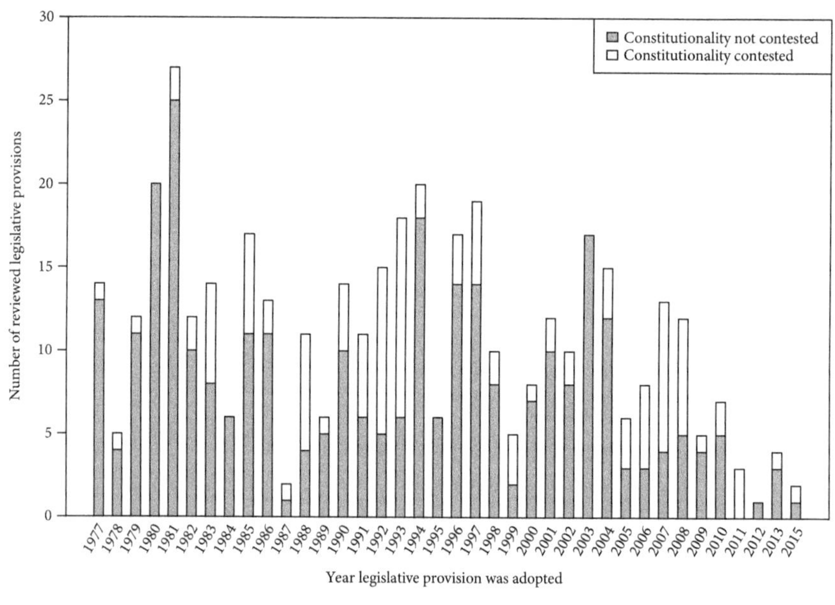

Figure 4.1 Legislative provisions reviewed by the GFCC 1977–2017 by their year of adoption. The figure distinguishes between provisions contested as unconstitutional by members of parliament and provisions that passed without contestation of their constitutionality

would seek to challenge a law at the GFCC if they had previously criticized its constitutional compatibility.

Digging a little deeper, Figure 4.2 subsets my data for provisions which saw their constitutionality contested by lawmakers and plots them conditional on their affiliation with the parliamentary opposition and governing coalition. While most of the contested provisions, roughly 71%, saw members of the parliamentary opposition voicing constitutional concerns, a non-negligible number of the contested provisions, 34 out of 116, also had members of the governing coalition caucus publicly going on record with their constitutional objections. In the following paragraphs, I will take a closer look at two illustrative examples of governing coalitions pushing controversial policy against the constitutional objections of the parliamentary opposition—and in the latter example against the advice of their own political allies.

I begin with an episode from 1983, specifically the *Act Amending the Law on Political Parties and Other Acts* of 22 December 1983. This act includes most of the legislative provisions passed in 1983 that were not only later challenged at the GFCC but had also raised constitutional concerns among lawmakers prior to their adoption. Various provisions of the act were challenged for infringing

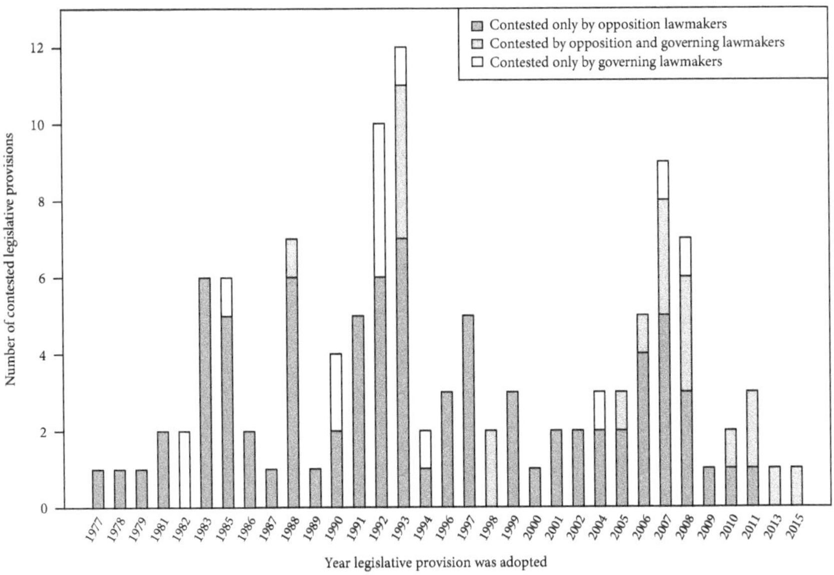

Figure 4.2 Contested legislative provisions reviewed by the GFCC 1977–2017 by their year of adoption. The figure distinguishes between provisions contested as unconstitutional by members of the parliamentary opposition parties and the governing coalition

a constitutionally guaranteed equality in opportunity among political parties and political associations, specifically with respect to their financing. These challenges concerned a denial of corporation and wealth tax exemptions for communal voter associations (see case *2 BvL 64/93*), the different treatment of political parties and communal voter associations with respect to the taxation of their income (see case *2 BvR 638/84*), and regulations concerning tax deductions for political parties that allegedly discriminated against smaller, less established political parties in Germany (see joined case *2 BvE 2/84, 2 BvR 442/84*). Notably, the latter case was brought by, among others, the board members of the Greens, then a relatively young party, which had managed to enter the Bundestag in 1983 for the first time. Unsurprisingly, several members of the Greens had already stated their constitutional concerns about the federal law's provisions at its final parliamentary debate. Consider the following statement by Otto Schily, a lawyer by training and then member of parliament for the Greens:

> Otto Schily (Greens): A point that has been picked up repeatedly here and which sits at the core of our discussion are the quite considerable constitutional concerns that must be asserted against this law. We firmly believe that what you delivered is constitutionally untenable. The key issue at stake is that you want to treat donations to political parties in the same way as donations to charitable associations. This reform favours in particular large donors, and in a way that clearly violates equal opportunities in political participation.[6]

Members of the Greens were not the only ones who went on record to express doubts about the constitutionality of the law and its impact on equal opportunities among political parties. Jürgen Schmude of the SPD, a former Minister of Interior, also noted that the new regulations would sit uneasily with the constitution.

> Jürgen Schmude (SPD): Whether these new regulations adequately address the constitutional concerns that were noted here is questionable. We can't rule out that a constitutional risk remains. That's what the experts told us in the committee hearings, and that was also apparent especially when we heard from the Minister of Justice and the Minister of Interior in the committee.[7]

[6] Translated from German, excerpt from the second reading of the Aviation Security Act in the German Bundestag, 1 December 1983, 2. Beratung: BT-PlPr 10/40.

[7] Translated from German, excerpt from the second reading of the Aviation Security Act in the German Bundestag, 1 December 1983, 2. Beratung: BT-PlPr 10/40.

In all three of the aforementioned cases, the GFCC eventually ruled that the challenged provisions were incompatible with the constitution and instructed the government to devise new rules that would respect the constitutionally guaranteed principle of equal opportunities. The governing coalition of the CDU/CSU and FDP had ignored advice that their reform would cross constitutional boundaries and had to return to the drawing board (for an in-depth discussion of the back-and-forth between the GFCC and the political branches over financing regulations for political parties, see Vanberg, 2005). While the 1983 *Act Amending the Law on Political Parties and Other Acts* is a typical example of legislation that caused constitutional concerns among the members of the political opposition, the next illustrative example captures a less frequent phenomenon, albeit one that is particularly important for my analysis in the next chapter: Legislation that saw members of parliament from the ranks of the governing coalition join the chorus of constitutional objections.

In the early 1990s, Germany experienced a rapid, since World War II unprecedented, influx of refugees. Roughly 440,000 applicants sought asylum in Germany in 1992, most of them unsuccessfully (the application approval rate sat at a mere 4.3%, see Bundeszentrale für politische Bildung, 2013). Along with this increase in mostly unsuccessful asylum applications came a wave of xenophobic assaults by far-right mobs in several German cities, targeting immigrants and Germans with an immigration background. Against the backdrop of these developments, a sentiment was stoked among several media outlets and conservative political parties that the German government's refugee policy had failed and that its lax asylum regulations were prone to abuse (Bundeszentrale für politische Bildung, 2013).

In this politically charged climate, the governing coalition of the CDU/CSU and FDP, supported by several members of the SPD, sought a fundamental reform of asylum regulations in Germany. In three key pieces of legislation, namely the *Act Amending Procedural Law concerning Asylum, Foreign Nationals and Citizenship* of 30 June 1993, the *Act on the Re-regulation of the Provision of Services to Asylum Seekers* of 30 June 1993, and the *Act on Amendments to the Basic Law (Article 16 and Article 18)* of 28 June 1993, the governing coalition chartered a new course in Germany's asylum policy. This package of legislation, known as the so-called 'asylum compromise', inter alia ushered in three new regulations. According to the newly established 'third-country regulation', asylum seekers who had entered Germany via one of its neighbouring countries or another EU Member State would see their application rejected. Further, refugees from ostensibly 'safe third-countries' would no longer be able to claim asylum in Germany. Finally, refugees who had reached Germany via an aeroplane could be detained at an airport for up to 19 days to process their asylum claims, prior to even entering German territory.

The 'asylum compromise' was one of the most intensely debated pieces of legislation in the Bundestag in the early 1990s, with more than 70 speakers going on record in its final debate. Notably, members of every party except the conservative CDU/CSU voiced constitutional concerns about the planned reforms, including several members of the governing coalition caucus. Consider for example the statement by Burkhard Hirsch of the FDP, who did not mince matters in his opening speech:

> Burkhard Hirsch (FDP): Dear colleagues, I am speaking for myself and my colleague Gerhart Baum. When this legislation was first submitted, we stated that despite some of the improvements it brings for refugees claiming German citizenship, we can't endorse it. Against our hopes, neither our own consultations nor the urgent advice of the experts heard in the committee sessions made any difference. Your plans violate humanitarian principles. They are incompatible with our obligations under international law and the Geneva convention. They infringe fundamental pillars of our constitution that have endured so far.[8]

Hirsch was certainly not alone in his criticism of the asylum compromise. More than 80 members of the SPD's parliamentary faction signed a written statement that objected to the 'asylum compromise':

> Katrin Fuchs and others (SPD): Not even if they are facing imminent danger can an asylum seeker turn to an administrative court in Germany, they are simply deported and at best can file their claim with a German court from a third country. This regulation leaves them with only one hope, the Federal Constitutional Court. Even the supporters of the asylum compromise admit that these regulations won't survive the Constitutional Court's scrutiny.[9]

These lawmakers were right that following the adoption of the 'asylum compromise' the treatment of asylum seekers would ultimately be subject to a

[8] Translated from German, excerpt from the second reading of the Act amending Procedural Law concerning Asylum, Foreign Nationals and Citizenship in the German Bundestag, 26 May 1993, 2. Beratung: BT-PlPr 12/160.

[9] Translated from German, excerpt from the second reading of the Act amending Procedural Law concerning Asylum, Foreign Nationals and Citizenship in the German Bundestag, 26 May 1993, 2. Beratung: BT-PlPr 12/160.

review by the GFCC. In 1995, the Court heard three cases that challenged various provision of the legislative package that lawmakers had adopted in June 1993 (see the joined case *2 BvR 1938/93, 2 BvR 2315/93*, joined case *2 BvR 1507/93, 2 BvR 1508/93*, and case *2 BvR 1516/93*). These cases concerned asylum seekers from Iraq, Ghana, and Togo, who had their asylum claims rejected after the new regulations had come into force, and subsequently filed constitutional complaints, inter alia challenging the controversial 'third-country regulation'. However, the GFCC eventually upheld the challenged provisions in its three separate rulings, and the judges in Karlsruhe declared key pillars of Germany's so hotly contested new asylum regime as compatible with the constitution.

Episodes like the one just discussed certainly stand out in my data and highlight that lawmakers are at times prepared to ignore constitutional concerns voiced by members of parliament from across the political spectrum and push for policies that ostensibly infringe fundamental constitutional rights. While I cannot provide a more in-depth discussion of every such instance, it is still worthwhile to take look at the legislative acts that caused constitutional concerns on both sides of the aisle. What types of policies are pushed through the legislative process despite opposition from both sides of the aisle, and which governing coalitions are driving these efforts?

Table 4.1 provides an overview over every federal law containing legislative provisions that had been contested for their constitutionality by members of the governing coalition caucus, along with the coalition in power at the time of adoption and the case numbers of the GFCC's reviews. Looking through this list of federal laws, several patterns stand out. First, almost all of these laws are linked to highly salient policy issues. Aside from several laws that deal with asylum regulations, the list provided in Table 4.1 inter alia contains policies concerning abortion regulations, German unification, fiscal austerity programmes, surveillance activities by law enforcement agents, EU measures adopted in the aftermath of the 2008 financial crisis, retroactive preventive detention of criminals, and regulations concerning Germany's public health insurance. Rather than deviating from party lines on relatively minor policies, it seems that lawmakers in the governing coalition are unafraid to publicly express their constitutional concerns about key policies within the government's political agenda.

Second, while every type of governing coalition (i.e. coalitions comprising the SPD/FDP, CDU/CSU/FDP, SPD/Greens, and the CDU/CSU/SPD) adopted federal laws that were objected by members of the governing coalition

Table 4.1 Federal laws objected as unconstitutional by members of the governing coalition caucus and corresponding cases heard by the German Federal Constitutional Court (with year of decision)

Federal law and governing coalition	GFCC case(s)
Act concerning Asylum Procedures of 16 July 1982 (BGBl. I S. 946); SPD/FDP	2 BvR 1413/83 (1984), 1 BvR 1470/82 (1983)
Act on Tax Adjustments of 19 December 1985 (BGBl. I S. 2436); CDU/CSU/FDP	1 BvL 2/04 (2008)
Fifth Act concerning Amendments to the Political Party Act and other Acts of 22 December 1988 (BGBl. I S. 946); CDU/CSU/FDP	2 BvR 1413/83 (1984), 1 BvR 1470/82 (1983)
Act of 23 September 1990 on the Treaty of 31 August 1990 between the Federal Republic of Germany and the German Democratic Republic on the Reunification of Germany and the Agreement of 18 September 1990 (BGBl. II S. 885); CDU/CSU/FDP	1 BvR 1341/90 (1991), 1 BvR 454/91 (1992), 1 BvR 1467/91 (1992), 1 BvR 1452/90 (1996), 2 BvL 6/95 (1997)
Act on the Regulation of Outstanding Property Issues as amended by the Second Law on Outstanding Property Issues of 14 July 1992 (BGBl I S. 1257); CDU/CSU/FDP	1 BvR 1452/90 (1996), 1 BvF 1/94 (1999), 2 BvR 955/00 (2004)
Act concerning the Protection of Pre-Natal Life, the Promotion of a Child-Friendly Society, for Support concerning Pregnancy Conflict and Regulations concerning the Termination of Pregnancy of 27 July 1992 (BGBl. I S. 1398); CDU/CSU/FDP	2 BvF 2/90 (1993)
Act on Amendments to the Basic Law (Article 16 and Article 18) of 28 June 1993 (BGBl. I S. 1002); CDU/CSU/FDP	2 BvR 1938/93 (1996)
Act amending Procedural Law concerning Asylum, Foreign Nationals and Citizenship of 30 June 1993 (BGBl. I S. 1062); CDU/CSU/FDP	2 BvR 1938/93 (1996), 2 BvR 1507/93 (1996), 2 BvR 1516/93 (1996), 2 BvL 2/98 (1999)
Act on the Re-regulation of the Provision of Services to Asylum Seekers of 30 June 1993 (BGBl. I 1993 S. 1074); CDU/CSU/FDP	1 BvR 293/05 (2006)
First Act on the Implementation of the Austerity-, Consolidation- and Growth-Programme of 21 December 1993 (BGBl. I S. 2353); CDU/CSU/FDP	1 BvL 16/95 (2002)
Act on Adjusting Contractual Law with regard to the Use of Property in Acceding Territories of 21 September 1994 (BGBl. I S. 2538); CDU/CSU/FDP	1 BvR 995/95 (1999)
Act on Amendments to the Basic Law (Article 13) of 26 March 1998 (BGBl I S. 610); CDU/CSU/FDP	1 BvR 1104/92 (2001), 1 BvR 2378/98 (2004)

Federal law and governing coalition	GFCC case(s)
Act on Improving Measures to Combat Organised Crime of 4 May 1998 (BGBl I S. 845); CDU/CSU/FDP	1 BvR 1104/92 (2001), 1 BvR 2378/98 (2004)
Act on the Introduction of a Retroactive Preventive Detention of 23 July 2004 (BGBl I S. 1883); SPD/Greens	2 BvR 2365/09 (2011)
First Act on the Amendment of the Claim- and Entitlement-Transfer Act of 21 June 2005 (BGBl I S. 1672); SPD/Greens	1 BvL 9/06 (2010)
Act concerning Tax Changes in 2007 of 19 July 2006 (BGBl I S. 1652); CDU/CSU/SPD	2 BvL 1/07 (2008)
Act concerning the Strengthening of Competition in Public Health Insurance of 26 March 2007 (BGBl I S. 378); CDU/CSU/SPD	1 BvR 825/08 (2009), 1 BvR 831/08 (2009), 1 BvR 706/08 (2009)
Act on the Re-regulation of Telecommunication Surveillance and other Covert Investigative Measures of 21 December 2007 (BGBl I S. 378); CDU/CSU/SPD	2 BvR 236/08 (2011), 1 BvR 256/08 (2010)
Act on the Lisbon Treaty of 13 December 2007 of 8 October 2008 (BGBl II S. 1038); CDU/CSU/SPD	2 BvR 2136/09 (2009), 2 BvE 2/08 (2009)
Act on Amendments to the Basic Law (Article 23, Article 45 and Article 93) of 8 October 2008 (BGBl I S. 1926); CDU/CSU/SPD	2 BvE 2/08 (2009)
Act on the Reform of Inheritance Tax Law of 24 December 2008 (BGBl I S. 3018); CDU/CSU/SPD	1 BvL 21/12 (2014)
Act on Prevention by the Federal Criminal Police Office of Threats from International Terrorism of 25 December 2008 (BGBl I S. 3083); CDU/CSU/SPD	1 BvR 966/09 (2016)
Act concerning the European Stabilisation Mechanism of 21 May 2010 (BGBl I S. 627); CDU/CSU/FDP	2 BvR 987/10 (2011)
Act concerning Amendments to the Second and Twelfth Social Security Statute Book of 24 March 2011 (BGBl I S. 453); CDU/CSU/FDP	1 BvL 10/12 (2014)
Thirteenth Act concerning Amendments to the Atomic Energy Act of 31 July 2011 (BGBl I S. 1704); CDU/CSU/FDP	1 BvR 2821/11 (2016)
Act concerning the Introduction of a Care Allowance of 15 February 2013 (BGBl I S. 254); CDU/CSU/FDP	1 BvF 2/13 (2015)
Act concerning Tariff Uniformity of 3 July 2015 (BGBl I S. 1130); CDU/CSU/SPD	1 BvR 1571/15 (2017)

caucus for their unconstitutionality, the frequency with which this phenomenon happens differs markedly between them. During the four consecutive terms in office for Chancellor Helmut Kohl between 1983 and 1998, his governing coalition of the CDU/CSU/FDP adopted 0.80 federal laws per year, that saw objections from within the government's ranks. In contrast, during Chancellor Gerhard Schröder's two terms from 1998 until 2005, the coalition of the SPD and Greens merely adopted 0.29 federal laws per year that were contested by members of the governing coalition caucus. The worst offender, in this regard, was the grand coalition of the CDU/CSU/SPD during Chancellor Merkel's first term in office between 2005 and 2009, which adopted 1.75 laws per year that saw their constitutionality contested by members of the governing parties. During Merkel's second term in office between 2009 and 2013, now in a coalition with the FDP, exactly one contested law was adopted per year.

On the one hand, seeing that lawmakers of the governing coalition were most likely to break party ranks during a grand-coalition of the conservative CDU/CSU and centre-left SPD is not all too surprising. For the most part of Germany's modern political history, these two parties had been political rivals, and often held opposing views on high-stakes policy issues. Yet, on the other hand, during the grand-coalitions term in office between 2005 and 2009 it was clear that at least one of the two incumbent parties would remain in office for the next term—forming a governing coalition without either the CDU/CSU or the SPD was simply unrealistic at the time. In line with the expectations of the game-theoretic model of Chapter 2 (see Figure 2.2), these are the types of governments that are most likely to muster the resolve to push for controversial policies even against the advice of their own political allies, given that they would have good shot at being in office long enough to respond to the Court's judgment. The opposite holds for governments, which struggle for electoral support, given that their chances of getting to respond to a court judgment that struck their policy are relatively dim. Arguably, this scenario applied to the governing coalition of the SPD and Greens between 1998 and 2005. The 2002 Bundestag elections were closely contested, with the SPD ultimately finishing ahead of the CDU/CSU by the narrowest of margins, securing just 6,027 more second votes (the votes that typically determine the distribution of seats in the Bundestag) than the CDU/CSU. In other words, observing a grand-governing coalition relatively frequently pushing for constitutionally controversial policies, and a coalition struggling for electoral support generally shying away from doing so, maps onto the equilibrium predictions of the game-theoretic model of Chapter 2.

4.3 Conclusion

In this chapter, I showed which of the federal laws that would later land in the GFCC's docket had previously been contested for their constitutionality—and by whom. Most of the provisions that were eventually referred to the GFCC for constitutional review had passed through legislative proceedings without causing concerns regarding their constitutionality. Nonetheless, a substantial number of federal laws still set off the alarm bells, and some of them even saw members of the governing coalition question their constitutional compatibility, highlighting the importance of the phenomenon addressed by this study.

Unsurprisingly, the data presented here shows that members of the opposition were far more likely than their colleagues in the ranks of the governing coalition to make their voices heard, accusing the government of passing policies they knew would fall foul of constitutional norms. It is reasonable to expect that the political opposition will seize every opportunity to challenge the constitutionality of government policies in an effort to discredit them among the electorate. However, seeing lawmakers from the governing coalition do the same is much rarer—and arguably carries more significant consequences. In the preceding chapters, I argued that governing coalitions ignoring the constitutional advice of their allies risk paying a high political price. Flouting these warning signs, only to then see their policies censored by the GFCC presents a welcome opportunity for their political rivals—within and beyond their own party—to discredit their political acumen. I argue that precisely for that reason, going against the advice of your political allies serves as a sign of a governing coalition's commitment to a policy, signalling a credible non-compliance threat to a court tasked with reviewing the policy in question. In the next chapter, I am putting the data presented here to work to find out how the GFCC responds when German lawmakers push constitutional boundaries in their policy choices.

5

Judicial Responses: When Constitutional Courts Back Down

The game-theoretical model developed in Chapter 2 claims that courts identify whether their constitutional review judgments are at risk of non-compliance by paying attention to the signals that lawmakers send. Lawmakers who risk paying a high political price for pursuing constitutionally controversial policies are more likely to be the ones prepared to evade compliance with courts' judgments. Put simply, lawmakers' political costs from confrontation signal a non-compliance threat to courts. Assuming courts face incentives to avoid conflict with the elected branches when non-compliance with their jurisprudence is on the horizon, we should be more likely to see courts display self-restraint in their judgments when lawmakers had provoked a potentially costly confrontation with them.

In this chapter, I offer an empirical test of this claim, employing a statistical analysis of original data on the German Federal Constitutional Court's (GFCC) constitutional review of federal laws between 1977 and 2017. I first describe how I operationalized the relevant parameters of my theoretical model to test key hypotheses developed in Chapter 2. I then define the statistical models I estimate and present the findings of my analysis, followed by a series of robustness checks. The chapter concludes with a discussion of my findings.

5.1 Hypotheses and data

The theoretical model's empirical implication at the centre of the statistical analysis in this chapter states that courts are more likely to show deference in their judgments to lawmakers who have instigated a confrontation that could be costly for them. This implication can be translated into a hypothesis tailored to the GFCC's review of the Bundestag's federal laws: *Ceteris paribus, the GFCC should be less likely to strike a law when lawmakers had risked suffering high political costs for provoking confrontation with the GFCC.*

Putting Courts Under Pressure. Philipp A. Schroeder, Oxford University Press. © Philipp A. Schroeder (2025).
DOI: 10.1093/9780198953265.003.0005

The second implication of the model that I consider in this chapter concerns the relationship between a court's decision-making and the likelihood that lawmakers who had authored the reviewed act would also control the implementation of a court's corresponding judgment. Hypothesis 2 discussed in Chapter 2 suggests that as we move across the theoretical model's equilibria, a higher likelihood of lawmakers controlling the implementation of judgments concerning their own policies comes with a higher likelihood of courts showing self-restraint in their exercise of constitutional review. Tailored to the GFCC's reviews, this hypothesis reads: *Ceteris paribus, the GFCC should be less likely to strike a law when the probability that the law's author controls implementation of the GFCC's decision is high.*

These hypotheses refer to the same outcome variable, the GFCC's decision to declare a challenged legislative provisions unconstitutional. My outcome variable *Strike* is binary and coded as 1 if the GFCC declared the challenged paragraphs unconstitutional, and coded as 0 otherwise. Between 1977 and 2017, the GFCC's Senates heard 417 challenges to the constitutionality of federal law provisions. Each year the GFCC's Senates collectively heard roughly 10.2 of these cases and struck the challenged paragraphs in about 51% of them.[1] In the following, I model the GFCC's decision to strike a challenged legislative provision as a function of a set of explanatory and control variables.

5.1.1 Explanatory variables

For the operationalization of my main explanatory variables, I draw on the data discussed at length in the preceding chapter. The variable *Constitutional objections by opposition MP(s)* is binary and coded 1 if at least one member of the parliamentary opposition objected to the law citing their constitutional concerns, and 0 otherwise. Similarly, the variable *Constitutional objections by governing MP(s)* is binary and coded 1 if at least one member of the governing coalition caucus objected to the law citing their constitutional concerns, and 0 otherwise. As previously discussed in Chapter 4, coding for lawmakers' objections and distinguishing between their affiliation with the governing coalition and parliamentary opposition allow me to capture variation in the costs that lawmakers risk paying when pushing constitutionally controversial

[1] It is worth noting here that, unlike Vanberg (2005) and Krehbiel (2016), I exclude decisions issued by any of the GFCC's Chambers on the admissibility of a challenge in my main analysis. These types of decisions are substantially different from Senate decisions, as they do not consider the constitutionality of a law. However, I include the decisions of the GFCC's Chambers in one of my robustness checks discussed in Section 5.2.3 with results provided in Table 5.4.

laws through parliament. It is reasonable to assume that not every law referred for review to the GFCC is violating constitutional norms, and I expect that laws which had been passed by parliament without stirring any controversy are unlikely to be struck down by the court. In contrast, I believe that laws which genuinely conflict with the constitution are more likely to be found among those that prompted lawmakers to raise constitutional concerns. By ignoring these concerns, whether raised by members of the parliamentary opposition or their own governing caucus, lawmakers risk facing political consequences if the GFCC ultimately strikes down the law. However, the repercussions are even more severe when lawmakers disregard constitutional concerns raised by members of their own governing coalition, as opposed to those voiced by the opposition. While members of the parliamentary opposition may attempt to score political points by accusing the governing majority of violating constitutional norms, members of the governing caucus should only go on record with their constitutional concerns if these are well-founded and genuine. Ignoring the latter kinds of concerns is then a particularly egregious step for the governing majority. Accordingly, although flouting the opposition's constitutional concerns is certainly not risk-free, dismissing the advice of their close colleagues comes with a higher price tag for lawmakers—ultimately sending a stronger signal to the GFCC.

To no surprise, the data suggests that members of the opposition are far more likely to argue that a federal law fails to conform with constitutional principles than their colleagues from the majority caucus. Out of the 417 legislative provisions of federal laws reviewed by the GFCC's Senates between 1977 and 2017, 102 (roughly 25%) involved provisions, which had been considered unconstitutional by the opposition in the Bundestag prior to their adoption. At the same time, only 34 of the challenged provisions (roughly 8%) had been considered unconstitutional by members of the governing coalition caucus. Again to no surprise, the two variables are not independent of each other and objections voiced by members of the governing caucus are usually accompanied by objections voiced by the parliamentary opposition (the corresponding χ^2-test statistic is highly significant with a p-value of roughly 0.01).

A critical factor concerning the variable *Constitutional objections by governing MP(s)* relates to the individuals voicing their constitutional concerns. It is possible that these lawmakers are typically backbenchers at the fringes of their political parties, criticizing their colleagues in the coalition caucus to pander to a particular electoral constituency. A pattern of the GFCC upholding laws, which had been objected by these backbenchers for their supposed unconstitutionality, may thus not reflect the GFCC's response to a signalled non-compliance threat but may simply be due to a lack of substance in backbenchers' claims.

To account for this possibility in my robustness checks, I re-run my analysis while distinguishing lawmakers of the governing coalition caucus voicing constitutional concerns according to their seniority. The variable *Seniority of objecting governing MP(s)* comprises three categories: *No objections* if no member of the governing coalition voiced constitutional concerns; *Senior governing MP(s)* if constitutional concerns are voiced by a cabinet member, a governing party's designated spokesperson for a policy area, a member of a governing party's executive board, or a governing party member serving as parliamentary committee chair; and *Junior governing MP(s)* if constitutional concerns are voiced by any other member of the governing coalition caucus. This operationalization follows from the assumption that lawmakers considered as senior require the support of their party colleagues to attain these positions and hence should not be considered backbenchers. Table 5.1 provides the distribution of the variable *Seniority of objecting governing MP(s)*.

Moving on to the second explanatory variable of interest for the analysis in this chapter, I require a measure that captures the likelihood that lawmakers who had authored the reviewed law would also take control of crafting the response to the GFCC's corresponding judgment. To capture this likelihood, I first identified whether the legislative paragraphs challenged at the GFCC were passed by the governing coalition in office at the time of the court's decision. The variable *Incumbent government* is binary and coded 1 either if the law containing the challenged paragraphs was passed during the current legislative period at the time of the court's decision, or if the law was passed during the previous legislative period, provided the then-governing coalition had won subsequent elections and was still in office at the time of the court's decision. Otherwise, the variable was coded 0. Of the 417 challenged provisions reviewed by the GFCC, 110 (roughly 26%) had been authored by the then-governing coalition.

Table 5.1 Distribution of the variable *Seniority of objecting governing MP(s)*

Category	Frequency	% of observations
No objections	383	92%
Junior governing MP(s)	12	3%
Senior governing MP(s)	22	5%

In a second step, I then specified an interaction term in my statistical model(s), involving the measure *Incumbent government* and a measure capturing the time left until the next federal parliamentary elections at the date of the court's decision, the variable *Years until election*. For the latter variable, I counted the exact number of days between the date of the GFCC's decision and the date of the next scheduled election, and then expressed this time period in years.[2] On average, the GFCC's Senates issued their decisions roughly 2.04 years prior to the next federal elections to the Bundestag (the variable's standard deviation is roughly 1.16 years).

The rationale underlying the interaction effect is as follows: When the GFCC issues a decision early on during a legislative period it can expect that the legislative response to a judicial veto (potentially evading compliance) would be authored by the current government. As elections draw closer, however, the probability that a different governing coalition would take charge of responding to the court's decision increases. I expect the court to be less likely to strike the challenged paragraphs when the time until the next elections is longer, provided the law was passed by the current governing coalition. In line with this expectation, the sign of the interaction term's regression coefficient should be negative.

One concern about this operationalization is that a court conscious of a non-compliance threat may simply choose to postpone a decision sufficiently long enough in the hope of finding a politically more favourable climate in the future. It seems difficult to generally rule this possibility out; however, there are also indications that the GFCC's discretion over the timing of its decisions is somewhat limited. In my interviews with members of the GFCC, I asked how much control justices enjoy over the timing of their decisions. In a telephone interview conducted on 14 April 2019, one former justice noted:

> When applications land on our desks then of course we have to decide them. As mentioned earlier, there is some degree of discretion and the publication of a decision can be pushed back by a couple of months. For example, the Federal Constitutional Court will not drop a political bombshell, so to speak, during an election season. But you have to understand, a lot of the scheduling at the court is done by the administration, of course we need to prioritise some things over others once in a while, but the decisions at the Federal Constitutional Court are subject to a preliminary planning cycle by the administration.

[2] To account for the early elections in September 2005, which were announced by Federal President Horst Köhler on 21 July 2005, I considered the GFCC's anticipated date of the next federal elections to be 1 October 2006, for decisions issued prior to President Köhler's announcement, and 18 September 2005 (the actual date of the elections) after the announcement.

Another factor likely to limit the GFCC's discretion in scheduling decisions according to political considerations is that in doing so the court may tarnish its institutional legitimacy among actors in Germany's political system that frequently interact with it. In cases involving the constitutional review of federal (or state) laws, the GFCC generally seeks the opinion of interested parties to a case, comprising relevant interest groups (e.g. the Federation of German Industries and trade unions) and non-governmental organizations. These interested parties are aware that the GFCC currently considers a constitutional question that is relevant to their operations and often require constitutional clarity over a law under review at the GFCC. Thus, deliberately delaying constitutional review decisions may come with costs for the court's reputation that may outweigh the costs of deferring to the elected branches in an individual case.

5.1.2 Control variables

Given that my empirical tests in this chapter rely on observational data, i.e. values on my independent variables of interest are not randomly assigned to individual observations, it is critical for my analysis to avoid omitted variable bias. I therefore include several control variables in my statistical models, which—if omitted from my analysis—may confound any observed effect of my explanatory variables.

Some of the challenged provisions in federal law were adopted by a grand-coalition of the two electorally strongest parties in Germany, the CDU/CSU and SPD, while others were explicitly authored by members of parliament from both the governing coalition and the parliamentary opposition. It is likely that the GFCC is more reluctant to challenge a law that secured widespread backing among members of parliament. Therefore, I control for the variable *Cross-party proposal* in my analysis, which is coded 1 if the federal law was authored by members of parliament from both sides of the aisle, and 0 otherwise. Similarly, to avoid confounding effects of laws passed by electorally stronger governing coalitions, my analysis includes an additional control variable, *Law by grand-coalition*, which is coded 1 if the reviewed law was adopted by a coalition of the CDU/CSU and SPD, and 0 otherwise. Further, as federal laws on some policy issues may be more likely to touch upon constitutional rights, and hence may be correlated with both instances of lawmakers objecting a law as unconstitutional and the court's decision-making, I control for the issue area of the challenged legislative paragraphs. The variable *Policy area* is categorical and draws on the designation of the parliamentary committee in the Bundestag formally in charge of the law. The variable distinguishes between ten policy areas, namely economic regulation, education policy, family law, healthcare, internal domestic policies, individual rights, social insurance regulations, public infrastructure, fiscal policy, and a residual category for any other types of policies.

While I avoid including control variables specifically related to the proceedings at the GFCC in my model estimating the effect of lawmakers' constitutional objections to avoid post-treatment bias, the model estimating the effect of the variables *Incumbent government* and *Years until election* can include these types of controls. First, the court may be less concerned about a non-compliance threat when a considerable amount of time lies between the reviewed law's adoption and the court's corresponding ruling, either because it took several years before an application challenging the law reached the court or because a case lingered on at the court for years. Therefore, I control for the time that had passed between the date the challenged law had been adopted and the date the court issued its corresponding ruling, *Years since adoption*, as well as the time it took the GFCC to issue its ruling since the corresponding application had been filed with the court's registrar, *Length of proceeding*.[3] On average, between 1977 and 2017 the GFCC's Senates issued their rulings roughly 6.5 years after the reviewed law had been adopted by the Bundestag (the standard deviation of the variable *Years since adoption* is 4.6 years), while their proceedings lasted on average 3.6 years (the standard deviation of the variable *Length of proceeding* is roughly 2.3). Finally, I control for the type of constitutional review procedure at the GFCC (e.g. concrete norm control, abstract norm control, or constitutional complaints).

5.2 Estimation and analysis

In the following, I consider each hypothesis in turn and first specify the statistical model I employ to test the hypothesis, followed by a brief discussion of how I estimated the models' coefficients. I then discuss the sign and uncertainty of the relevant regression coefficients, and finally provide an intuition of what

[3] While I can pin down the time that had passed between a law's adoption and the court's corresponding decision to the exact number of days (then expressed in years), I can only identify the year an application was lodged with the GFCC, yet not its exact date. Hence, the variable *Length of proceeding* reports only an approximate time the GFCC spent on a particular proceeding. However, lacking access to the files submitted by individual applicants (e.g. lower courts or individuals filing a constitutional complaint) that would allow me to identify the exact date the GFCC received an application, referring to the year seems to be the best option.

these coefficients mean in substantive terms. Throughout this section, I will make an effort to visualize the relevant results of my analysis rather than providing lengthy tables displaying a myriad of regression coefficients (although the latter will make an appearance in the appendix to this chapter). The specification of my statistical models requires a fair bit of notation and I will stick to the type of notation used by Gelman and Hill (2007), while occasionally resorting to matrix notation. To save on notation for nominal variables with more than two categories, I express regression coefficients for these variables through a single coefficient.[4]

5.2.1 Costly signalling and judicial deference

I first consider my theoretical model's core claim: The GFCC is more likely to show deference to lawmakers who have initiated a confrontation that could be costly for them. The dependent variable *Strike* is binary, accordingly I estimate a logistic regression model. Since paragraphs challenged in different court cases are nested in federal laws, I allow intercepts to vary across federal laws. Throughout this section, let i indicate the individual challenged paragraphs and j indicate federal laws. Model 1 to test this claim is then defined as follows:

$$
\begin{aligned}
\Pr(\text{Strike}_i = 1) = \text{logit}^{-1}(\beta_0 + \beta_1 \cdot \text{Opposition MPs}_i + \beta_2 \cdot \text{Governing MPs}_i + \\
\beta_3 \cdot \text{Law by grand-coalition}_i + \beta_5 \cdot \text{Policy area}_i + \\
\beta_6 \cdot \text{Cross-party proposal}_i + \beta_7 \cdot \text{Senate}_i + \alpha_{j[i]}^{\text{Law ID}}) \\
\alpha_j^{\text{Law ID}} \sim N(0, \sigma^2_{\text{Law ID}}), \quad \text{for} \quad j = 1, \ldots, J \quad \text{(number of laws)}
\end{aligned}
$$

All statistical models in this chapter are estimated using the statistical computing environment R. In light of the large number of parameters to estimate for a relatively small dataset, I follow advice by Gelman and Hill (2007) and employ a Bayesian approach to estimate the model parameters. Throughout this chapter, the Bayesian estimation of the models' parameters relies on the **rstanarm** package (Stan Development Team, 2016). For each model, I specify **rstanarm's** weakly informative default (normal) prior distributions (i.e. normal priors of regression coefficients for explanatory variables are centred at 0 with a standard deviation of 2.5, the default prior for the intercept has a mean

[4] For instance, the nominal variable *Policy area* comprises ten categories and would require coefficients for seven dummy variables, one for each category save the reference category. For convenience, I write down only one regression coefficient for the variable *Policy area*.

of 0 and a standard deviation of 10). For each model estimated in this chapter, I run four chains with 1,000 warm-up iterations and 5,000 sampling iterations, yielding a total of 20,000 draws describing the model parameters' posterior distributions. Across all models estimated in this chapter, none of the parameters' $\hat{R}$ values exceed 1.01, well below the critical threshold of 1.2 defined by Gelman and Rubin (1992).

My interpretation focuses on the regression coefficients for the main explanatory variables of interest, *Constitutional objections by opposition MP(s)* and *Constitutional objections by governing MP(s)*. Results for the remaining coefficients of Model 1 are displayed in Table 5.2 in the chapter's appendix. Figure 5.1 reports posterior distributions and their respective means of the coefficients for the two explanatory variables of interest. We can quickly spot an interesting pattern in the relationship between lawmakers' constitutional objections and the GFCC's decision-making. The posterior mean of the coefficient for *Constitutional objections by opposition MP(s)* is positive and its highest posterior density (HPD) effectively allows us to be confident that the coefficient is not negative (note that the coefficient's 95% HPD interval just overlaps zero). The coefficient suggests that the GFCC was more likely to invalidate a federal law (or parts thereof) if members of the opposition in the Bundestag had objected the law as unconstitutional just prior to its adoption.

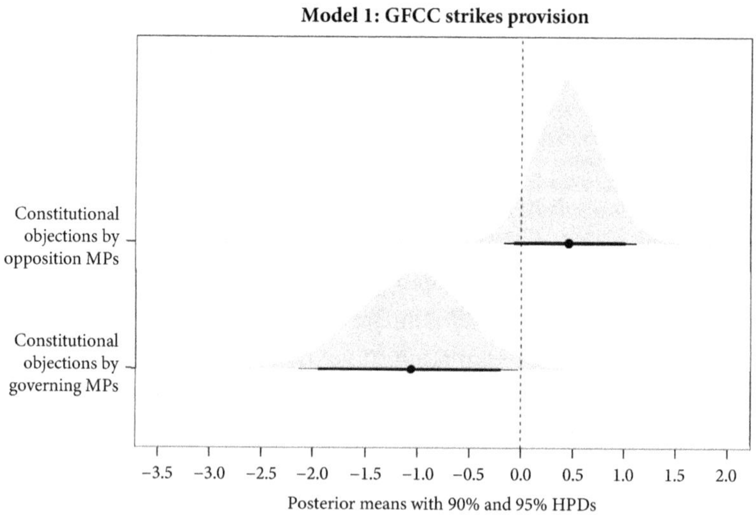

Figure 5.1 Posterior means, 90% and 95% highest posterior densities for main fixed-effects coefficients of Model 1; posterior distributions are illustrated in grey

This result seems hardly surprising. While controlling for objections voiced by members of the governing coalition caucus, the reference category for the variable *Constitutional objections by opposition MP(s)* by and large captures laws, which did not attract any constitutional concerns at the final stage of the legislative process. Notwithstanding the possibility that members of the opposition declare government policy as unconstitutional to score political points, the measure may still come somewhat close to an 'objective' evaluation of the constitutionality of a law. Laws which did not attract constitutional objections in the Bundestag may simply be more likely the ones which actually do not infringe on any constitutional norms. At the same time, it seems plausible to assume that at least some of the laws, which were objected by members of the parliamentary opposition, indeed conflict with the constitution. Accordingly, we should expect the GFCC to be more likely to strike (parts of) these types of laws.

Interestingly, the opposite appears to be the case if members of the governing coalition caucus had objected a federal law as unconstitutional. The coefficient's posterior mean for the variable *Constitutional objections by governing MP(s)* is negative (as well as every point within the coefficient's 95% HPD), suggesting that the court was less likely to strike federal law as unconstitutional when lawmakers in government had ignored constitutional concerns from their own political allies. The theoretical model presented in Chapter 2 provides an explanation for this otherwise counter-intuitive finding. Insisting on pursuing a constitutionally controversial policy while dismissing the concerns of political allies can be costly for lawmakers in government if a constitutional court strikes down the policy. However, since this choice carries political risks, lawmakers signal their readiness to defend the policy against a judicial veto and, if necessary, avoid complying with the court's ruling. When a court detects such signals and becomes concerned about non-compliance, it is incentivized to adopt a more deferential approach in its decision-making.

I now illustrate the substantive effects for variation on the variables *Constitutional objections by opposition MP(s)* and *Constitutional objections by governing MP(s)*. Given the random effects bear on the results, I predict average marginal probabilities, indicating the average change in the probability of *Strike* = 1 across all laws in my data while manipulating values on the main independent variables of interest.[5] I predict the difference in average

[5] Specifically, I hold an independent variable of interest k in the data-matrix $\mathbf{X}$ constant at a specific value x to create the matrix $\mathbf{X_i}$. Let $\mathbf{B}$ denote a matrix containing fixed-effect coefficient estimates and $\boldsymbol{\Gamma}$ denote a matrix containing random-effect coefficient estimates from the Bayesian model's sampling iterations, I then calculate $\mathbf{H_i} = \alpha + \mathbf{X_i}\mathbf{B} + \mathbf{Z}\boldsymbol{\Gamma}$. The matrix $\mathbf{H_i}$ contains the predicted log-odds for each

marginal probabilities between the two variables' levels (i.e. 0 and 1), respectively. Figure 5.2 shows that the model predicts that the GFCC was on average about 9 percentage-points more likely to strike federal law paragraphs if the federal law had been objected by members of the parliamentary opposition as unconstitutional than if no opposition members had raised concerns. On the other hand, when constitutional concerns had been raised by members of the governing majority, the model predicts that the GFCC was on average about 19 percentage-points less likely to strike the challenged paragraphs, a substantial decrease in the court's use of its constitutional veto. The GFCC is more likely to back-off from challenging lawmakers if the latter had signalled determination in their pursuit of controversial policy by taking the risk of ignoring constitutional objections from their own political allies. This evidence is consistent with the theoretical model's claim that courts are more likely to respond with deference to lawmakers, who had provoked a potentially costly confrontation.

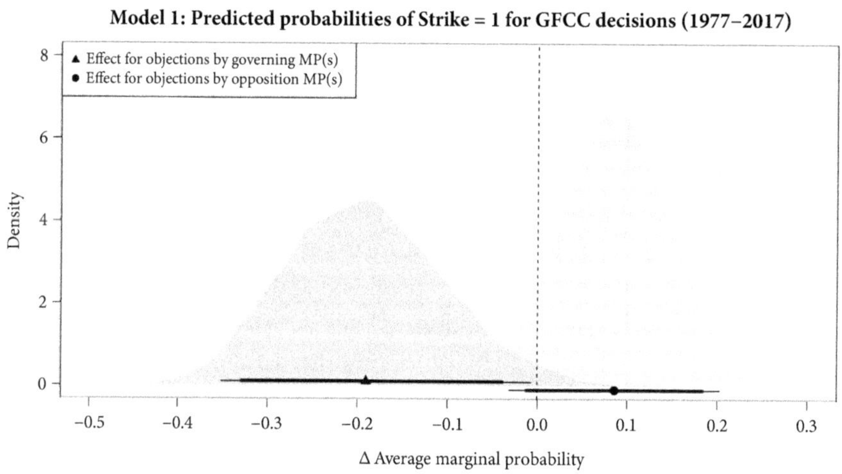

Figure 5.2 First difference in predicted average marginal probabilities for *Constitutional objections by opposition MP(s)* and *Constitutional objections by governing MP(s)* with 5.0th–90th and 2.5th–97.5th percentiles of predictions

sampling iteration across the observations in $\mathbf{X_i}$. I can transform these into predicted probabilities through $\mathbf{M_i} = \frac{exp(\mathbf{H_i})}{1+exp(\mathbf{H_i})}$. I can then calculate the expectation of average marginal probabilities across the sampling iterations and their 2.5th and 97.5th percentiles.

5.2.2 Anticipation of elections

Next, I provide an empirical test of the claim that the GFCC should be less likely to strike a federal law when it is likely that the lawmakers responsible for the reviewed act would also be in charge of crafting the response to the GFCC's judgment (see Hypothesis 2 in Chapter 2). At the heart of my empirical test is an interaction effect involving the variables *Incumbent government* and *Years until election*. Again, given the dependent variable *Strike* is binary, while challenged paragraphs are nested in federal laws, I estimate a multi-level logistic regression model, allowing intercepts to vary across federal laws. Model 2 is then defined as:

$$\begin{aligned}
\Pr(\text{Strike}_i = 1) = \text{logit}^{-1}(&\beta_0 + \beta_1 \cdot \text{Years until election}_i + \\
&\beta_2 \cdot \text{Incumbent government}_i + \\
&\beta_3 \cdot \text{Years until election}_i \cdot \text{Incumbent government}_i + \\
&\beta_4 \cdot \text{Policy area}_i + \beta_5 \cdot \text{Court proceeding}_i + \\
&\beta_6 \cdot \text{Years since adoption}_i + \\
&\beta_7 \cdot \text{Length of proceeding}_i + \alpha_{j[i]}^{\text{Law ID}})
\end{aligned}$$

$$\alpha_j^{\text{Law ID}} \sim N(0, \sigma^2_{\text{Law ID}}), \quad \text{for} \quad j = 1, \ldots, J \quad (\text{number of laws})$$

Figure 5.3 illustrates the posterior means, 90% and 95% HPDs for the coefficients of the variables *Years until election* and *Current government*, as well as their interaction term. Results for all coefficients of Model 2 are displayed in Table 5.3 in the appendix to this chapter. The posterior mean, 90% and 95% HPDs of the coefficient for the variable *Years until election* suggest that the GFCC appears more likely to strike federal law as the time left until the next election to the Bundestag increases—provided the reviewed law was *not* authored by the current governing coalition. In other words, when considering laws that were not adopted by the current incumbent, the GFCC tends to avoid striking federal laws when elections are around the corner. Evidence from interviews with former justices and law clerks at the GFCC provides an explanation for this pattern. In a telephone interview conducted on 18 April 2019, one of the justices noted:

> Something that is rarely mentioned when people cover the Federal Constitutional Court is that we do pay attention to the timing of our decisions. For

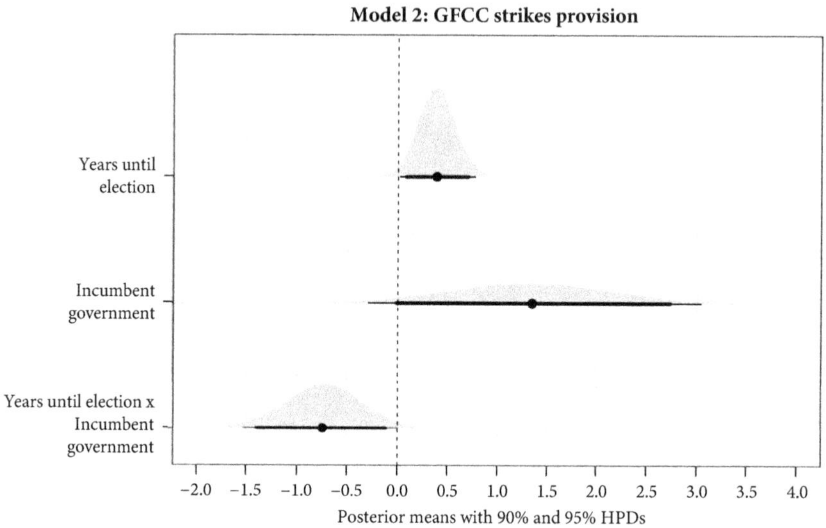

Figure 5.3 Posterior means, 90% and 95% highest posterior densities for main fixed-effects coefficients of Model 2; posterior distributions are illustrated in grey

instance, the court will not issue a politically sensitive decision during an election season, we don't do that.

Accordingly, the GFCC may generally be less likely to strike a law as the next elections are drawing closer simply because the court carefully avoids playing a proactive role in the electorates' decision-making at the ballot box. At the same time, the coefficient of the interaction term suggests that another timing-related factor influences the Court's decision-making, provided the GFCC reviews laws passed by the incumbent governing coalition. The posterior mean for the interaction term's coefficient is negative and distinguishable from zero. This suggests that the GFCC on average appears less likely to strike a law as the time until the next election increases, provided the court reviews a law adopted by the incumbent governing coalition.

In the following, I consider whether these coefficients translate into a substantially discernible effect. Again, I predict average marginal probabilities, indicating the average change in the probability of *Strike* = 1 across all groups (i.e. laws) in my data while manipulating values on the main explanatory variables of interest, *Years until election* and *Incumbent government*.[6] Figure 5.4

[6] Specifically, I allow the variable *Years until election* to vary from its minimum value 0.01 to its maximum value 3.98 in the data, and consider its effect for both cases of *Incumbent government* = 0 and *Incumbent government* = 1.

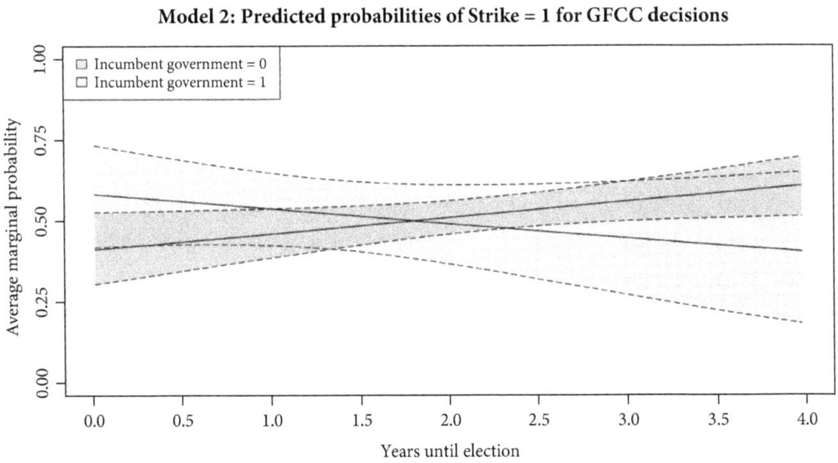

Figure 5.4 Predicted average marginal probabilities for *Current government* across range of *Years until election* (solid lines indicate mean values of predicted probabilities, shaded areas indicate 2.5–97.5th percentiles of predictions)

illustrates average marginal predicted probabilities across the range of *Years until election* for *Incumbent government* = 0 (dark grey) and *Incumbent government* = 1 (light grey). Figure 5.4 shows that the effect of the time left until the next elections on the Court's decision-making is conditional on whether or not it reviews a law authored by the incumbent government. The average predicted probability of a judicial veto for laws authored by the incumbent government slopes downwards as the time until the next election increases, yet upwards for laws *not* authored by the incumbent government. The GFCC appears more careful when reviewing incumbent governments' laws when the latter have more time left in office until the next election. However, Figure 5.4 also shows that the predictions' 2.5th and 97.5th percentiles for each scenario are at no point clearly distinguishable from each other across the range of the variable *Years until election*. In other words, while there is tentative support for the claim that the GFCC is less likely to strike a federal law when it is likely that the lawmakers responsible for the law would also be in charge of implementing the court's decision (see Hypothesis 2 in Chapter 2), uncertainty surrounding the model's estimates, particularly for *Incumbent government* = 1, is relatively high.

What does this mean for the empirical evaluation of the theoretical model presented in Chapter 2 in a more general sense? Hypothesis 2 draws on the observation from the formal analysis that—holding everything else constant—increasing the likelihood of the policy's authors controlling implementation of the court's judgment corresponds to movement across the model's equilibria. This movement starts at the model's pooling equilibrium showing that all types of lawmakers 'auto-limit' their policy choices knowing the court would strike every policy it considers unconstitutional, and it eventually ends at a pooling equilibrium where all types of lawmakers ignore constitutional jurisprudence knowing that the court will never challenge them. The justification for selecting Germany as the case for the model's empirical evaluation in this chapter centred on the assumption that the GFCC exercises constitutional review in an environment matching the conditions of the model's partial-pooling equilibrium: a court enjoying high levels of public support reviewing the acts of lawmakers controlling (at least for long periods within the timeframe of the analysis) government office for several consecutive terms. It is these kinds of environments in which the costs lawmakers appear willing to pay from confrontation with the court signal a non-compliance threat and the evidence presented in Section 5.2.1 appears consistent with this claim.

However, it is also these kinds of environments in which the likelihood that lawmakers responsible for the reviewed law would also control the implementation of the courts' judgment does not directly reflect in the court's decision-making but in the choices of lawmakers (i.e. otherwise 'compliant' lawmakers are more likely to risk confrontation with the court as their chance at getting a shot at controlling implementation increases). It is possible that—particularly in light of the GFCC's high public support—German lawmakers' chances of controlling implementation of the GFCC's judgments on their own policies are never high enough to move from an environment characterized by the model's partial-pooling equilibrium to a scenario in which the GFCC consistently exercises self-restraint (the model's final pooling equilibrium).

5.2.3 Robustness checks

In addition to the statistical models estimated for the main analyses discussed in Sections 5.2.1 and 5.2.2, I implement several robustness checks to dig a little deeper regarding the results from Model 1, which shows that the GFCC is less likely to strike a federal law if it had been objected as unconstitutional by members of the governing coalition caucus prior to its adoption. While the theoretical model of Chapter 2 provides one possible explanation for this counter-intuitive pattern, another explanation appears consistent with this evidence. Some lawmakers in the governing coalition caucus may use constitutional objections in the Bundestag to send a highly visible signal of their position on a policy issue to pander to a particular constituency. Several former members of the German government highlighted in my interviews that every new legislative initiative is carefully screened by constitutional lawyers working for two of the federal government's ministries, the Justice Ministry and the Ministry for Internal Affairs (the so-called 'constitutional ministries'). One lawmaker noted in a telephone interview conducted on 11 November 2017:

> Generally, it seems to me that the Ministry for Internal Affairs tries to make as much use as possible of the scope of action the constitution leaves us, while my feeling always was that the Justice Ministry tends to make the case that some initiatives go too far. What then follows is a close exchange among these ministries and every initiative is subject to their joint scrutiny.

Following the ministries' screenings of federal laws' constitutional compatibility, any subsequent objections voiced by members of the governing coalition at the end of the legislative process may reflect opportunistic political motivations rather than genuine constitutional concerns. We should then expect the court to be less likely to strike these types of laws, an expectation that appears consistent with the evidence discussed in Section 5.2.1.

To evaluate this alternative explanation for the empirical pattern shown by Model 1, I first turn to the decisions the GFCC makes about the admissibility of constitutional review cases. The GFCC can refuse to admit constitutional complaints directed against laws for decision in its Senates if applicants fail to show that the challenged law affects them personally, presently, and directly. In addition, when considering laws referred for review by lower courts, the GFCC can rule a case as inadmissible if the lower court fails to demonstrate which constitutional norm the challenged act appears to violate and how it arrived at this conclusion. In other words, a lower court has to show that the law referred for review harbours a violation of constitutional norms that merits the GFCC's scrutiny.

The GFCC's rules concerning the admissibility of cases allow the court to avoid overburdening its Senates with cases which do not require scrutiny of the challenged act's constitutional compatibility on the merits, and dismiss these cases through so-called Chamber decisions instead, with sets of three justices hearing the cases. Given the GFCC enjoys some discretion over the cases it hears in its Senates and dismisses the kinds of cases that do not involve a substantive constitutional question mitigates concerns that the empirical pattern shown by Model 1 reflects governing lawmakers voicing constitutional for purely political motivations. All of the GFCC's cases included in the analysis of

Model 1 made it past the court's admissibility test, suggesting that they involve substantial constitutional questions that merit the GFCC's scrutiny.

Nonetheless, it is still worthwhile to evaluate whether governing lawmakers' constitutional objections of laws play a discernible role in the GFCC's choice to admit constitutional review cases for decision. For the analysis below, I extend my dataset to cases in which the GFCC eventually ruled that a challenge of a federal law's constitutionality was inadmissible, increasing the number of observations in my data to 716 challenges of legislative provisions from 404 federal laws. If members of the governing coalition caucus voice constitutional concerns about federal laws for purely political reasons rather than legal motivations, applications challenging these laws should not be more likely to be admitted for decision at the GFCC than any other applications. Vice versa, if all constitutional concerns voiced by governing lawmakers indeed speak to constitutional issues meriting the GFCC's scrutiny, the court should also be more likely to admit hearing cases involving laws subject to these concerns.

To test these arguments, I consider the effect of the variable *Constitutional objections by governing MP(s)* on an outcome variable capturing whether the GFCC admitted a case for decision (*Admission* = 1) or not (*Admission* = 0). The multi-level logistic regression model, Model 3, includes the same control variables as Model 1 in Section 5.2.1 and is defined as follows:

$$\begin{aligned}
\Pr(\text{Admission}_i = 1) = \text{logit}^{-1}(\beta_0 &+ \beta_1 \cdot \text{Opposition MPs}_i \\
&+ \beta_2 \cdot \text{Governing MPs}_i \\
&+ \beta_3 \cdot \text{Law by grand-coalition}_i + \beta_5 \cdot \text{Policy area}_i \\
&+ \beta_6 \cdot \text{Cross-party proposal}_i + \alpha_{j[i]}^{\text{Law ID}}) \\
\alpha_j^{\text{Law ID}} \sim N(0, \sigma_{\text{Law ID}}^2), \quad \text{for} \quad j &= 1, \ldots, J \quad \text{(number of laws)}
\end{aligned}$$

Figure 5.5 reports posterior means, 90% and 95% HPDs for the regression coefficients of the variables *Constitutional objections by opposition MP(s)* and *Constitutional objections by governing MP(s)*. Results for the remaining coefficients of Model 3 are provided in Table 5.4 in the chapter's appendix. Figure 5.5 shows a highly interesting pattern. First, we can see that the coefficient estimate for the variable *Constitutional objections by opposition MP(s)* is negative and clearly distinguishable from zero. The evidence suggests that challenges of legislative provisions that had been objected as unconstitutional by members

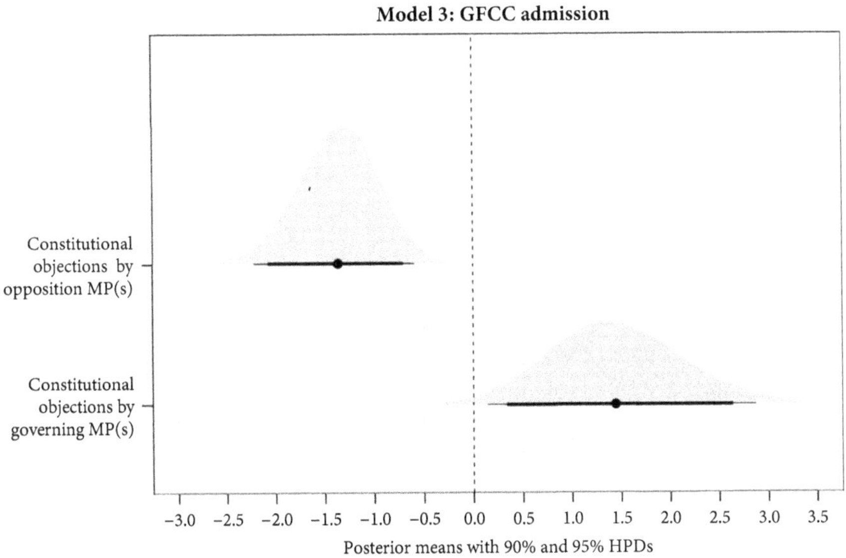

Figure 5.5 Posterior means, 90% and 95% HPDs for coefficients for main fixed-effects coefficients of Model 3; posterior distributions are illustrated in grey

of the parliamentary opposition are less likely to be admitted for a decision by the GFCC's Senates on the merits than any other challenges. In fact, out of the 299 inadmissible challenges in my data (i.e. *Admission* = 0), 96 challenges concerned legislative paragraphs that the parliamentary opposition had considered as unconstitutional. This pattern fits an assumption that members of the opposition use constitutional objections opportunistically to discredit government policy, even when the legal merits of their objections are at best questionable.

The exact opposite, however, is the case once we turn our attention to constitutional objections voiced by members of the governing coalition caucus. The coefficient estimate for the variable *Constitutional objections by governing MP(s)* is positive and again clearly distinguishable from zero. Challenges of legislative paragraphs that members of the governing majority had considered constitutionally problematic stand a higher chance to be admitted for a decision on the merits by the GFCC's Senates—only 12 of the 299 inadmissible challenges concerned legislative provisions objected by governing MPs. This evidence corroborates the assumption that governing MPs' constitutional objections to government policy reflect legal rather political motivations, and that the results of Model 1 reflect the GFCC's strategic responses to credible non-compliance threats.

A second robustness check for the results obtained from Model 1 involves substituting the dichotomous variable *Constitutional objections by governing MP(s)* with the variable *Seniority of objecting governing MP(s)*. As discussed in Section 5.1.1 above, it is possible that lawmakers of the governing coalition caucus voicing constitutional concerns are backbenchers at the fringes of their political parties, criticizing government to pander to a particular electoral constituency. Similar to the motivation underlying the previous robustness check, a pattern of the GFCC upholding laws which had been objected by government backbenchers may thus not reflect the GFCC's response to a credible non-compliance threat but may simply be due to a lack of substance in backbenchers' claims of unconstitutionality.

Recall that the variable *Seniority of objecting governing MP(s)* comprises three categories: *No objections* if no member of the governing coalition voiced constitutional concerns; *Senior governing MP(s)* if constitutional concerns are voiced by a cabinet member, a governing party's designated spokesperson for a policy area, a member of a governing party's executive board, or a governing party member serving as parliamentary committee chair; and *Junior governing MP(s)* if constitutional concerns are voiced by any other member of the governing coalition caucus. In the following, I estimate a multi-level logistic regression model, Model 4, including the same set of control variables as Model 1, yet replacing the explanatory variable *Constitutional objections by governing MP(s)* with the variable *Seniority of objecting governing MP(s)*. Model 4 is then defined as:

$$\begin{aligned}\Pr(\text{Strike}_i = 1) = \text{logit}^{-1}(&\beta_0 + \beta_1 \cdot \text{Obj. opposition MP(s)}_i + \\ &\beta_2 \cdot \text{Senior gov. MP(s)}_i + \beta_3 \cdot \text{Junior gov. MP(s)}_i + \\ &\beta_4 \cdot \text{Law by grand-coalition}_i + \beta_5 \cdot \text{Policy area}_i + \\ &\beta_6 \cdot \text{Cross-party proposal}_i + \alpha_{j[i]}^{\text{Law ID}}) \\ \alpha_j^{\text{Law ID}} \sim N(0, \sigma^2_{\text{Law ID}}), \quad &\text{for} \quad j = 1, \ldots, J \quad \text{(number of laws)}\end{aligned}$$

The category *No objections by governing MP(s)* serves as the reference category for the variable *Seniority of objecting governing MP(s)* in Model 4. If the empirical pattern uncovered by Model 1 was driven by backbenchers' constitutional concerns lacking legal substance, the coefficient for the category *Junior governing MP(s)* should be negative and clearly distinguishable from zero, while the same should not be the case for the coefficient for the category *Senior governing MP(s)*.

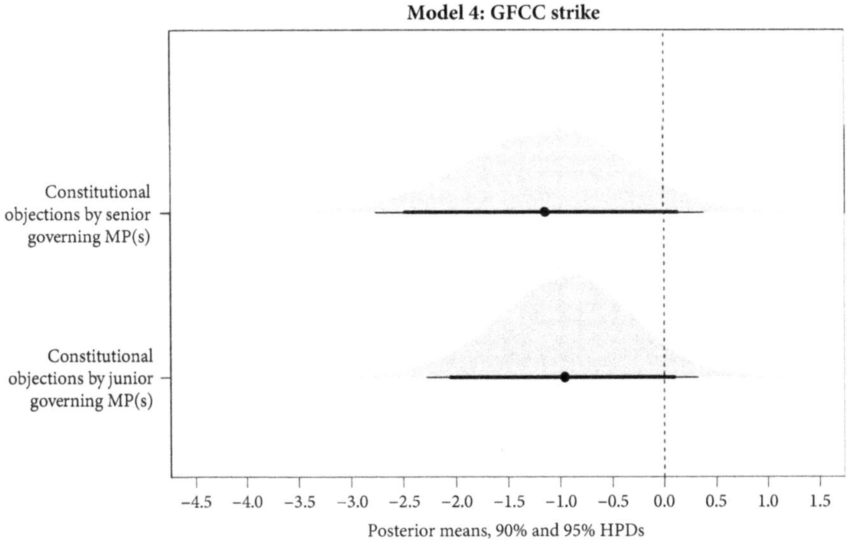

Figure 5.6 Posterior means, 90% and 95% HPDs for coefficients for main fixed-effects coefficients of Model 4; posterior distributions are illustrated in grey

Figure 5.6 reports the posterior distributions, their means as well as 90% and 95% HPDs for the coefficients of the categories *Senior governing MP(s)* and *Junior governing MP(s)* of the variable *Seniority of objecting governing MP(s)*. Results for the remaining coefficients of Model 4 are displayed in Table 5.5 in the appendix. With the caveat in mind that the inference from Model 4 is driven by a very small number of observations in the categories *Senior governing MP(s)* and *Junior governing MP(s)* (22 and 12 observations, respectively), there is no conclusive evidence suggesting that the seniority of the governing lawmakers voicing constitutional concerns about a law makes a difference in the GFCC's decision-making. The coefficients' posterior means reported in Figure 5.6 are both clearly negative, and while their 95% HPDs indicate that the coefficient estimates are not distinguishable from zero at conventional levels of confidence, wide uncertainty intervals surrounding the estimates seem not surprising given the few number of observations the inference relies on. Overall, the results obtained from Model 4 show the same general pattern as Model 1 in my main analysis. The GFCC appears less likely to strike federal laws as unconstitutional if lawmakers of the governing coalition caucus (irrespective of their seniority) had objected the reviewed laws as unconstitutional prior to their adoption in the Bundestag.

5.3 Conclusion

In this chapter, I set out to test the core empirical implication derived from the theoretical model presented in Chapter 2: I expect courts to be more likely to show self-restraint in their jurisprudence when lawmakers send costly and thus credible signals of a non-compliance threat. I identified Germany's constitutional politics between 1977 and 2017 and the GFCC's constitutional review of federal law as a suitable case to empirically test this claim. Within this timeframe, both the GFCC and lawmakers in the elected branches occupied (at least during certain legislative terms) powerful positions in Germany's political system, setting the stage for constitutional confrontations over policy. The empirical analysis presented in this chapter suggests that the GFCC was indeed less likely to strike parts of federal laws when members of the governing coalition had previously objected these laws as unconstitutional. Ignoring their colleagues' constitutional concerns may backfire for lawmakers in government once a constitutional court actually invalidates their policies. However, because this choice is politically risky, it also signals lawmakers' determination to courts, which according to my theoretical model explains the GFCC's propensity to exercise self-restraint when considering these types of cases.

While this empirical pattern may raise normative concerns, which will be further discussed in the concluding chapter of this book, it is worth mentioning here what the empirical evidence presented in this chapter does not suggest. First, the data I have collected suggests that, at least in Germany, it is rare for constitutional concerns raised by members of the governing coalition to be ignored (this occurs in less than 10% of the GFCC's constitutional review cases involving federal laws). In other words, there is little evidence to support the idea that governing majorities often disregard credible warnings that their actions might conflict with constitutional norms, regularly pushing constitutional boundaries and provoking clashes with the GFCC. Unsurprisingly, it happens far more often that government disregards claims of constitutional incompatibility voiced by the parliamentary opposition, although it is difficult to assess the credibility of each of these claims. In addition, if anything, the results of my analysis show that the GFCC is indeed more likely to strike federal laws when members of the opposition rang the constitutional alarm bells.

Even when lawmakers in government occasionally do flout their political allies' concerns, the evidence considered in this chapter does not suggest that the GFCC *always* backs off from challenging them. The interpretation I give to the main empirical finding presented in this chapter suggests that lawmakers' costly signalling of a non-compliance threat effectively allows the GFCC to avoid the kinds of confrontations that would visibly rattle at the pillars of systems of limited government, with courts invalidating the elected branches' act and the latter failing to comply. In systems of limited government, the competences that can shape policy are distributed across the elected and judicial branches, with the branches' 'ambition counteracting ambition' (Madison, 1961). After all, lawmakers' costly signalling may help courts to navigate the tension in their role as effective checks on the elected branches and their reliance on the latter for the efficacy of their jurisprudence.

5.4 Appendix

In the following, I tabulate results for fixed-effect coefficient estimates of each model estimated in Chapter 3. Each table reports the coefficient estimates' posterior means, posterior distributions' standard deviation as well as 95% HPD intervals. Further, the tables report the number of laws (i.e. groups in the multi-level models), the total number of observations, and the variance of their random-effect, $\sigma^2_{\text{Law ID}}$. Replication files for all analyses presented in this chapter are available upon request.

Main analyses

Table 5.2 Posterior means, standard deviations, and 95% HPDs of fixed-effects coefficients of Model 1—GFCC strike of federal laws, 1977–2017

Variable	Mean	SD	2.5%	97.5%
Constitutional objections by opposition MP(s)	0.46	0.32	−0.16	1.11
Constitutional objections by governing MP(s)	−1.06	0.53	−2.13	−0.03
Law by grand-coalition	1.31	0.74	−0.10	2.80
Policy area: Education	2.05	1.17	−0.09	4.50
Policy area: Family law	1.27	1.27	−1.09	3.91
Policy area: Healthcare	−1.19	0.80	−2.81	0.32
Policy area: Interior	−0.29	0.65	−1.60	0.98
Policy area: Social insurance	−0.29	0.63	−1.52	0.95
Policy area: Other	−0.47	0.82	−2.10	1.14
Policy area: Budgets/Fiscal policy	0.09	0.62	−1.13	1.31
Policy area: Individual rights	−0.48	0.62	−1.73	0.74
Policy area: Public infrastructure	−1.38	0.88	−3.14	0.32
Cross-party proposal	−0.25	0.63	−1.51	0.98
$\sigma^2_{\text{Law ID}}$: 0.17				
Number of groups (Law ID): 275				
Number of observations: 417				

Table 5.3 Posterior means, standard deviations, and 95% HPDs of fixed-effects coefficients of Model 2—GFCC strike of federal laws, 1977–2017

Variable	Mean	SD	2.5%	97.5%
Years until election	0.38	0.19	0.02	0.77
Incumbent government	1.35	0.84	−0.29	3.04
Years until election × Current government	−0.74	0.39	−1.53	0.00
Policy area: Education	2.17	1.52	−0.67	5.27
Policy area: Family law	1.28	1.62	−1.80	4.55
Policy area: Healthcare	−1.67	1.09	−3.85	0.41
Policy area: Interior	−0.30	0.89	−2.01	1.47
Policy area: Social insurance	−0.65	0.88	−2.37	1.09
Policy area: Other	−0.74	1.17	−3.01	1.59
Policy area: Budgets/Fiscal policy	0.18	0.83	−1.44	1.81
Policy area: Individual rights	−0.63	0.83	−2.26	0.98
Policy area: Public infrastructure	−1.81	1.24	−4.28	0.63
Court proceeding: Concrete norm control	0.61	0.67	−0.69	1.93
Court proceeding: Constitutional complaints	0.55	0.64	−0.70	1.82
Years since adoption	0.06	0.05	−0.04	0.17
Length of proceeding	−0.04	0.09	−0.23	0.13
$\sigma^2_{\text{Law ID}}$: 1.69				
Number of groups (Law ID): 275				
Number of observations: 417				

Robustness checks

Table 5.4 Posterior means, standard deviations, and 95% HPDs of fixed-effects coefficients of Model 3—GFCC admission of challenges to federal laws, 1977–2017

Variable	Mean	SD	2.5%	97.5%
Constitutional objections by opposition MP(s)	−1.36	0.41	−2.21	−0.60
Constitutional objections by governing MP(s)	1.44	0.69	0.14	2.86
Law by grand-coalition	−2.34	0.59	−3.59	−1.26
Policy area: Education	2.14	1.13	−0.06	4.40
Policy area: Family law	0.45	0.90	−1.36	2.16
Policy area: Healthcare	6.37	1.28	4.09	9.11
Policy area: Interior	7.28	1.23	5.12	9.88
Policy area: Social insurance	0.60	0.53	−0.45	1.60
Policy area: Other	1.95	0.79	0.41	3.51
Policy area: Budgets/Fiscal policy	3.06	0.58	1.95	4.24
Policy area: Individual rights	1.40	0.51	0.40	2.40
Policy area: Public infrastructure	5.22	1.40	2.65	8.17
Cross-party proposal	2.08	0.63	0.93	3.37
$\sigma^2_{\text{Law ID}}$: 1.77				
Number of groups (Law ID): 404				
Number of observations: 716				

Table 5.5 Posterior means, standard deviations, and 95% HPDs of fixed-effects coefficients of Model 4—GFCC strike of federal laws, 1977–2017

Variable	Mean	SD	2.5%	97.5%
Constitutional objections by opposition MP(s)	0.46	0.32	−0.16	1.11
Constitutional objections by junior governing MP(s)	−1.14	0.80	−2.76	0.39
Constitutional objections by senior governing MP(s)	−0.96	0.66	−2.28	0.32
Law by grand-coalition	1.35	0.77	−0.10	2.92
Policy area: Education	2.07	1.18	−0.09	4.56
Policy area: Family law	1.31	1.28	−1.09	3.95
Policy area: Healthcare	−1.20	0.82	−2.86	0.37
Policy area: Interior	−0.29	0.67	−1.61	1.01
Policy area: Social insurance	−0.28	0.64	−1.54	0.97
Policy area: Other	−0.46	0.83	−2.08	1.17
Policy area: Budgets/Fiscal policy	0.10	0.63	−1.13	1.35
Policy area: Individual rights	−0.49	0.63	−1.74	0.74
Policy area: Public infrastructure	−1.38	0.90	−3.20	0.37
Cross-party proposal	−0.28	0.65	−1.58	0.97
$\sigma^2_{\text{Law ID}}$: 0.19				
Number of groups (Law ID): 275				
Number of observations: 417				

6
Pushing Boundaries: The Case of State Surveillance in Germany

Throughout this book, I argue that the shadow of constitutional review cannot always deter lawmakers from pursuing policies that are pushing constitutional boundaries. Especially when it is politically costly for lawmakers to have their policies struck down by a court, lawmakers' dogged pursuit of constitutionally controversial policies sends credible signals that they are prepared to evade compliance with unfavourable jurisprudence. Courts concerned about protecting their institutional integrity but lacking the 'power of the purse and sword' to coerce the political branches into compliance should therefore be more likely to defer to lawmakers when they receive costly signals of non-compliance threats. Consequently—and counter-intuitively—courts face incentives to leave the kinds of policies on the statute books that had sparked widespread constitutional concerns and controversy.

The theoretical model introduced in Chapter 2 demonstrates these dynamics and predicts how courts and lawmakers navigate their interactions in systems of limited government amid varying conditions of their political environment. So far, I have presented empirical evidence from a statistical analysis of the German Federal Constitutional Court's (GFCC) review of federal laws between 1977 and 2017, which uncovered patterns consistent with the expectations of the theoretical model.

This chapter complements the statistical analysis with a qualitative case study of German lawmakers' tug of war with the GFCC over law enforcement's surveillance powers to combat terrorism and organized crime. It offers an analytic narrative of the story told by the theoretical model in Chapter 2 and provides the kinds of insights into the motivations of lawmakers and nuance in the GFCC's jurisprudence that a statistical analysis simply cannot deliver. Drawing on evidence from legislative preparatory works and parliamentary debate transcripts along with GFCC judgment texts, interviews with law clerks at the GFCC, and contemporary media coverage, the chapter shows how German lawmakers repeatedly tried to expand law enforcement's

Putting Courts Under Pressure. Philipp A. Schroeder, Oxford University Press. © Philipp A. Schroeder (2025).
DOI: 10.1093/9780198953265.003.0006

authority to monitor the activities of crime suspects—and how they repeatedly found themselves defending their policies before the GFCC.

The case study captures this *repeated* nature of legislative-judicial encounters. Where jurisprudence defines narrow boundaries for lawmakers' discretion, the latter's efforts to make full use of their limited room for manoeuvre often trigger new litigation, in turn allowing the GFCC to adjust, tightening or loosening, the constraints placed on the political branches' policymaking. The chapter's qualitative evidence traces how this back-and-forth unfolded in the domain of state surveillance legislation in Germany over nearly two decades. In the late 1990s, lawmakers adopted—amid much controversy—a policy package aptly billed as the 'great eavesdropping operation' (in German, 'Großer Lauschangriff') that would allow law enforcement agents to plant acoustic surveillance devices in the private homes of crime suspects. Striking down several of the policy's provisions in 2004, the GFCC's review of the policy in *1 BvR 2378/98* defined stringent rules for the implementation of these measures and how law enforcement authorities could use the intercepted information. A few years later, these rules were evidently stretched when a coalition government of the CDU/CSU and SPD passed the 2008 Federal Criminal Police Office Act (in German, the Bundeskriminalamtgesetz, in the following BKAG). With the objective to provide federal law enforcement agents the tools to effectively combat international terrorism, the act allowed for the interference with individuals' fundamental rights to the inviolability of their home, secrecy of telecommunication, as well as the confidentiality and integrity of information technology systems.

Similar to the adoption of the 'Lauschangriff' in 1998, several prominent members of the governing coalition publicly protested against the BKAG's adoption, citing serious constitutional concerns. This time around, in its review of the policy the GFCC again declared several provisions of the act as unconstitutional, but it notably 'consolidated' existing jurisprudence regarding law enforcement's use of surveillance data for purposes other than those determining the original data collection. Specifically, the court chose to 'revoke former requirements' for law enforcement's use of data for new purposes, which had been developed by the court's jurisprudence in *1 BvR 2378/98* in 2004. Put simply, the GFCC chose to—at least partially—overrule its previous, relatively recent, jurisprudence on this issue.

The chapter's case study of German state surveillance legislation offers an excellent illustration of the back-and-forth that is characteristic of legislative-judicial interactions in systems of separation of power. Further, following the expectations of the theoretical model in Chapter 2, it provides an explanation for the GFCC's otherwise puzzling decision to ease constraints on lawmakers' policymaking discretion in its review of the BKAG. Existing scholarship highlights that courts generally avoid overruling legal precedents they had specified in their recent case law. Zink et al. (2009, 911) argue that '[r]ather than adjudicating disputes on a case-by-case basis, the Court invokes precedent in part to demonstrate its use of fair and neutral decision-making procedures, whereby similar cases are consistently treated according to similar legal principles, thus bolstering the public's acceptance of judicial outcomes and its confidence in the Court itself' (see also Hansford and Spriggs, 2006). The coalition government's decision to push the BKAG through parliament despite vehement constitutional objections voiced by prominent members of the SPD signalled government's willingness to evade compliance with jurisprudence. Again facing a grand-coalition when issuing their decision on the BKAG in April 2016, justices at the GFCC had an incentive to show self-restraint in their jurisprudence and re-evaluate some of the constitutional constraints on lawmakers.

The remainder of the chapter is structured into two sections. I begin by outlining German lawmakers' adoption of the controversial legislative package in 1998 allowing law enforcement agents to plant acoustic surveillance devices in private homes, which set the tone for German lawmakers' repeated attempts to expand state surveillance powers at the expense of individuals' right to privacy throughout the following years. Subsequently, I discuss the GFCC's constitutional review of the corresponding legislative acts in *1 BvR 2378/98*, which defined key parameters for the constitutionality of law enforcement's surveillance activities. In the chapter's second section, I turn to the BKAG, the legislative act at the centre of this case study. I provide evidence from the German parliament's documentation of committee proceedings and plenary debates to highlight the governing coalition's internal conflict over the BKAG's constitutionality throughout legislative proceedings. An in-depth analysis of the GFCC's review of the BKAG in *1 BvR 966/09* then links the constitutional controversy that had unfolded in the Bundestag to key elements of the GFCC's judgment. The chapter concludes with a discussion of the costs that German lawmakers risked (and arguably paid) with their adoption of the BKAG, and the Bundestag's response to the GFCC's judgment in *1 BvR 966/09*.

6.1 Persistence amid controversy

Citing an increasing incidence of organized crime in Germany, the parliamentary factions of the then-governing CDU/CSU and FDP as well as the SPD as the largest opposition party jointly tabled a policy package in October 1997 that promised the effective prosecution of individuals pulling the strings in criminal gangs. The initiative, at its core comprising the 1998 Fight Against Organised Crime Act and the 1998 Act Amending the Basic Law (Article 13), was aptly billed as the 'Großer Lauschangriff' (the 'great eavesdropping operation'), as it envisioned a substantial albeit controversial expansion of state surveillance powers. While law enforcement's acoustic surveillance of private homes had previously only been allowed in cases of an emergency response to *prevent* serious danger for individuals, members of the CDU/CSU, FDP, and SPD sought to expand law enforcement's use of such surveillance measures for the purposes of *investigation* and *prosecution*. Subject to obtaining a judicial warrant, law enforcement agents would be authorized to plant electronic devices in private homes to listen in on conversation between individuals suspected of committing a catalogue of crimes.

6.1.1 Debating the 'Lauschangriff' in the Bundestag

The policy package sparked heated debates in the German Bundestag and was harshly criticized by several lawmakers despite their own parliamentary factions supporting the reform. Critics highlighted that the policy's provisions conflicted with the constitutionally guaranteed inviolability of the home enshrined in Article 13 of the German constitution. In the Bundestag's first plenary debate of the corresponding acts, the FDP's former justice minister Sabine Leutheusser-Schnarrenberger lamented a 'sad day for liberal legal policy',[1] while Hermann Bachmeier, the SPD's legal policy spokesperson, noted:

> Hermann Bachmeier (SPD): We all know that the planned extensive use of acoustic surveillance measures will affect a great number of entirely uninvolved individuals and that the right to refuse to give evidence granted to suspects' relatives, medical professionals, journalists, priests and attorneys will be severely undermined.[2]

Given members of parliament across the political spectrum voiced serious reservations against the 'Lauschangriff', its passage proved to be anything but smooth for its supporters. Adding to the latter's headaches, the state government of Bremen led by the SPD, whose consent to the reform was

[1] Translated from German, excerpt from the first reading of the Fight Against Organised Crime Act, German Bundestag, 9 October 1997, 1. Beratung: BT-PlPr 13/197.

[2] Translated from German, excerpt from the first reading of the Fight Against Organised Crime Act, German Bundestag, 9 October 1997, 1. Beratung: BT-PlPr 13/197.

needed in the Bundesrat (i.e. Germany's upper parliamentary chamber comprising representatives of its state governments), publicly proclaimed its intent to reject the policy package unless substantial concessions were made.[3] Bremen's mayor insisted on adding protections that would ensure that journalists and attorneys would not become subjects of state surveillance measures, a concern shared by the German Federation of Journalists as well as the chairmen of two of Germany's largest publishing houses.[4] A mediation committee comprising selected members of the Bundestag and leaders of Germany's state governments eventually tabled a compromise solution stating that the collection of evidence based on suspects' conversations with individuals enjoying a right to refuse to give evidence—including journalists, doctors, and attorneys—would be illegal.[5]

Despite these concessions, given the policy still allowed law enforcement agents to plant acoustic surveillance devices in private homes, prominent members of the FDP continued to express their concerns that the reform was at its core unconstitutional. Burkhard Hirsch, Sabine Leutheusser-Schnarrenberger, and Gerhart Baum, three senior members of the FDP's parliamentary faction, used the Bundestag's final consideration of the 'Lauschangriff' to publicly reiterate their reservations. Summarizing the trio's concerns, Burkhard Hirsch stated:

> Burkhard Hirsch (FDP): The mediation committee's proposal cannot change my conviction that this act is conflicting with the spirit and substance of our constitution. First, because the state can literally break into important relationships of trust even if there is only the slightest suspicion against someone; second, because the state will be able listen in on a married couple's private conversations within their own home; [...] because the question of whether human dignity will be violated by such provisions is not a question of statistical frequency. Instead, the constitution should and must provide protection in every single case. And finally, because you cannot protect our fundamental values by constantly undermining them.[6]

[3] Spiegel Online (original in German), 2 February 1998. *'Eine fast neurotische Beziehung'*, https://www.spiegel.de/spiegel/a-3596.html, accessed 27 September 2024.

[4] Spiegel Online (original in German), 2 February 1998. *HAUSMITTEILUNG 2. Februar 1998 Lauschangriff*, https://www.spiegel.de/politik/hausmitteilung-2-februar-1998-lauschangriff-a-2bcf4c0e-0002-0001-0000-000008365313, accessed 27 September 2024.

[5] Beschlußempfehlung des Ausschusses nach Artikel 77 des Grundgesetzes (Vermittlungsau sschuß), 3 March 1998, BT-Drucksache 13/10004.

[6] Translated from German, excerpt from the final reading of mediation committee's proposal on the Fight Against Organised Crime Act, German Bundestag, 5 March 1998, BT-PlPr 13/222.

These concerns, however, fell on deaf ears. With the votes of the CDU/CSU and a majority of members of the FDP and SPD's parliamentary factions, the Bundestag eventually adopted the Act Amending the Basic Law (Article 13) in January 1998 and the Fight Against Organised Crime Act in March 1998.

6.1.2 Partial success for both sides

The adoption of the 'Lauschangriff' in early 1998 led to a rather unusual development. A little over a year after their own party facilitated the adoption of the 'Lauschangriff', its prominent critics in the FDP, Burkhard Hirsch, Sabine Leutheusser-Schnarrenberger, and Gerhart Baum, filed a constitutional complaint against the policy with the GFCC. The complainants argued that the policy allowed law enforcement authorities to interfere with the core area of individuals' private lives (in German, 'Kernbereich privater Lebensgestaltung') and constituted a severe infringement of their general right of personality (see paragraph 62 of *1 BvR 2378/98*). Further, they considered the policy incompatible with the constitution given the use of acoustic surveillance measures was not limited to the investigation of the most serious crimes and included loopholes relieving law enforcement from obligations to retrospectively inform suspects of the surveillance measures taken against them in a timely fashion (see paragraphs 63 and 64 of *1 BvR 2378/98*).

The GFCC took nearly five years to complete its constitutional review of the 1998 Fight Against Organised Crime Act and the 1998 Act Amending the Basic Law (Article 13). The Court's judgment in *1 BvR 2378/98* of 3 March 2004 offered partial successes for both the complainants and supporters of the 'Lauschangriff'. On the one hand, the GFCC declared that the '[a]coustic surveillance of private homes for law enforcement purposes does not *generally* violate the human dignity content of Art. 13(1) of the Basic Law and Art. 2(1) in conjunction with Art. 1(1) of the Basic Law' (paragraph 114 of *1 BvR 2378/98*, emphasis added). Specifically, the Court highlighted that 'conversations that contain information on crimes that have been committed do not fall within the inviolable core of private life' (paragraph 137 of *1 BvR 2378/98*), and thus were not beyond the reach of law enforcement authorities' surveillance measures. Nonetheless, the justices insisted that a statutory basis must exist that requires law enforcement authorities to assess the likelihood that an intercepted conversation in a private home 'falls within the part of private life that is inviolable or—if this is not the case—within the social domain' (paragraph 136 of *1 BvR 2378/98*).

While the GFCC thus upheld a key element of the 'Lauschangriff'—the acoustic surveillance of conversations in private homes to investigate crimes—it also found that a series of the 1998 Fight Against Organised Crime Act's provisions failed to meet the standards for a statutory basis that would make such surveillance measures compatible with the constitution. The GFCC declared that lawmakers had 'failed to sufficiently specify the prohibitions to carry out surveillance measures and to collect data that are required under constitutional law in cases where the core of private life is affected' (paragraph 170 of *1 BvR 2378/98*). The judgment inter alia pointed out that the policy's provisions neither ensured the illegality of intercepting private conversations when only the suspect's immediate family or other close confidants were present (see paragraph 175 of *1 BvR 2378/98*), nor 'that surveillance measures are discontinued if a situation unexpectedly arises which relates to the inviolable core of private life' (paragraph 179 of *1 BvR 2378/98*).

The GFCC also specified rules on the further use of information gathered from surveillance measures, for example in law enforcement authorities' subsequent criminal investigations. Itself noting that it was opting for a restrictive interpretation of the constitution, the Court declared that the already collected information could only be used in further investigations of equally serious crimes and only to *prevent* damage to so-called high-ranking legally protected interests (in German 'hochrangige Rechtsgüter', see paragraph 342 of *1 BvR 2378/98*). In other words, the GFCC defined that law enforcement authorities could rely on already collected information in further investigations only if they had sufficient reason to believe that its use allowed them to avert an imminent risk (in German, 'dringende Gefahr') to a high-ranking legally protected right. What may have seemed like a minor legal detail, had significant implications for the work of law enforcement authorities in practice. While the GFCC could have permitted the further use of existing information if it creates a so-called specific basis for further investigations (in German, 'konkreter Ermittlungsansatz'), it instead opted for a much more stringent threshold by tying an information's further use to the prevention of an imminent risk. As we will see in the chapter's second section below, this distinction proved relevant again when the GFCC reviewed yet another controversial piece of state surveillance legislation, the BKAG.

Before I turn to the discussion of the legislative procedure that led to the adoption of the aforementioned BKAG and the Court's subsequent review, I briefly reflect on the evidence presented in this first section in light of the theoretical model's expectations. Several of the formal model's equilibria expect that certain lawmakers are prepared to pursue highly controversial policies despite a high risk of being censored by a court. The governing coalition's decision to ignore the constitutional concerns voiced by senior members of the FDP and others is an excellent illustration of this type of behaviour. Supporters of the policy within the governing coalition knew that the 'Lauschangriff' would be reviewed by the GFCC, and they knew that there was a high risk that their plans fell foul of constitutional norms—after all, prominent constitutional law experts in their own parties had told them as much. To what extent the GFCC responded with deference in its review of the 'Lauschangriff' in light of the evident risks that lawmakers were willing to take and the potential political fallout from a judicial veto is difficult to assess. The GFCC struck down several of the policy's provisions and defined strict rules for the statutory basis of state surveillance measures and the use of intercepted information. At the same time, the Court notably conceded that covert surveillance measures carried out in private homes to investigate crimes can be compatible with the constitution, albeit in a tightly regulated space. In other words, while the GFCC may have sent lawmakers back to the drawing board on how to appropriately design the statutory basis for covert surveillance, it also cleared the way for law enforcement's unprecedented reach into the most private refuges of crime suspects.

While the GFCC's ruling on the 'Lauschangriff' in *1 BvR 2378/98* may appear as the conclusion of a particular legislative-judicial interaction, it merely set the stage for another episode of constitutional controversy. As German lawmakers turned their attention to effective strategies to combat international terrorism in the mid-2000s, the stringent rules defined by the GFCC in *1 BvR 2378/98* soon proved to be a sticking point throughout the legislative negotiations over the BKAG.

6.2 Pushing for deference

In light of the terrorist attacks of 11 September 2001 on the World Trade Center in New York and the U.S. Department of Defense headquarters in Virginia, the bombings of commuter trains in Madrid on 11 March 2004, as well as coordinated bombings of London's public transport system on 7 July 2005, lawmakers in many Western democracies, including Germany, sought to equip law enforcement agencies with effective tools to combat the security threat from international terrorism.

In June 2008, Chancellor Angela Merkel's coalition cabinet of the CDU/CSU and SPD submitted a draft version of the BKAG to parliament. Survey data from the German Politbarometer suggests that, at least at the time, the German public did not consider terrorist security threats to rank among the most pressing issues in Germany: Less than 1% of the nearly 30,000 surveyed respondents listed terrorism or terrorist attacks as the most important issue facing Germany in 2008, far behind concerns about unemployment (40.7% in East Germany, 27.4% in West Germany), living expenses (10.4% in East Germany, 12.2% in West Germany), and the state of the economy (4.3% in East Germany, 5.5% in West Germany, see Forschungsruppe Wahlen, 2008a, and Forschungsgruppe Wahlen, 2008b). Nonetheless, the government's plans to mandate a federal law enforcement agency, the BKA, with the prosecution and prevention of acts of terrorism certainly caught the public eye.

6.2.1 Committee proceedings

The contents of the BKAG's draft were first debated in the Bundestag's designated leading Committee for Internal Affairs. The committee scheduled a hearing on the draft act in September 2008, inviting statements from representatives of the BKA and state law enforcement agencies as well as academic experts on constitutional law, the Federal Data Protection Commissioner and civil rights campaigners. The hearing was covered by several media outlets, reporting that opinions on the constitutionality of several provisions of the planned BKAG were divided.[7] The newspaper *ZEIT* reported from the hearing that law enforcement officials considered the envisioned competences for the BKA as 'absolutely necessary' in light of a growing threat of terrorist attacks, while a majority of academic experts argued that the plans failed to respect the constitutionally protected core area of private life.[8]

Much of the criticism was directed at the BKAG's provisions allowing law enforcement officials at the BKA to remotely access information technology systems, a measure coined as 'online searches'. In his statement, Hansjörg Geiger, a law professor at the Goethe University Frankfurt and former director of Germany's foreign intelligence service, noted that '[t]he draft act does not respect the balance between freedom and security, which had been repeatedly demanded by the Federal Constitutional Court, and which needs to observed even in the face of the most heinous attacks on the liberal, democratic and

[7] See Heise Online (original in German), 15 September 2008. *Für und Wider im Bundestag zur geplanten Novelle des BKA-Gesetzes*, https://www.heise.de/news/Fuer-und-Wider-im-Bundestag-zur-geplanten-Novelle-des-BKA-Gesetzes-205693.html, accessed 30 April 2019.

[8] ZEIT (original in German), 15 September 2008. *Teilweise verfassungswidrig*, https://www.zeit.de/online/2008/38/bka-gesetz-anhoerung, accessed 30 April 2019.

constitutional state order as well as human life'.[9] Geiger added that '[e]ven though parts of the draft act's text are clearly leaning on the wording of recent Federal Constitutional Court decisions, this does not necessarily mean that the act respects the 'spirit of the constitution' that can be deduced from these decisions'.[10]

Geiger referred to the GFCC's ruling in *1 BvR 370/07* concerning a state law of North-Rhine Westphalia, the Act on the Protection of the Constitution in North Rhine-Westphalia of 20 December 2006. The act originally allowed certain law enforcement agents of North-Rhine Westphalia to carry out investigative measures involving the secret monitoring of suspects' online activities and to secretly access information technology systems. On 27 February 2008, less than four months before the federal government submitted its draft of the BKAG, the GFCC had ruled that the act's provision allowing law enforcement 'access to information technology systems ('online searches') violates the general right of personality in its particular manifestation as a fundamental right to the guarantee of the confidentiality and integrity of information technology systems', adding that '[t]he provision in particular does not meet the requirements of the principle of proportionality' (see the GFCC's press release No. 22/2008 of 27 February 2008).

Following weeks of deliberations, several committee members echoed the sentiment that the federal government's plans for the BKAG paid lip service to constitutional constraints on law enforcement's use of intrusive investigative powers in the fight against terrorism, yet in practice ignored the spirit of the court's recent jurisprudence. In the committee's recommended resolution submitted to the Bundestag's plenary session in November 2008, representatives of the opposition parties, the FDP, the Green party, and Die Linke, announced that their factions would vote against the BKAG in the Bundestag, with committee members of the FDP arguing that 'it is not enough to quote the Federal Constitutional Court verbatim, when the semantic content of its decisions is not actually taken into account'.[11]

[9] Translated from German, excerpt from statement delivered by Prof Dr Hansjörg Geiger on the draft Act on Prevention by the Federal Criminal Police Office of Threats from International Terrorism at the German Bundestag's Committee for Internal Affairs, 15 September 2008, Innenausschuss: A-Drs 16(4)460 H.

[10] Translated from German, excerpt from statement delivered by Prof Dr Hansjörg Geiger on the draft Act on Prevention by the Federal Criminal Police Office of Threats from International Terrorism at the German Bundestag's Committee for Internal Affairs, 15 September 2008, Innenausschuss: A-Drs 16(4)460 H.

[11] Translated from German, excerpt from the recommended resolution and report of the Committee for the Interior on the Act on Prevention by the Federal Criminal Police Office of Threats from International Terrorism, German Bundestag, 10 November 2008, BT-16/10822.

To see representatives of opposition parties voicing concerns that the BKAG's draft proposed by the governing factions failed to respect constitutional constraints seems hardly surprising. After all, evidence presented in Chapters 4 and 5 suggests that this is a fairly common phenomenon characteristic of legislative proceedings in the Bundestag. Even the government's dismissal of constitutional concerns raised by some academic experts at committee hearings does not seem too unusual. Notably, not all academic experts invited to the Committee on Internal Affairs' hearing considered the BKAG's provisions as unconstitutional.[12] Diverging opinions among experts were to be expected given that the core issue governing lawmakers sought to address with the BKAG (i.e. law enforcement's prevention of terrorist attacks) pitted two constitutionally protected norms—the state's responsibility to protect life and limb of its citizens and the individual's freedom from state interference with the core area of private life—against each other.

6.2.2 Constitutional controversy at plenary debates

What makes the Bundestag's legislative proceedings on the BKAG and government's persistence in its pursuit of the act unusual is the fact that several members of the governing coalition caucus echoed lawmakers of the opposition and shared their constitutional concerns.

In the course of the Bundestag's final ordinary plenary debate on the BKAG, ten members of the SPD's parliamentary faction, including former Federal Minister of Justice Herta Däubler-Gmelin and Jörg Tauss, then-member of the parliamentary faction's executive board, issued a statement explaining that they would vote against the BKAG. Drawing on the GFCC's decision of 27 February 2008, on North-Rhine Westphalia's Constitution Protection Act, they argued that law enforcement's 'secret access to computers and other information technology systems not only produces data related to a specific threat but also provides deep insights into individuals' 'digital personal privacy' and their communications, adding that 'it is practically unavoidable that investigations would routinely violate individuals' constitutionally protected core area of private life'.[13]

[12] See Stern (original in German), 15 September 2008. *Staatsrechtler geben Okay für BKA-Gesetz*, https://www.stern.de/politik/deutschland/expertenanhoerung-im-bundestag-staatsrechtler-geben-okay-fuer-bka-gesetz-3760034.html, accessed 30 April 2019.

[13] Translated from German, excerpt from the second reading of the Act on Prevention by the Federal Criminal Police Office of Threats from International Terrorism, German Bundestag, 12 November 2008, 2. Beratung: BT-PlPr 16/186.

While the group claimed that the empowerment of law enforcement to remotely access information technology systems 'should be questioned in principle alone', they also lamented that the BKAG's provisions to protect individuals' core area of private life through a data protection officer employed by the BKA were insufficient, that the BKAG did not specify whether or how law enforcement agents would ensure that the 'correct' computer was targeted by a remote search, and that the government's plans failed to show that such intrusive measures were indispensable in light of the existing means available to law enforcement.[14] Despite 20 members of the SPD's parliamentary faction joining the FDP, the Green party and Die Linke in voting against the act, with a further six SPD members abstaining, a sufficient number of CDU/CSU and SPD lawmakers supported the BKAG's draft, and the Bundestag adopted the act at its third reading on 12 November 2008.[15]

Nonetheless, the constitutional controversy surrounding the BKAG did not end with the vote in the Bundestag. Since the act's provisions touched upon state competences, the BKAG required the consent of parliament's upper chamber, the Bundesrat, comprising representatives of Germany's 16 federal states. Several SPD-controlled state governments decided to withdraw their support for the BKAG. Karl Peter Bruch, the SPD's State Minister for Internal Affairs of Rhineland-Palatine, voiced concerns 'that it would be the Federal Criminal Police Office itself, which would assess what constitutes an individual's core area of private life', while Gisela Aue of the SPD and Senator of Berlin noted that 'the covert access to information technology systems envisioned by the act implies further severe interferences with fundamental rights'.[16] The decision of several SPD-led state governments to withhold their support for the BKAG meant that the act failed to garner enough votes to pass the Bundesrat.

Following state governments' rejection of the BKAG, the federal government called for a conciliation committee comprising a selection of representatives from both the Bundestag and the Bundesrat to hammer out a compromise that would see the BKAG across the finish line. The conciliation committee made several substantial amendments to the BKAG's draft

[14] Translated from German, excerpt from the second reading of the Act on Prevention by the Federal Criminal Police Office of Threats from International Terrorism, German Bundestag, 12 November 2008, 2. Beratung: BT-PlPr 16/186.

[15] See roll call vote count at the third reading of the Act on Prevention by the Federal Criminal Police Office of Threats from International Terrorism, German Bundestag, 12 November 2008, 3. Beratung: BT-PlPr 16/186.

[16] Translated from German, excerpt from the Bundesrat's second reading of the Act on Prevention by the Federal Criminal Police Office of Threats from International Terrorism, 28 November 2008, 2. Durchgang: BR-PlPr 851.

version. First, law enforcement's remote access to telecommunications systems now generally required a judge's authorization. Second, whether investigations would violate an individual's core area of private life would be assessed by a data protection officer employed by the BKA at the 'direction' of a judge.[17]

While these compromises were enough to get a sufficient number of state governments on board to shuttle the BKAG through the Bundesrat, some SPD lawmakers in the Bundestag reiterated concerns that the act failed to respect constitutional norms. At the Bundestag's hearing of the conciliation committee's compromise on 18 December 2008, SPD members Jörg Tauss and Monika Griefahn issued a joint statement, arguing:

> Jörg Tauss (SPD): The BKA's new powers include the secret access to information technology systems, or so-called online searches. The Federal Constitutional Court established strict requirements for intrusions into individuals' digital privacy in its decision on the Constitution Protection Act of North-Rhine Westphalia, requirements that this draft act—even after the agreement found in the conciliation committee—fails to consider.[18]

Despite these persisting constitutional objections, the Bundestag adopted the BKAG on 25 December 2008 and the act entered into force on 1 January 2009.

The previous sections have demonstrated that concerns about the act's constitutional compatibility were raised at every stage of the Bundestag's legislative proceedings. The federal government addressed some of these concerns by amending the BKAG's draft during the legislative process, including measures to introduce a degree of judicial oversight over law enforcement's use of highly intrusive investigative methods. However, some of the core constitutional objections, based on the GFCC's recent case law against law enforcement's use of covert searches of information technology systems, were ultimately ignored, despite being raised by members of the governing coalition.

[17] Spiegel ONLINE, 17 December 2008. *Vermittlungsausschuss: Einigung bei BKA-Gesetz*, accessed May 2, 2019.

[18] Translated from German, excerpt from the reading on the conciliation committee's recommended resolution of the Act on Prevention by the Federal Criminal Police Office of Threats from International Terrorism, German Bundestag, 18 December 2008, Abstimmung über Vermittlungsvorschlag: BT-PlPr 16/196.

6.2.3 Balancing protection by and against the state

Merely weeks after the BKAG's adoption, a group of plaintiffs including the editor of the German newspaper *ZEIT*, a former Federal Minister for Internal Affairs as well as the director of the Berlin Regional Association of German Lawyers had filed constitutional complaints directed against two sets of provisions of the act. The first set of complaints concerned provisions granting various investigative powers to the Federal Criminal Police Office (in German, the Bundeskriminalamt, in the following BKA). These included (1) the covert recording of non-public speech and images, the application of tracking devices, and the use of police informants pursuant to paragraph 20g sec. 1 to 3 BKAG, (2) the power to carry out visual and acoustic surveillance of private homes pursuant to paragraph 20h BKAG, (3) the power to access information technology systems (so-called 'online searches') pursuant to paragraph 20k BKAG, and (4) the power to monitor and collect on-going telecommunications data pursuant to paragraph 20l and 20m BKAG (see preamble in *1 BvR 966/09*).

The second set of challenged provisions related to the BKA's further use of the data obtained in the course of its investigations. These provisions comprised (1) the use of data by the BKA itself, specifically concerning the use of data beyond the original incident and beyond the reason justifying the original data collection pursuant to paragraph 20v sec. 4 BKAG, (2) the transfer of surveillance data to other domestic public authorities pursuant to paragraph 20v sec. 5 BKAG, and (3) the transfer of surveillance data to authorities in third countries pursuant to paragraph 14 sec. 1 and sec. 7 BKAG (see preamble in *1 BvR 966/09*). When considering the constitutional compatibility of an act pursued by a public authority, the GFCC first establishes the constitutional principles the challenged act needs to meet. These principles are derived from Germany's constitution and substantiated in the court's case law. The court then considers whether or not the challenged act meets the principles applicable in a specific case (see for example Kommers, 1994; Landfried, 1995). In the following, I briefly discuss the benchmarks the GFCC considered in *1 BvR 966/09* and its evaluation of the constitutionality of both sets of the BKAG's challenged provisions in light of these (for more comprehensive evaluations of the GFCC's decision in *1 BvR 966/09*, see Darnstädt, 2017; Rusteberg, 2017).

The BKA's investigative powers

The GFCC centred its evaluation of the constitutional compatibility of investigative powers granted to law enforcement through the BKAG on two separate principles: (1) the principle of proportionality, noting that 'the granting of these powers must always pursue a legitimate aim and must be suitable, necessary and, in the strict sense, proportionate to achieving this aim' (see paragraph 93 of *1 BvR 966/09*), and (2) the principle of legal clarity and specificity, which aim 'to increase the predictability of interferences for citizens, constitute an effective limit to administrative powers and enable effective judicial review' (see paragraph 94 of *1 BvR 966/09*).

The application of the principle of proportionality, in particular, reflects the fundamental constitutional tension accompanying lawmakers' attempts to bestow the BKA with effective powers to protect the public from threats of international terrorism. The investigative powers granted to law enforcement officials at the BKA allowed for serious interferences with the privacy of suspects as well as the individuals who interacted with these suspects. At the same time, the GFCC reiterated in its decision that the security of the state as well as the safety of the population it is bound to guarantee 'rank equally with other highly valued constitutional rights' (see paragraph 100 of *1 BvR 966/09*). In other words, given the BKAG sought to offer protections against acts of terrorism, lawmakers and the court were tasked to strike the right balance in protecting the public by and from the state.

Defining the principle of proportionality as well as the principle of legal clarity and specificity, the GFCC drew closely on its existing jurisprudence (for example the GFCC's decision on the sharing of telecommunications data with law enforcement agencies in *1 BvR 330/96* of 12 March 2003, and its decision on the acoustic surveillance of private homes in *1 BvR 2378/98* of 3 March 2004). It is beyond the scope of this chapter to consider every detail of the requirements the challenged provisions of the BKAG had to meet (note that the court substantiated the principles in 54 paragraphs in *1 BvR 966/09*). Yet, overall, the GFCC's reasoning on proportionality as well as legal clarity and specificity can be summarized by its assertion that '[t]he more seriously the surveillance measures interfere with privacy and thwart legitimate expectations of confidentiality, the stricter the requirements must be' (see paragraph 105 of *1 BvR 966/09*).

The GFCC found that several aspects of the investigative powers granted to the BKA did not meet the constitutional requirements it had defined. The court found that (1) provisions on the use of special means of surveillance outside of homes, including the application of tracking devices or the use of police informants, were not sufficiently limited, (2) provisions on the surveillance of private homes, including data collection via acoustic surveillance, only partially satisfied the requirement of proportionality, (3) powers granting access to information technology systems did not come with adequate measures to protect the core area of individuals' private life, while (4) the powers allowing surveillance of on-going telecommunications were too unspecific and broad (see preamble in *1 BvR 966/09*). Overall, the GFCC found that aspects of every challenged investigative power conflicted with the constitution and ruled them unconstitutional, much in line with its existing jurisprudence.

The BKA's use of surveillance data

While the GFCC showed little self-restraint and stuck to its existing jurisprudence when considering the constitutional (in-)compatibility of law enforcement's investigative powers granted by the BKAG, the picture changes somewhat when turning to the BKA's use of surveillance data. The two principles at the centre of the GFCC's evaluation of the constitutionality of the BKA's further uses of data were (1) purpose limitation, i.e. the use of data in the same context as the original purpose of the data, and (2) changes in purpose, i.e. the use of data for new purposes (see paragraph 277 of *1 BvR 966/09*).

With regard to purpose limitation, the GFCC noted that '[t]he legislature may permit the use of data extending beyond the original investigation procedure in the context of the original purpose of this data (further use), provided that the authority empowered to collect that data uses it within the same field of activity, for the protection of the same legally protected interests, and the enforcement or prevention of the same criminal offences, as authorised by the relevant data collection provision' (see the GFCC's press release No. 19/2016 of 20 April 2016).

On requirements for changes in the purpose of data, the GFCC wrote that 'as far as data that results from particularly intrusive surveillance and investigative measures is concerned, such as the data at issue in these proceedings, it is necessary to determine whether it would be permissible, by constitutional standards, to also collect the relevant data for the changed purpose with comparably weighty means' (see paragraph 287 of *1 BvR 966/09*). Crucially, the court added that while a use of data for new purposes must serve the protection of legally protected rights or aim to investigate criminal offences of such a weight that hypothetically re-collecting them would be justified, it is ' necessary but generally also sufficient that the data—either as such or in combination with the authority's additionally available information—results in a specific evidentiary basis for further investigations' (see paragraph 289 of *1 BvR 966/09*).

The GFCC explicitly revoked a requirement for changes in the purpose of data contained in its existing jurisprudence with this statement (see paragraph 292 in *1 BvR 966/09*). As discussed in the chapter's first section, in *1 BvR 2378/98* of 3 March 2004, and *1 BvR 2226/94* of 14 July 1999, the GFCC had established that a change of purpose of data is permissible only if a temporal proximity threshold regarding the risk situation is met. The GFCC kept this requirement in place for data obtained through the surveillance of private homes or remote searches of information technology systems. However, for data obtained through less intrusive means, the GFCC eased constraints on lawmakers willing to allow law enforcement officials to use surveillance data for purposes other than the one justifying their original collection.

The GFCC still found that several of the BKAG's provisions did not meet its requirements for purpose limitation and changes in purpose. To summarize, the court found that (1) provisions relating to the use of data obtained from the surveillance of private homes and remote searches were disproportionate, (2) provisions on the use of data for the protection of witnesses or other persons were too unspecific, and (3) provisions allowing the transfer of data were unconstitutional insofar as they covered transfers for the general prevention of terrorist offences, irrespective of a specific evidentiary basis for further investigations (see preamble in *1 BvR 966/09*). Nonetheless, lawmakers keen on providing law enforcement with more flexibility in their use of surveillance data walked away with a significant achievement. The court may have sent lawmakers back to the drawing board for several provisions originally contained in the 2008 BKAG, but the constitutional requirements lawmakers then had to respect for changes in purposes of data had been eased.

Revoking constitutional requirements the court had further substantiated only four years prior to the Bundestag's adoption of the 2008 BKAG is unusual for the GFCC. Existing scholarship suggests that courts make a conscious effort not to break with precedent all too frequently (see Rasmusen, 1994; Knight and Epstein, 1996). Spriggs and Hansford (2001, 1092) note that '[t]he overruling of a precedent, despite its infrequency, is a significant political and legal event, most notably because it represents a dramatic form of legal change'. Similarly, evidence from my interviews with former members of the GFCC implies that it is critical for the court to stay consistent in its case law. In a telephone interview conducted on 18 May 2017, a former clerk of the GFCC noted:

> To look back at how cases have been decided in the past is really important, it provides continuity and the court decides its cases in a consistent fashion.

> Whenever consistency is lacking, you quickly see the lower specialised courts issue strange opinions. You know, you can think of the Federal Constitutional Court as a tank ship, it does not take a zigzag route, instead things are steered very carefully and slowly. When something needs correcting, you take a long, slow turn, this does not happen abruptly.

What makes the GFCC's decision to revoke previous requirements on law enforcement's use of surveillance data for new purposes even more surprising is that two of the court's Justices published dissenting opinions, in large parts referring to the GFCC's approach to changes in purpose of surveillance data. Yet, neither of these two Justices objected to the decision to revoke existing jurisprudence—instead, both of them argued that the court should have eased constraints on lawmakers even further. Regarding the court's decision to keep the requirement of a temporal proximity threshold in place for data obtained through the surveillance of private homes and searches of information technology systems, Justice Eichberger wrote:

> I cannot back the exception called for by this concept, whereby every further use and change in purpose with regard to data from the surveillance of private homes or remote searches must be justified by an imminent or a sufficiently specific danger, just as for the initial collection of the data. Even in the context of the surveillance of private homes, the actual massive interference with privacy takes place when the investigation accesses the protected area. A further use—even one with a change in purpose—does indeed perpetuate this interference, but, even with regard to the surveillance of private homes (and similarly with remote searches), it does not reach the level of severity of the initial interference. The further use and change in purpose of intelligence obtained from surveillance measures must thus be subject to the general rules. The Senate should have corrected its existing case law accordingly.[19]

Justice Schluckebier's dissenting opinion goes a step further and suggests that for data obtained through the use of certain, less intrusive surveillance methods, the requirement of a protection of comparably weighty legal interests when hypothetically re-collecting this data should have been revoked as well. In his dissenting opinion, Justice Schluckebier wrote:

[19] An excerpt (in English) of Justice Eichberger's dissenting opinion on *1 BvR 966/09* is available at https://www.bundesverfassungsgericht.de/SharedDocs/Entscheidungen/EN/2016/04/rs2016 0420_1bvr096609en.html.

> The judgement predicates the transfer and use of the data for other purposes on whether, even after a change in purpose, this data serves to protect legally protected interests or to uncover criminal offences of such a weight that this could, by constitutional standards, justify collecting them again with comparably weighty means (criterion of a hypothetical re-collection of data). This perspective may be justified with regard to findings that were obtained through highly intrusive, particularly significant interferences, which is the case, for example, when measures such as the surveillance of private homes and remote searches were employed. However, with regard to other interferences, which result in so-called coincidental findings, this can, in my opinion, lead to hardly tolerable results since it requires the rule-of-law order to accept the occurrence of crimes and damage to legally protected interests. On condition that such coincidental findings were obtained through a lawful and constitutional interference, my view is that it is an unacceptable consequence that a state under the rule of law is forced to deliberately 'look away'.[20]

Justice Eichberger and Justice Schluckebier's dissenting opinions indicate that the court was under pressure to ease the constitutional constraints on lawmakers trying to provide law enforcement with effective tools to respond to tangible security threats. For most of its judgment in *1 BvR 966/09*, the GFCC stuck to its existing jurisprudence and it invalidated a series of provisions contained in the BKAG for their constitution incompatibility. However, the GFCC's decision to revoke requirements for changes in purpose of surveillance data suggests that the court—at least to some extent—gave in to this pressure. Why did the GFCC feel the need to self-restrain and revoke parts of its own, relatively recent, jurisprudence? Why did two justices feel the need to go on record and state that they would have liked to see the GFCC provide lawmakers with even more room to breathe?

6.2.4 Linking lawmakers' objections to the court's demands

The earlier sections' discussion of the GFCC's decision in *1 BvR 966/09* on the BKAG suggests that the constitutional concerns voiced by some members of the SPD were well-founded. Recall that the GFCC eventually ruled that

[20] An excerpt (in English) of Justice Schluckebier's dissenting opinion on *1 BvR 966/09* is available at https://www.bundesverfassungsgericht.de/SharedDocs/Entscheidungen/EN/2016/04/rs20160420_1bvr096609en.html.

several of the act's provisions conflicted with constitutional norms, including provisions concerning the use of remote, covert searches of information technology systems. Specifically, in its press release accompanying its decision in *1 BvR 966/09*, the court singled out the BKAG's provision aimed at ensuring that those searches would not violate the protection of individuals' core area of private life (see the GFCC's press release No. 19/2016 of 20 April 2016):

> Sufficient protection of the core area of private life is lacking with regard to access to information technology systems (paragraph 20k BKAG). In this case, the body tasked with viewing the collected data is not sufficiently independent. It is necessary that the control essentially be carried out by external persons not charged with security tasks. While the recourse to personnel from the Federal Criminal Police Office for the purpose of involving staff with investigation-specific or technical expertise is not ruled out, the actual carrying out and decision-making responsibility must lie in the hands of persons independent from the Federal Criminal Police Office. By attributing the task of screening mainly to employees of the Federal Criminal Police Office, however, paragraph 20k sec. 7 sentences 3 and 4 BKAG falls short of these requirements.

The GFCC's demand that external persons had to effectively control decisions over law enforcement's use of online searches means the court hardly showed self-restraint when considering the issue at the centre of persistent constitutional objections voiced by members of the governing coalition caucus.

A strict reading of the empirical implications of the theoretical model presented in Chapter 2 would lead us to expect that the court faced incentives to show deference to lawmakers on this issue, instead. After all, the federal government's dismissal of their political allies' constitutional concerns would suggest that lawmakers in government were prepared to take high political risks in their pursuit of constitutionally controversial policies, signalling a credible non-compliance threat to the court.

While the GFCC did not seem to respond with deference on issues at the heart of the constitutional controversy in the Bundestag, the discussion of the GFCC's decision in *1 BvR 966/09* above shows that the court was indeed more lenient in its constitutional requirements concerning law enforcement's further uses of surveillance data. The empirical evidence presented in this chapter does not allow for a definitive conclusion that the GFCC chose to revoke its existing jurisprudence concerning requirements on the further use of surveillance data in response to a credible non-compliance threat. However, evidence from a telephone interview with a former law clerk at the GFCC, conducted on 20 May 2017, suggests that lawmakers' choice to disregard the GFCC's jurisprudence was not lost on the court. Asked how the GFCC can assess how lawmakers would respond to its jurisprudence, the clerk noted:

> We also take a look at the laws the federal and state legislatures recently passed. For example, on issues like data protection or covert surveillance through law enforcement, it became quite clear that the concept of protecting the core area of private life simply hadn't been properly applied by the legislature. So what do you in these situations? One option is to simplify the jurisprudence and to work with simple statements. The simpler the language, the easier it is for others to follow it. A second option is to openly address it. There is jurisprudence that hasn't been properly implemented by the legislature, you acknowledge that, consolidate and scale back. It's sign of goodwill and then you hope that the legislature complies with the new jurisprudence.

The theoretical model presented in Chapter 2 highlights a factor behind the GFCC's decision to ease some of the constitutional constraints lawmakers had to consider in their attempts to equip law enforcement with effective tools to combat a tangible terrorist threat. By ignoring several warning signs that provisions included in the BKAG were at odds with the GFCC's recent decisions, lawmakers in government made it clear that they were prepared to evade compliance with the requirements the court had established in its jurisprudence.

Arguably, the GFCC did not respond to this signal with outright deference but made concessions to lawmakers, striking several of the BKAG's provisions that would entail violations of individuals' core area of private life, while simultaneously easing constraints on law enforcement's further use of surveillance data.

In the remainder of this chapter, I consider two further empirical implications of the theoretical model. Since the GFCC struck the BKAG's provisions that had been at the centre of constitutional concerns voiced by members of the governing coalition caucus, we should expect lawmakers to bear the political costs for insisting on these provisions. In addition, given the court invalidated several of the BKAG's provisions despite a credible non-compliance threat, it appears worthwhile to assess how lawmakers actually responded to the GFCC's decision in *1 BvR 966/09*.

6.3 The costs of provoking confrontation

The theoretical model presented in Chapter 2 states that lawmakers who support a policy despite anticipating that it would transgress constitutional norms risk to pay a price for their choice once a court actually strikes the policy as unconstitutional. In the following, I present evidence from news media coverage and debates in the Bundestag in the aftermath of the GFCC's ruling in *1 BvR 966/09* to illustrate that the reputation of those who had championed the BKAG indeed came under fire following the court's ruling.

The GFCC's decision on the BKAG's constitutional incompatibility was covered by every major German newspaper and media network.[21] While most reports centred on the text of the GFCC's ruling and its implications for law enforcement officials tasked with preventing terrorist attacks, some of the coverage took aim at the constitutional controversy that had accompanied the BKAG's adoption in the first place. The day after the GFCC's ruling, the nationwide network Deutschlandfunk broadcast an interview with the deputy chair of the SPD's parliamentary faction, Eva Högl.[22] The following exchange from the interview illustrates that journalists were well-aware that lawmakers of grand-coalition had missed opportunities to avoid confrontation with the GFCC over the BKAG:

> Interviewer: It is clear that the law needs correcting. The legislature now has two years to do so. And your party, the SPD, was also responsible for the law. Basically, you suffered a defeat yesterday as well.
>
> Eva Högl (SPD): Yes that is exactly right, and you need to handle these situations with self-confidence, it's the job of the Federal Constitutional Court to keep an eye on what the legislature is doing. And yes, the law was adopted with the votes of the SPD. We were part of the grand-coalition. Some of the criticism directed at parts of the law came from members of the SPD. So we feel that our concerns were validated by the Federal Constitutional Court. [...]

[21] See for example Spiegel ONLINE (original in German), 20 April 2018. *Polizisten murren über Verfassungsgericht*, https://www.spiegel.de/politik/deutschland/bundesverfassungsgericht-karlsruhe-bremst-bka-gesetz-a-1088298.html, accessed 3 May 2019; Frankfurter Allgemeine Zeitung (original in German), 20 April 2018. *BKA-Befugnisse zur Terrorabwehr zum Teil verfassungswidrig*, https://www.faz.net/aktuell/politik/inland/bundesverfassungsgericht-bka-befugnisse-zur-terrorabwehr.html, accessed 3 May 2019; tagesschau.de (original in German), 20 April 2018. *Verfassungsgericht urteilt über BKA-Gesetz*, https://www.tagesschau.de/inland/bka-gesetz-109.html, accessed 3 May 2019.

[22] Deutschlandfunk (original in German), 21 April. *Bundesverfassungsgericht hat Grundrechte gestärkt*, https://www.deutschlandfunk.de/bka-gesetz-bundesverfassungsgericht-hat-grundrechte.694.de.html, accessed 3 May 2019.

Interviewer: I'd like to come back to my previous point. Critics now ask, why is it that time and again the Federal Constitutional Court has to explain to government and legislature what's allowed and what's not?

Eva Högl (SPD): Well, that is the normal balance between the different branches in our democracy. [. . .] I don't see a problem with the Federal Constitutional Court taking a look at one of our laws, giving us, the legislature, advice.

Interviewer: But every law is reviewed by in-house legal counsel, at least in the Bundestag. It is remarkable that the legislature and court can arrive at so fundamentally different conclusions.

Eva Högl (SPD): Look, lawyers have different opinions. You know how the saying goes, two lawyers, twenty-five different opinions. In the end it's always a question of interpretation.[23]

The lawmaker's latter statement offers an alternative perspective on the governing faction's decision to dismiss constitutional concerns regarding the BKAG in 2008 and push the act through the Bundestag: Even legal experts often disagree over the constitutional compatibility of policy and lawmakers of the governing coalition believed that their plans for the BKAG would live up to the requirements of the GFCC's jurisprudence yet simply misjudged. However, this sentiment was not shared by commentators in other media outlets. Wolfgang Janisch, correspondent of the *Süddeutsche Zeitung* (one of Germany's most prominent and widely read newspapers) at the GFCC, commented on the court's ruling in *1 BvR 966/09*:

The play that we've seen in the Federal Constitutional Court's courtroom this Wednesday has been performed, with some exceptions, for more than a decade. The legislature picks up the pace in combating terrorism, civil rights activists litigate, justices at the constitutional court pick the law apart and call for 'privacy rights' and 'proportionality'. You could almost get used to this ritual if it wasn't actually a defiant strategy: Government and governing coalition factions create paragraphs, even though they anticipate that they are unconstitutional, and then see what's left after the court reviewed them. This sarcastic conclusion was evident again this Wednesday in some of the responses of the federal government. In fact: The Federal Criminal Police

[23] Deutschlandfunk (original in German), 21 April. *Bundesverfassungsgericht hat Grundrechte gestärkt*, https://www.deutschlandfunk.de/bka-gesetz-bundesverfassungsgericht-hat-grundrechte.694.de.html, accessed 3 May 2019.

> Office Act of 2009, the centre-piece of the so-called fight against terror, is an act created clearly beyond the boundaries of the Basic Law. Everyone who had read the court's earlier decisions would have known that.[24]

These examples illustrate that even though the GFCC issued its decision on the BKAG more than seven years after the act's adoption, journalists recalled that lawmakers in the elected branches took an arguably calculated gamble and had passed an act they knew would transgress constitutional norms. Having their commitment to the principles of the constitution and the GFCC's jurisprudence openly questioned in the media is unlikely to help lawmakers' reputation among the electorate, particularly in light of the GFCC's comfortable public support (see Gibson et al., 1998; Vanberg, 2005). Vanberg (1998, 305) argues 'that in democratic systems, citizens are likely to care not only about *policy*, but also *process*, that is, they expect politicians and parties to "play by the rules"'. Lawmakers of the CDU/CSU and SPD's grand-coalition had been warned that their plans for the BKAG would violate the constitution, but took their chances and were called out for it once the GFCC actually struck several provisions of the law.

Several members of the opposition factions in the Bundestag seized the opportunity of the GFCC striking parts of the BKAG and argued that the governing coalitions had wilfully passed a law at odds with the constitution in 2008. On 17 February 2017, the Bundestag held its first reading of the Act on the Amendment of the Federal Criminal Police Office Act, the CDU/CSU and SPD's response to the GFCC's ruling in *1 BvR 966/09*.[25] Members of the opposition rang the debate in with scathing attacks on the grand-coalition:

> Ulla Jelpke (Die Linke): Minister, I believe you should have mentioned that about a year ago you received a ruling by the Federal Constitutional Court, which confirmed that significant parts of the old BKAG were unconstitutional and instructed you to find remedies for these transgression in a new law. I believe that this was a humiliating defeat for the government, which in the name of 'combating terrorism' wilfully accepted a breach of the constitution.[26]

[24] Süddeutsche Zeitung (original in German), 20 April 2018. *Wer durch das BKA-Urteil nun besser vor Überwachung geschützt ist*, https://www.sueddeutsche.de/politik/anti-terror-gesetze-wer-durch-das-bka-urteil-nun-besser-1.2957910, accessed 3 May 2019.

[25] See first reading of the Act on the Amendment of the Federal Criminal Police Office Act, German Bundestag, 17 February 2017, 1. Beratung: BT-PlPr 18/219.

[26] Translated from German, excerpt from the first reading of the Act on the Amendment of the Federal Criminal Police Office Act, German Bundestag, 17 February 2017, 1. Beratung: BT-PlPr 18/219.

> Konstantin von Notz (Greens): But in 2008, as well as today, the grand-coalition chose to downplay our law enforcement agencies, only to wildly reallocate their competences—against the widespread constitutional concerns from law enforcement experts, but also from the opposition, academia and civil society. As had been expected, the law was challenged in Karlsruhe, and Karlsruhe invalidated exactly those parts as incompatible with the constitution and void, which we had criticised. That was a proper hammering, Mr. de Maizière.[27]

Existing scholarship argues that lawmakers face electoral costs when their non-compliance with court's constitutional jurisprudence is uncovered, highlighting the role of the media and the political opposition for communicating lawmakers' failure to comply to the public (see Vanberg, 2005; Staton, 2010; Krehbiel, 2016, see also Whittington, 2003). Admittedly, it is difficult to gauge to what extent the CDU/CSU and SPD's reputation among the electorate suffered following the GFCC's ruling in *1 BvR 966/09*. Nonetheless, this section provided evidence from news media coverage and debates in the Bundestag in the aftermath of the GFCC's ruling on the BKAG, showing that governing lawmakers' non-compliance with the court's jurisprudence was publicized in the media and the legislature. In other words, following the GFCC's ruling in *1 BvR 966/09*, the conditions for lawmakers' electoral reputation costs to take effect were in place.

6.4 The response in the Bundestag

Much of this chapter covered how lawmakers of the CDU/CSU and SPD's grand-coalition faced down constitutional objections voiced from within the governing coalition caucus and supported the BKAG despite clear warning signs that the law was at odds with the constitution. According to the theoretical model presented in this book, lawmakers' choice to pass a law despite anticipating that it would conflict with the GFCC's jurisprudence (and the risks this choice entailed) made it clear that lawmakers were unwilling to see their policymaking curtailed by the court. In other words, lawmakers had signalled a credible threat of non-compliance. Reviewing the BKAG, the GFCC indeed eased constitutional constraints on lawmakers and revoked

[27] Translated from German, excerpt from the first reading of the Act on the Amendment of the Federal Criminal Police Office Act, German Bundestag, 17 February 2017, 1. Beratung: BT-PlPr 18/219.

requirements it had established in its previous decisions. But the court did not fully cede the field to lawmakers and struck several provisions of the BKAG. Lawmakers of the grand-coalition again controlled government office at the time the GFCC issued its ruling on the BKAG in *1 BvR 966/09*. How did they respond to the court's ruling?

As briefly indicated above, about a year after the GFCC's ruling, the parliamentary factions of the CDU/CSU and SPD submitted a new draft of the BKAG to the Bundestag, the Act on the Amendment of the Federal Criminal Police Office Act. In their explanatory statement submitted along the new draft act, the governing coalitions referenced the GFCC's requirements for law enforcement's further use of surveillance data, stating:

> The Federal Constitutional Court delivered a judgement concerning law enforcement's data protection that consolidates existing jurisprudence concerning covert investigative measures, systematises this jurisprudence in overarching principles, further develops constitutional requirements regarding limitations in purpose and changes in purpose of data, and for the first time issues statements regarding the transfer of data to state agencies in third countries. In particular, the judgement states that the requirements for further uses and transfer of data are linked to the principles of purpose limitation and changes in purpose, and that the proportionality requirements concerning changes in purpose are to be assessed in light of the criterion of a hypothetical re-collection of data. The principles of purpose limitation and changes in purpose are also applicable to the transfer of data to state agencies in third countries. The Federal Criminal Police Office's existing IT-infrastructure, particularly its information network INPOL, is not suited to match the standards of the Federal Constitutional Court's judgement of April 20, 2016, and therefore requires a fundamental re-structuring.[28]

In other words, rather than amending the BKAG by addressing the GFCC's demands regarding law enforcement's further uses of surveillance data one-by-one, the governing coalition instead opted for a comprehensive overhaul of how German law enforcement agencies would administer their data inventories. In June 2017, Matthias Bäcker, law professor at Johannes-Gutenberg-University Mainz, wrote a commentary on the amended BKAG on

[28] Translated from German, excerpt from the explanatory statement on the draft of the Act on the Amendment of the Federal Criminal Police Office Act, German Bundestag, 14 February 2018, BT-Drs 18/11163 (Gesetzentwurf).

Verfassungsblog, a journalistic and academic debate forum on German constitutional law and politics supported by the WZB Berlin Social Science Center. Bäcker noted that the amended BKAG was nothing short of a 'revolution' in the way law enforcement agencies at the federal and state levels would administer, store, and share their data, allowing the different agencies to link up their data inventories to facilitate the identification of patterns in criminal or terrorist activities.[29] Given that decisions about access rights to the now centralized data inventory would rest with the BKA, Bäcker added that '[t]he law therefore lacks clarity on fundamental issues: It is possible that the administration of law enforcement's information systems would be by and large at the discretion of the BKA; this would be incompatible with our constitutional rights'.[30]

In my interviews with former members of the elected branches, I asked lawmakers about the options available to the government and legislature when responding to the GFCC's jurisprudence. In a telephone interview conducted on 4 April 2019, one lawmaker specifically referred to the governing coalition's decision to pursue an overhaul of law enforcement's administration of its databases:

> Usually the court doesn't declare legislative texts as void but gives the legislatures instructions, which then have to be implemented by a certain date. And that creates work for the legislative branch. I can tell you, there is certainly little desire on behalf of the government to swiftly get to work on some of these decisions. Often, you then wait as long as you can and see just how little you can do to still match the court's requirements. With the Federal Criminal Police Office Act, you could see a different kind of strategy. Here, the legislature chose a fundamentally different legal construct in the act, and then people were able to say 'well, the Federal Constitutional Court didn't say anything on this new construct'.

Despite the governing coalition's change in course, restructuring how law enforcement officials would handle surveillance data rather than addressing the GFCC's requirements for further uses of such data head on, concerns emerged that the court's jurisprudence was once again acknowledged yet not

[29] Verfassungsblog (original in German), 8 June 2017. *Der Umsturz kommt zu früh: Anmerkungen zur polizeilichen Informationsordnung nach dem neuen BKA-Gesetz*, https://verfassungsblog.de/der-umsturz-kommt-zu-frueh-anmerkungen-zur-polizeilichen-informationsordnung, accessed 9 May 2019.

[30] Verfassungsblog (original in German), 8 June 2017. *Der Umsturz kommt zu früh: Anmerkungen zur polizeilichen Informationsordnung nach dem neuen BKA-Gesetz*, https://verfassungsblog.de/der-umsturz-kommt-zu-frueh-anmerkungen-zur-polizeilichen-informationsordnung, accessed 9 May 2019.

faithfully implemented. In the Committee for Internal Affair's recommendation to the Bundestag's plenary session concerning the BKAG's new draft, representatives of Die Linke wrote:

> Almost all of the experts confirmed in the committee's hearing that the coalition factions simply copy-pasted passages from the Federal Constitutional Court's judgement of April 20, 2016, without making their own considerations or making an effort to tailor certain terms to police or regulatory law.[31]

These concerns were echoed in the Bundestag's plenary session at the final reading of the BKAG's draft. Irene Mihalic of the Green party noted:

> Irene Mihalic (Greens): The new linking up of data is essentially the same as a re-collection of data. That's why this is indeed important. To be honest, I don't understand why you are willing to take the constitutional risks that come with this approach. The only thing you will achieve with this is continued litigation in Karlsruhe. Instead, you should tackle the known issues in the context of the existing systems. [...] The Federal Constitutional Court objected to several competences in the previous BKAG and defined strict boundaries for our decision-making. Your draft act consistently scrapes these guardrails. What the Federal Constitutional Court considered as barely compatible with the constitution, you then copy-pasted into the act. But copy-and-paste is not only poor in style for a legislature, it also fails to recognise your mandate to ensure proportionality in a broader sense.[32]

Notably, this time members of the SPD's parliamentary faction did not share the constitutional concerns of their colleagues on the opposition benches. The amended BKAG shuttled through the Bundestag and Bundesrat without further constitutional controversy and entered into force on 25 May 2018. Nonetheless, once again concerns had been raised that lawmakers of the CDU/CSU and SPD had paid lip service to the GFCC's decision in *1 BvR 966/09* but effectively evaded compliance with the judgment by opting for an overhaul of law enforcement's data administration system, something the

[31] Translated from German, excerpt from the recommended resolution and report of the Committee for Internal Affairs on the Act on the Amendment of the Federal Criminal Police Office Act, German Bundestag, 25 April 2017, BT-Drs 18/12141.

[32] Translated from German, excerpt from the second reading of the Act on the Amendment of the Federal Criminal Police Office Act, German Bundestag, 27 April 2017, 2. Beratung: BT-PlPr 18/231.

court's judgment did not call for. Matthias Bäcker concluded his commentary on the amended BKAG by stating:

> Perhaps, practitioners in law enforcement will find a way to organise the BKA's administration of data in an useful manner, in ways not envisioned by the act. Otherwise, we can expect that the new provisions will either lead to dysfunctional results or will be brought down with reference to constitutional rights.[33]

6.5 Conclusion

This chapter provided an analytic narrative of the theoretical model's main argument through a case study on the GFCC's decision on the BKAG. Citing from the GFCC's case law, the Bundestag's legislative proceedings, media coverage on the BKAG, and interviews with former members of the GFCC and lawmakers, this chapter showed that the theoretical model provides a useful lens to analyse the interactions between courts and lawmakers, and can explain otherwise surprising patterns in judicial decision-making.

Shortly after submitting their draft of the BKAG, lawmakers of the CDU/CSU and SPD faced concerns that the act was at odds with the GFCC's jurisprudence concerning law enforcement's data protection duties and their respect for privacy rights. The grand-coalition's decision to push the BKAG through parliament despite these concerns signalled their willingness to evade compliance with a subsequent judgment that would constrain their decision-making on security policy, especially given that some of these concerns had been voiced by members of the governing coalition caucus. In line with the theoretical model's expectations, the GFCC offered concessions to lawmakers in its ruling on the BKAG by taking the rare step of revoking constitutional requirements contained in its existing jurisprudence. Since the GFCC simultaneously struck several provisions of the BKAG, the reputation of those who had supported the act despite widespread constitutional concerns nonetheless came under fire. Again in line with expectations of the theoretical model, there are also indications that lawmakers made good on their non-compliance threat and opted for a response to the GFCC's ruling that would allow them to evade faithful compliance with the court's jurisprudence.

[33] Verfassungsblog (original in German), 8 June 2017. *Der Umsturz kommt zu früh: Anmerkungen zur polizeilichen Informationsordnung nach dem neuen BKA-Gesetz*, https://verfassungsblog.de/der-umsturz-kommt-zu-frueh-anmerkungen-zur-polizeilichen-informationsordnung, accessed 9 May 2019.

This chapter's case study also highlighted two facets of the interactions between lawmakers and courts the statistical analysis of Chapter 5 could not capture. First, the discussion of the GFCC's ruling in *1 BvR 966/09* shows that it is useful to look beyond the dichotomous outcome of an individual case—for instance, did the court strike a provision or not—and to pay close attention to the reasoning in the text of the court's decision. Clark and Lauderdale (2010, 871) note that 'decisions are often most important because of the qualitative changes in law that they effect, rather than because of the decision they provide on the case facing the Court' (see also Tiller and Cross, 2006). The GFCC invalidated several provisions of the BKAG, yet to conclude that the court hence did not self-restrain its decision-making would miss the fact that the court simultaneously eased constitutional constraints on lawmakers.

Second, for the sake of parsimony, the theoretical model presented in Chapter 2 captures a single interaction between lawmakers and a court, yet its mechanism rests on the assumption that both lawmakers and the court are forward-looking actors, anticipating how the other would react to their own decisions. This chapter's case study was able to highlight the dynamic nature of the interaction between lawmakers of the elected branches and the GFCC in Germany's system of limited government. The chapter shows that in order to explain how a court decided in a particular case, it is useful to evaluate how lawmakers had responded to the court's previous, similar decisions and what this information might tell the court about lawmakers' behaviour in the future.

6.6 Appendix

The following provides bibliographical information on the GFCC's case law and press releases (where available in English) cited in this chapter.

Case law

German Federal Constitutional Court, Order of the First Senate of 14 July 1999 – 1 BvR 2226/94, http://www.bverfg.de/e/rs19990714_1bvr222694en.html.

German Federal Constitutional Court, Urteil des Ersten Senats vom 12. März 2003 – 1 BvR 330/96, http://www.bverfg.de/e/rs20030312_1bvr033096.html.

German Federal Constitutional Court, Beschluss des Ersten Senats vom 20. April 2005 – 1 BvR 2378/98, http://www.bverfg.de/e/rs20050420_1bvr237898.html.

German Federal Constitutional Court, Judgement of the First Senate of 27 February 2008 – 1 BvR 370/07, http://www.bverfg.de/e/rs20080227_1bvr037007en.html.

German Federal Constitutional Court, Judgement of the First Senate of 20 April 2016 – 1 BvR 966/09, http://www.bverfg.de/e/rs20160420_1bvr096609en.html.

Press releases

German Federal Constitutional Court: Provisions in the North-Rhine Westphalia Constitution Protection Act (Verfassungsschutzgesetz Nordrhein-Westfalen) on online searches and on the reconnaissance of the Internet null and void. Press Release No. 22/2008 of 27 February 2008, https://www.bundesverfassungsgericht.de/SharedDocs/Pressemitteilungen/EN/2008/bvg08-022.html.

German Federal Constitutional Court: Constitutional complaints against the investigative powers of the Federal Criminal Police Office for fighting international terrorism partially successful. Press Release No. 19/2016 of 20 April 2016, https://www.bundesverfassungsgericht.de/SharedDocs/Pressemitteilungen/EN/2016/bvg16-019.html.

7

Putting Courts under Pressure: Normative Repercussions

In constitutional democracies, courts with the authority to exercise their constitutional veto by striking down legislative and executive actions play a pivotal political role. These courts are expected to delineate constitutional boundaries in their rulings and compel lawmakers to revisit their policies when they overstep those boundaries. The judiciary's crucial role in systems of limited government is underscored by the increasing volume of scholarship dedicated to understanding the factors that influence judicial decision-making (see for example Epstein and Knight, 1998; Cross and Nelson, 2001; Rogers, 2001; Staton and Vanberg, 2008; Bailey and Maltzman, 2011; Epstein et al., 2013).

About two decades ago, some scholars lamented that 'comparative political scientists have traditionally devoted surprisingly little attention to studying courts' (Vanberg, 2005, 168), a sentiment that would appear wholly unwarranted today. The judiciary occupies a prominent spot in the minds of scholars interested in identifying the factors that shape the laws that govern our societies (see Ginsburg, 2003; Hirschl, 2009; Hall, 2011; Kelemen, 2011; Staton et al., 2022). Whereas much of the early literature on courts' influence in politics and the determinants of their decision-making had focused on the U.S. Supreme Court (see for example Dahl, 1957; Handberg and Hill Jr., 1980; Segal, 1984; Segal and Cover, 1989; Caldeira and Gibson, 1992; Mondak, 1992), scholars' interests have since diversified beyond the American experience (see Volcansek, 2000; Trochev, 2004; Stone Sweet, 2007; Dyevre, 2011; Hanretty, 2012; Brouard and Hönnige, 2017).

Inter alia, scholars of judicial politics have shed light on the role courts play in Asia's emerging democracies (Ginsburg, 2003), the South African Constitutional Court's struggles to translate its legitimacy into acquiescence with unpopular rulings (Gibson and Caldeira, 2003), the Argentine Supreme Court's navigation of tense relationships with autocratic and democratic rulers in the executive branch (Helmke, 2005), and the Mexican Supreme Court's interactions with the media to defuse the threats of non-compliance with its jurisprudence (Staton, 2010). Some scholars have turned their attention

Putting Courts Under Pressure. Philipp A. Schroeder, Oxford University Press. © Philipp A. Schroeder (2025).
DOI: 10.1093/9780198953265.003.0007

from the domestic arena to international courts, particularly the Court of Justice of the European Union (CJEU), showing that many of the determinants shaping the decision-making of national courts are at work at the international level as well (see Carrubba, 2005; Carrubba et al., 2008; Alter, 2014; Larsson and Naurin, 2016; Ovádek, 2021).

Collectively, this literature has contributed to our understanding of how courts influence politics in systems of limited government. Existing scholarship suggests that once courts are able to rely on comfortable reservoirs of diffuse support among their constituents, courts can place constraints on the actions of lawmakers in the legislative and executive branches, often without actively intervening in the political process (see Stone, 1992; Rogers and Vanberg, 2007; Carrubba, 2009). However, even courts enjoying high levels of institutional legitimacy are themselves not free from constraints in their review of lawmakers' actions. Lawmakers frustrated by courts obstructing the pursuit of their preferred policies face an incentive to clip away at courts' jurisdiction and gradually undermine their institutional integrity, an incentive that is not lost on courts (Clark, 2010; Mark and Zilis, 2019). In addition, just as much as the shadow of constitutional review leaves its mark on lawmakers' choices during the legislative process, scholars have shown that the prospects of lawmakers' non-compliance with courts' jurisprudence affect the latter's decision-making (see Vanberg, 2005; Carrubba and Zorn, 2010; Hall, 2014).

In this book, I presented a theoretical model that highlights how courts' compliance dilemma and the external constraints on their exercise of constitutional review identified in the existing literature help us explain an otherwise puzzling phenomenon: Even courts with high levels of public support, which should typically encourage the legislative and executive branches to avoid confrontation with the judiciary, cannot always prevent lawmakers from pursuing policies that clearly contradict the courts' jurisprudence. Existing scholarship suggests that when lawmakers face courts that are widely supported by the public, they have strong incentives to steer clear of the political and reputational costs associated with having their policies overturned. As a result, they should pre-emptively adjust their policy choices to align with the standards set by the courts' jurisprudence (see Landfried, 1992; Stone, 1992; Vanberg, 1998; Rogers and Vanberg, 2007). Why, then, would lawmakers choose to risk the costs of clashing with courts that have the power to overturn their policies?

Offering an explanation for this puzzle, this book opened up a new perspective on how the constraints on courts' exercise of constitutional review reflect in the behaviour of lawmakers, and how the mutual interdependence among the judiciary and the elected branches translates into jurisprudence establishing the constitutional guardrails for lawmakers' policy-making. This book makes a simple claim, that nonetheless has wider implications for the definition of the constitutional limits to policy in systems of limited government: Lawmakers' decisions made under the threat of constitutional review send signals to courts about how they might react to future rulings that restrict their policy-making discretion.

7.1 Looking forwards, looking backwards

Like many prominent contributions by scholars of judicial politics, the theoretical approach employed in this book perceives courts and lawmakers as strategic actors (see for example Ferejohn and Weingast, 1992; Epstein and Knight, 1998; Rogers, 2001; Stephenson, 2003; Vanberg, 2005; Clark, 2009, see also Tsebelis, 2002). In systems of limited government, courts and lawmakers recognize that the realization of their preferences depends not only on their own choices but also on the preferences of others and the actions they expect them to take (Epstein and Knight, 1998, 12).

This book follows in the footsteps of this strand of scholarship. The theoretical model presented in Chapter 2 assumes that courts and lawmakers are forward-looking, anticipating the actions of their counterparts, which are then reflected in their own choices. Some of the model's equilibria replicate existing scholarship's expectations about the inter-branch dynamics in systems of limited government, including lawmakers' 'auto-limitation' in the shadow of constitutional review (see Landfried, 1992; Vanberg, 1998; Rogers and Vanberg, 2007; Stone Sweet, 2007). However, beyond the phenomenon of 'auto-limitation', the book uncovers an additional effect of lawmakers' anticipated costs from constitutional review, which has so far received little attention in the existing literature (see Staton et al., 2022, for an exception).

The book highlights that both courts and lawmakers anticipate each others' responses to their own actions by turning to the past. Lawmakers draw on rules courts established in previous decisions to identify policy choices at risk of a judicial veto. Courts, on the other hand, consider the political risks lawmakers took when they adopted policies flouting jurisprudence to assess the likelihood of non-compliance with their decisions. Courts shape their expectations of lawmakers' future actions by analysing their past behaviour. Lawmakers prepared to bear the costs of confrontation with courts are more likely to be the kinds of lawmakers prepared to evade compliance with courts' decisions censoring their policies. Courts keen to avoid issuing decisions that are ultimately not enforced then are more likely to respond with self-restraint when lawmakers had risked a costly confrontation.

The innovation of the theoretical model presented in this book lies within the link it establishes between lawmakers' willingness to bear the costs that come with a judicial veto and their willingness to evade compliance with courts' jurisprudence. For the sake of parsimony, the model abstracts from reality and captures only a snapshot of lawmakers and courts' repeated interactions. Nonetheless, despite limiting its attention to a single encounter, the model still shows that lawmakers and courts' choices are shaped by each other's past behaviour and the anticipation that their paths will cross again in the future. Some lawmakers avoid transgressing constitutional norms substantiated in existing jurisprudence to pre-empt courts' censure in the future. Yet, other lawmakers show the courage of risking a 'bloody nose' at the court and call existing constitutional rules into question in their policy choices. The model makes a simple claim: When tied to costs, lawmakers' past non-compliance with jurisprudence foreshadows lawmakers' future non-compliance. Given courts are incentivized to avoid issuing jurisprudence that ultimately goes unenforced, it is lawmakers who take the risk of enacting policies that conflict with prior court rulings who play a crucial role in driving the evolution of constitutional jurisprudence.

7.2 Empirical findings

In this book, I present both quantitative and qualitative empirical evidence from the German Federal Constitutional Court's (GFCC) constitutional review to test the implications of the theoretical model. Chapter 5 featured a statistical analysis of the GFCC's review of federal laws between 1977 and 2017, revealing that the court is less likely to strike down a challenged law if members of the governing coalition in the Bundestag had previously raised constitutional objections to the law before its adoption. The theoretical model provides an explanation for this otherwise counter-intuitive finding. Dismissing constitutional concerns voiced during the legislative process can come back to bite lawmakers. Existing scholarship suggests that lawmakers evading compliance with courts' jurisprudence risk paying a price at the ballot box, although non-compliance is generally difficult to observe for the electorate (Vanberg, 2001; Staton, 2006; Krehbiel, 2016). We can assume that lawmakers' flouting of advice that their policy choices conflict with jurisprudence—particularly advice from their own political allies—followed by a court's censure is an easily observable instance of non-compliance: It is the court itself, which highlights that lawmakers failed to respect the boundaries of the constitution.

The statistical analysis provided evidence consistent with the core claim of the theoretical model. Lawmakers risking a costly confrontation signal a credible non-compliance threat and induce courts to exercise self-restraint. To conduct this analysis, I identified every federal law reviewed by the GFCC between 1983 and 2017 (both by the court's Chambers and Senates) and read every corresponding final parliamentary debate to code whether members of the Bundestag had objected laws as unconstitutional.

Complementing the quantitative data analysis, Chapter 6 provided evidence through a case study of the GFCC's review of several federal laws aimed at expanding law enforcement powers to combat organized crime and international terrorism. Focusing on the court's review of the 2008 Federal Criminal Police Office Act (BKAG), the chapter illustrated how the theoretical model effectively explains the GFCC's atypical decision in this case. The case study presented an analytic narrative demonstrating the core claim of the theoretical model in action. Lawmakers from the CDU/CSU and SPD governing coalition dismissed concerns raised by members of their own caucus that the BKAG conflicted with constitutional limits on state surveillance, limits the GFCC had reaffirmed just months before the Bundestag's vote on the act. In its subsequent review, the GFCC invalidated several provisions of the BKAG but also overturned parts of its own precedent, relaxing restrictions on law enforcement's use of surveillance data to counter terrorist threats. This case study thus illustrated how the theoretical model provides valuable insights into the decisions made by both lawmakers and the court during their interactions over the BKAG.

7.3 Links to existing scholarship

The lessons we can draw from the theoretical and empirical analysis presented in this book speak to some of the views held in the existing literature on inter-branch dynamics in systems of limited government. Existing scholarship suggests that lawmakers pursue certain policies despite knowing that courts will eventually censor them to delegate the resolution of contested political issues to courts and hence shift any blame for unpopular decisions on to the judiciary (see Graber, 1993; Salzberger, 1993; Whittington, 2005).

The implications of the theoretical model in this book further differentiate this argument. Lawmakers know that key decisions shaping the effects of their policies are eventually taken by courts. In practice, the decisions courts reach in constitutional review cases are much more complex than the simple dichotomy of striking down or upholding policy presented in the formal model of Chapter 2. The legal rules that courts establish in their jurisprudence are crucial for shaping lawmakers' future policy-making decisions (an observation highlighted by the case study in Chapter 6, see also Clark and Lauderdale, 2010). By accepting the political fallout of having their policies censored by a court, lawmakers signal the point at which they are no longer willing to accept rules that impose strict limits on their policy-making discretion. In other words, lawmakers understand that not every provision of their legislation will survive constitutional review and recognize that courts' jurisprudence sets the constitutional boundaries for their policies. However, by provoking costly confrontations with the courts, lawmakers create a credible risk of non-compliance, thereby gaining leverage over the legal rules established in the court's jurisprudence.

Furthermore, studies examining the relationship between the level of support legislative acts enjoyed in the legislature and the likelihood of courts challenging the constitutionality of these acts have produced mixed empirical results (see for example Harvey and Friedman, 2009;Bailey and Maltzman, 2011; Segal et al., 2011). These studies draw on previous scholarship showing that courts' decisions are driven by justices' ideological preferences (see Segal and Spaeth, 1993, 2002), and often rely on an estimation of the ideological distance between the median justice and median lawmaker as well as current lawmakers' estimated support for an act reviewed by the court (see Segal et al., 2011; Hall and Ura, 2015, see also Poole, 1998).

A potential limitation of such approaches is that, beyond ideology, acts clearly at odds with constitutional norms may be less likely to receive support from lawmakers, which could explain why courts are more likely to strike down acts with little legislative backing. The theoretical and empirical approach in this book shifts the focus to lawmakers' perceptions of the constitutional compatibility of the policies they debate. It demonstrates that it is the political risks lawmakers are willing to take in pursuit of their policy goals that signal the strength of their support for an act ultimately reviewed by a court, influencing the court's decision-making. When lawmakers in power push through policies amid widespread constitutional concerns and in defiance of their own political allies, they face high political costs if a court strikes down their policy. In doing so, they also signal a credible threat of non-compliance.

Finally, the theoretical model outlines the political environments where lawmakers' costly signalling of a non-compliance threat is likely to influence courts' decision-making: specifically, when courts with strong institutional legitimacy face lawmakers who can stay in power long enough to challenge the courts' decisions on their own policies. At first glance, these conditions might suggest frequent, intense clashes between the elected branches and the courts, with neither side willing to back down. However, the central argument of this book shows that lawmakers signalling a non-compliance threat actually helps courts avoid all too frequent standoffs with the elected branches and recognize when to exercise self-restraint to prevent issuing decisions that will ultimately go unenforced.

7.4 Beyond Germany

The evaluation of the theoretical model's empirical implications centred on the case of Germany, given that the GFCC has consistently enjoyed high levels of approval among the public yet has also faced governing majorities controlling government for several consecutive terms. While much of the quantitative and qualitative evidence from the German case presented in this book appears consistent with the expectations of the theoretical model, it appears worthwhile to study whether effects of lawmakers' costly signalling are discernible in environments with similarly influential courts, including the U.S. Supreme Court's review of Congressional acts and the CJEU's decisions in preliminary reference procedures and infringement proceedings.

The U.S. Supreme Court has enjoyed similar levels of diffuse support as the GFCC, albeit experiencing more variation in levels of support over time (see Caldeira and Gibson, 1992; Durr et al., 2000; Gibson and Nelson, 2016). However, existing scholarship documents that the court's institutional legitimacy could not stop officials in Congress and the executive branch from occasionally flouting its jurisprudence (see for example Fisher, 1993; Carrubba and Zorn, 2010; Hall, 2011). Future research may analyse whether politically costly instances of public officials' non-compliance on a particular issue (e.g. where non-compliance misaligns with dominant state or nationwide public opinion) reflect in the U.S. Supreme Court's subsequent jurisprudence.

Further, existing scholarship has highlighted that governments in the European Union's Member States and the CJEU vie over the path of European integration, with Member States often failing to comply with European law (see Alter, 1998; Zürn and Joerges, 2005; Börzel et al., 2010). In line with the theoretical insights discussed in this book, we may expect the CJEU to become more likely to avoid antagonizing governments in Member States in its interpretation of European law following periods of Member States' governments opting for politically costly non-compliance with supranational rules.

7.5 Normative implications

In the final section of this book, I turn my attention to a normative question that has so far taken the back seat against the positive theoretical discussion and empirical evaluation: Should lawmakers' influence over the legal rules courts establish in their jurisprudence worry us?

Scholars' analysis of the drivers of courts' decision-making has been accompanied by a normative debate concerning the influence courts wield over politics and the constraints they place on lawmakers in the elected branches. Some see courts as fundamentally 'countermajoritarian' institutions, with justices acting as lawmakers in robes, who 'thwart the will' of the representatives of the people (Bickel, 1986; Friedman, 1998, 2002; Waldron, 2006). Scholars subscribing to these views of courts have cautioned against a judicialization of politics and government through courts (Tate, 1995; Stone Sweet, 2000b; Hirschl, 2009).

At the other end of the debate, scholars have argued that influential courts capable of obstructing the actions of the elected branches are an essential feature of constitutional democracies. Courts ensure that the constitutional rights of minorities are protected against the 'tyranny' of political majorities (see Kaufman, 1980; Riker and Weingast, 1988), and should stand tall when their decisions precipitate outrage among dominant segments of society (Sunstein, 2007).

The findings of this book may cause concern among those considering courts as necessary institutions to keep the politically powerful in check. Here, the logic that lawmakers in government are capable of pushing the constitutional limits defined in courts' jurisprudence after facing down widespread constitutional concerns would appear particularly alarming. Results of the formal analysis in Chapter 2 suggest that lawmakers consistently pushing the boundaries of the constitution ultimately succeed in undermining a court's protection of constitutional rights.

However, the empirical evidence presented in this book mitigates these concerns. The data I collected for the statistical analysis in Chapter 5 suggests that (at least in Germany) instances of lawmakers taking high political risks when pushing constitutional limits and hence inducing the court to show deference to the elected branches are relatively rare events. Further, the partial-pooling equilibrium harbouring the theoretical model's core claim shows that courts are more likely to respond with self-restraint to lawmakers costly signalling only under a certain set of circumstances: when courts are not at risk of suffering high costs from court-curbing and when lawmakers have a strong grip on government office. Provided the latter condition is not in place, courts face no incentive to show self-restraint in their decision-making. Hence, rather than highlighting how lawmakers can undermine constitutional rights, the book shows how electorally accountable lawmakers enjoying consecutive spells in office and powerful courts enjoying comfortable reservoirs of public support resolve their differences over policy, while avoiding frequent, bruising conflict.

The book shows that courts' jurisprudence defining the constitutional guardrails to lawmakers' policy-making is not rigid, with new judgments continually piling on further constraints on the actions of the elected branches. Instead, constitutional jurisprudence evolves over time, with legal rules varying the constraints lawmakers have to adhere to in their policy-making. Crucially, the book shows that it is not just justices serving on the highest benches who have a hand in writing these rules. By questioning the rules justices defined in their jurisprudence and provoking constitutional review, lawmakers set the premise for the evolution of jurisprudence and indirectly influence its direction.

This dynamic should not be viewed as an unwelcome, unintended anomaly in systems of limited government. Instead, it is born out of the institutional design of systems of checks and balances. To ensure the functioning of systems of checks and balances, 'ambition must be made to counteract ambition' (Madison, 1961), and this logic applies to courts as well. In other words, lawmakers' signalling of a political constraint on courts' exercise of constitutional review is an observable implication of a system of limited government at work.

Bibliography

Alter, K. J. (1998). Who are the "Masters of the Treaty"?: European Governments and the European Court of Justice. *International Organization*, 52(1):121–147.

Alter, K. J. (2001). *Establishing the Supremacy of European Law: The Making of an International Rule of Law in Europe*. Oxford: Oxford University Press.

Alter, K. J. (2014). *The New Terrain of International Law. Courts, Politics, Rights*. Princeton: Princeton University Press.

Alter, K. J. and Vargas, J. (2000). Explaining variation in the use of European litigation strategies: European community law and British gender equality policy. *Comparative and General Pharmacology*, 33(4):452–482.

Bailey, M. A., and Maltzman, F. (2011). *The Constrained Court: Law, Politics, and the Decisions Justices Make*. Princeton: Princeton University Press.

Bartels, B. L., and Johnston, C. D. (2013). On the ideological foundations of Supreme Court legitimacy in the American public. *American Journal of Political Science*, 57(1):184–199.

Bergara, M., Richman, B., and Spiller, P. T. (2003). Monitoring Supreme Court strategic decision making: The congressional constraint. *Legislative Studies Quarterly*, 28(2): 247–280.

Bickel, A. M. (1986). *The Least Dangerous Branch: The Supreme Court at the Bar of American Politics*, 2nd edn. New Haven, CT: Yale University Press.

Blauberger, M. (2012). With Luxembourg in mind . . . the remaking of national policies in the face of ECJ jurisprudence. *Journal of European Public Policy*, 19(1):109–126.

Blauberger, M., Heindlmaier, A., Kramer, D., *et al.* (2018). ECJ Judges read the morning papers. Explaining the turnaround of European citizenship jurisprudence. *Journal of European Public Policy*, 25(10):1422–1441.

Blauberger, M. and Schmidt, S. K. (2017). The European Court of Justice and its political impact. *West European Politics*, 40(4):907–918.

Börzel, T. A., Hofmann, T., Panke, D., *et al.* (2010). Obstinate and inefficient: Why Member States do not comply with European Law. *Comparative Political Studies*, 43(11): 1363–1390.

Brouard, S. and Hönnige, C. (2017). Constitutional courts as veto players: Lessons from the United States, France and Germany. *European Journal of Political Research*, 56(3): 529–552.

Bueno de Mesquita, E. and Stephenson, M. C. (2002). Informative precedent and intrajudicial communication. *American Political Science Review*, 96(4):755–766.

Bundeszentrale für politische Bildung (2013). Vor zwanzig Jahren: Einschränkung des Asylrechts 1993.

Burley, A. -M. and Mattli, W. (1993). Europe before the court: A political theory of legal integration. *International Organization*, 47(1):41–76.

Caldeira, G. A. and Gibson, J. L. (1992). The etiology of public support for the Supreme Court. *American Journal of Political Science*, 36(3):635–664.

Callander, S. (2011). Searching for good policies. *American Political Science Review*, 105(4):643–662.

Callander, S. and Clark, T. S. (2017). Precedent and doctrine in a complicated world. *American Political Science Review*, 111(1):184–203.

Capelletti, M. (1989). *The Judicial Process in Comparative Perspective*. Oxford: Clarendon Press.

Carrubba, C. J. (2005). Courts and compliance in international law. *Journal of Politics*, 67(3):669–689.

Carrubba, C. J. (2009). A model of the endogenous development of judicial institutions in federal and international systems. *The Journal of Politics*, 71(1):55–69.

Carrubba, C. J. and Clark, T. S. (2012). Rule creation in a political hierarchy. *American Political Science Review*, 106(3):622–643.

Carrubba, C. J. and Gabel, M. (2015). *International Courts and the Performance of International Agreements. A General Theory with Evidence from the European Union*. New York: Cambridge University Press.

Carrubba, C. J., Gabel, M., and Hankla, C. (2008). Judicial behavior under political constraints: Evidence from the European Court of Justice. *American Political Science Review*, 102(4):435–452.

Carrubba, C. J., Helmke, G., Gabel, M., *et al.* (2015). When parchment barriers matter: De jure judicial independence and the concentration of power. https://www.gretchenhelmke.com/uploads/7/0/3/2/70329843/parchment.pdf.

Carrubba, C. J. and Zorn, C. (2010). Executive discretion, judicial decision making, and separation of powers in the United States. *The Journal of Politics*, 72(3):812–824.

Casillas, C. J., Enns, P. K., and Wohlfarth, P. C. (2011). How public opinion constrains the U.S. Supreme Court. *American Journal of Political Science*, 55(1):74–88.

Chavez, R. B., Ferejohn, J. A., and Weingast, B. R. (2011). A theory of the politically independent judiciary. In: G. Helmke and J. Ríos-Figueroa (eds), *Courts in Latin America*, 219–247. New York: Cambridge University Press.

Clark, T. S. (2009). The separation of powers, court-curbing and judicial legitimacy. *American Journal of Political Science*, 53(4):971–989.

Clark, T. S. (2010). *The Limits of Judicial Independence*. Cambridge: Cambridge University Press.

Clark, T. S. (2016). Scope and precedent: Judicial rule-making under uncertainty. *Journal of Theoretical Politics*, 28(3):353–384.

Clark, T. S. and Carrubba, C. J. (2012). A theory of opinion writing in a political hierarchy. *The Journal of Politics*, 74(2):584–603.

Clark, T. S. and Lauderdale, B. E. (2010). Locating Supreme Court opinions in doctrine space. *American Journal of Political Science*, 54(4):871–890.

Clark, T. S. and Lauderdale, B. E. (2012). The genealogy of law. *Political Analysis*, 20(3): 329–350.

Clarke, K. A. and Primo, D. M. (2012). *A Model Discipline: Political Science and the Logic of Representations*. Oxford: Oxford University Press.

Conant, L. (2001). Europeanization and the courts: Variable patterns of adaption among national judiciaries. In: M. Green Cowles, J. Caporaso and T. Risse (eds), *Transforming Europe: Europeanization and Domestic Change*, 97–115. Ithaca, NY: Cornell University Press.

Craig, P. and de Búrca, G. (2020). *EU Law: Text, Cases, and Materials*. Oxford: Oxford University Press.

Cross, F. B. and Nelson, B. J. (2001). Strategic institutional effects on Supreme Court decisionmaking. *Northwestern University Law Review*, 95(4):1437.

Dahl, R. A. (1957). Decision-making in a Democracy: The Supreme Court as a national policy-maker. *Journal of Public Law*, 6:279–295.

Darnstädt, T. (2017). Ein personenbezogener Gefahrbegriff – Analyse der Bedingungen des Bundesverfassungsgerichts an Vorfeld-Ermächtigungen im BKA-Gesetz. *Deutsches Verwaltungsblatt*, 132(2):88–96.

De Vries, C. E. and Hobolt, S. B. (2020). *Political Entrepreneurs. The Rise of Challenger Parties in Europe*. Princeton: Princeton University Press.

Durr, R. H., Martin, A. D., and Wolbrecht, C. (2000). Ideological divergence and public support for the Supreme Court. *American Journal of Political Science*, 44(4): 768–776.

Dyevre, A. (2011). The German Federal Constitutional Court and European judicial politics. *West European Politics*, 34(2):346–361.

Easton, D. (1965). *A Systems Analysis of Political Life*. New York: Wiley.

Emnid Institute (1995). Vertrauen in Institutionen: Umfrage und Analyse Nr.1/2:72–8.

Engst, B. G. (2021). *The Two Faces of Judicial Power. Dynamics of Judicial-Political Bargaining*. Cham: Palgrave Macmillan.

Engst, B. G., Gschwend, T., Hönnige, C., *et al.* (2019). The Constitutional Court Database: Conceptualizing a relational database. (Manuscript prepared for the workshop "Multi-User Databases on Judicial Decision-Making", Florence, Italy, 10–11 October 2019).

Epstein, L. and Jacobi, T. (2010). The strategic analysis of judicial decisions. *Annual Review of Law and Social Science*, 6(1):341–358.

Epstein, L. and Knight, J. (1998). *The Choices Justices Make*. Washington, D.C: CQ Press.

Epstein, L., Knight, J., and Martin, A. D. (2001a). The Supreme Court as a strategic national policymaker. *Emory Law Review*, 55:583–611.

Epstein, L., Knight, J., and Shvetsova, O. (2001b). The role of constitutional courts in the establishment and maintenance of democratic systems of government. *Law and Society Review*, 35(1):117–164.

Epstein, L., Landes, W. M., and Posner, R. A. (2013). *The Behavior of Federal Judges: A Theoretical and Empirical Study of Rational Choice*. Cambridge, Mass: Harvard University Press.

Ervin, S. J. (1970). Separation of powers: Judicial independence. *Law and Contemporary Problems*, 35(1):108–127.

Fearon, J. D. (1997). Signaling foreign policy interests: Tying hands versus sinking costs. *Journal of Conflict Resolution*, 41(1):68–90.

Feld, L. P. and Voigt, S. (2003). Economic growth and judicial independence: Cross-country evidence using a new set of indicators. *European Journal of Political Economy*, 19(3): 497–527.

Ferejohn, J. A. and Weingast, B. R. (1992). A positive theory of statutory interpretation. *International Review of Law and Economics*, 12(2):263–279.

Fisher, L. (1993). The legislative veto: Invalidated, it survives. *Law and Contemporary Problems*, 56:273–292.

Forschungsruppe Wahlen (2008a). Politbarometer Ost 2008. Köln: GESIS Datenarchiv.

Forschungsruppe Wahlen (2008b). Politbarometer West 2008. Köln: GESIS Datenarchiv.

Forschungsruppe Wahlen (2019). Politbarometer 1977–2017 (Partielle Kumulation). Köln: GESIS Datenarchiv.

Fox, J., and Stephenson, M. C. (2011). Judicial review as a response to political posturing. *American Political Science Review*, 105(2):397–414.

Fox, J. and Vanberg, G. (2014). Narrow versus broad judicial decisions. *Journal of Theoretical Politics*, 26(3):355–383.

Friedman, B. (1998). The history of the countermajoritarian difficulty, part one: The road to judicial supremacy. *New York University Law Review*, 73(2):333–433.

Friedman, B. (2002). The birth of an academic obsession: The history of the countermajoritarian difficulty. *Yale Law Journal*, 112:153–259.

Gandhi, J. (2008). *Political Institutions under Dictatorship*. Cambridge: Cambridge University Press.

Garrett, G., Kelemen, R. D., and Schulz, H. (1998). The European Court of Justice, national governments, and legal integration in the European Union. *International Organization*, 52(1):149–176.

Gelman, A. and Hill, J. (2007). *Data Analysis Using Regression and Multilevel/Hierarchical Models*. Cambridge: Cambridge University Press.

Gelman, A. and Rubin, D. B. (1992). Inference from iterative simulation using multiple sequences. *Statistical Science*, 7(4):457–472.

Gely, R. and Spiller, P. T. (1990). A rational choice theory of Supreme Court statutory decisions with applications to the State Farm and Grove City cases. *Journal of Law, Economics, and Organization*, 6(2):263–300.

Gerring, J. (2004). What is a case study and what is it good for? *American Political Science Review*, 98(2):341–354.

Gessler, T. and Hunger, S. (2022). How the refugee crisis and radical right parties shape party competition on immigration. *Political Science Research and Methods*, 10(3): 524–544.

Gibson, J. L. and Caldeira, G. A. (1995). The legitimacy of transnational legal institutions: Compliance, support, and the European Court of Justice. *American Journal of Political Science*, 39(2):459–489.

Gibson, J. L. and Caldeira, G. A. (2003). Defenders of democracy? Legitimacy, popular acceptance, and the South African Constitutional Court. *Journal of Politics*, 65(1):1–30.

Gibson, J. L., Caldeira, G. A., and Baird, V. A. (1998). On the legitimacy of National High Courts. *The American Political Science Review*, 92(2):343–358.

Gibson, J. L., Caldeira, G. A., and Spence, L. K. (2005). Why do people accept public policies they oppose? Testing legitimacy theory with a survey-based experiment. *Political Research Quarterly*, 58(2):187–201.

Gibson, J. L. and Nelson, M. J. (2016). Change in institutional support for the US Supreme Court. *Public Opinion Quarterly*, 80(3):622–641.

Ginsburg, T. (2003). *Judicial Review in New Democracies: Constitutional Courts in Asian Cases*. Cambridge: Cambridge University Press.

Ginsburg, T. and Versteeg, M. (2014). Why do countries adopt constitutional review? *Journal of Law, Economics, and Organization*, 30(3):587–622.

Goertz, G. and Mahoney, J. (2012). *A Tale of Two Cultures: Qualitative and Quantitative Rsearch in the Social Sciences*. Princeton: Princeton University Press.

Graber, M. A. (1993). The nonmajoritarian difficulty: Legislative deference to the judiciary. *Studies in American Political Development*, 7(1):35–73.

Grimm, D. (2016). *Europa ja - aber welches? Zur Verfassung der europäischen Demokratie*. Munich: C.H. Beck.

Hackenesch, C., Högl, M., Öhler, H., *et al.* (2022). Populist radical right parties' impact on European foreign aid spending. *Journal of Common Market Studies*, 60(5):1391–1415.

Hall, M. E. (2011). *The Nature of Supreme Court Power*. Cambridge, Mass: Cambridge University Press.

Hall, M. E. (2014). The semiconstrained court: Public opinion, the separation of powers, and the U.S. Supreme Court's fear of nonimplementation. *American Journal of Political Science*, 58(2):352–366.

Hall, M. E. and Ura, J. D. (2015). Judicial majoritarianism. *Journal of Politics*, 77(3):818–832.

Hamilton, A. (1961). The Federalist 78. In: B. Fletcher Wright (eds), *The Federalist*, 489–496. Cambridge, Mass: Harvard University Press.

Handberg, R., and Hill Jr., H. F. (1980). Court curbing, court reversals, and judicial review: The Supreme Court versus Congress. *Law and Society Review*, 14(2):309–322.

Hanretty, C. (2012). Dissent in Iberia: The ideal points of justices on the Spanish and Portuguese Constitutional Tribunals. *European Journal of Political Research*, 51(5):671–692.

Hansford, T. G. and Spriggs, J. F. (2006). *The Politics of Precedent on the U.S. Supreme Court*. Princeton: Princeton University Press.

Harvey, A. and Friedman, B. (2009). Ducking trouble: Congressionally induced selection bias in the Supreme Court's agenda. *Journal of Politics*, 71(2):574–592.

Helmke, G. (2002). The logic of strategic defection: Courts and executive relations in Argentina under dictatorship and democracy. *American Political Science Review*, 96(2):291–303.

Helmke, G. (2005). *Courts under Constraints: Judges, Generals, and Presidents in Argentina*. Cambridge: Cambridge University Press.

Hirschl, R. (2008). The judicialization of politics. In: G. A. Caldeira, R. D. Kelemen, and K. E. Whittingdon (eds), *The Oxford Handbook of Law and Politics*, 119–141. Oxford: Oxford University Press.

Hirschl, R. (2009). *Towards Juristocracy: The Origins and Consequences of the New Constitutionalism*. Cambridge, Mass: Harvard University Press.

Hjorth, F. and Larsen, M. V. (2022). When does accommodation work? Electoral effects of mainstream left position taking on immigration. *British Journal of Political Science*, 52(2):949–957.

Hönnige, C. and Gschwend, T. (2010). Das Bundesverfassungsgericht im politischen System der BRD - ein unbekanntes Wesen? *Politische Vierteljahresschrift*, 51(3):507–530.

Humphreys, M. (2016). *Political Games: Mathematical Insights on Fighting, Voting, Lying, & Other Affairs of State*. New York: W.W. Norton & Company, Inc.

Ishiyama Smithey, S. and Ishiyama, J. (2002). Judicial activism in post-communist politics. *Law and Society Review*, 36(4):719–742.

Kapiszewski, D., Silverstein, G., and Kagan, R. A. (2013). *Consequential Courts: Judicial Roles in Global Perspective*. Cambridge: Cambridge University Press.

Kapiszewski, D. and Taylor, M. M. (2013). Compliance: Conceptualizing, measuring, and explaining adherence to judicial rulings. *Law and Social Inquiry*, 38(4):803–835.

Kaufman, I. R. (1980). The essence of judicial independence. *Columbia Law Review*, 80(4):671–701.

Kelemen, R. D. (2006). Suing for Europe. *Comparative Political Studies*, 39(1):101–127.

Kelemen, R. D. (2011). *Eurolegalism: The Transformation of Law and Regulation in the European Union*. Cambridge, Mass: Harvard University Press.

Knight, J. and Epstein, L. (1996). The norm of stare decisis. *American Journal of Political Science*, 40(4):1018–1035.

Kommers, D. P. (1994). The Federal Constitutional Court in the German political system. *Comparative Political Studies*, 26(4):470–491.

Krause, W., Cohen, D., and Abou-Chadi, T. (2023). Does accommodation work? Mainstream party strategies and the success of radical right parties. *Political Science Research and Methods*, 11(1):172–179.

Krehbiel, J. N. (2016). The politics of judicial procedures: The role of public oral hearings in the German Constitutional Court. *American Journal of Political Science*, 60(4): 990–1005.

Krehbiel, J. N. (2021). Strategic delay and the use of incompatibility rulings at the German Constitutional Court. *Journal of Politics*, 83(3):821–833.

Krehbiel, K. (2007). Supreme court appointments as a move-the-median game. *American Journal of Political Science*, 51(2):231–240.

Laffont, J. J. and Meleu, M. (2001). Separation of powers and development. *Journal of Development Economics*, 64(1):129–145.

Landa, D., and Lax, J. R. (2009). Legal doctrine on collegial courts. *The Journal of Politics*, 71(3):946–963.

Landfried, C. (1992). Judicial policy-making in Germany: The Federal Constitutional Court. In: M. L. Volcansek (ed.), *Judicial Politics and Policy-Making in Western Europe*, 50–67. London: Routledge.

Landfried, C. (1995). Germany. In: C. N. Tate and T. Vallinder (eds), *The Global Expansion of Judicial Power*, 307–324. New York: New York University Press.

Larsson, O. and Naurin, D. (2016). Judicial independence and political uncertainty: How the risk of override affects the Court of Justice of the EU. *International Organization*, 70(2):377–408.

Lax, J. R. (2007). Constructing legal rules on appellate courts. *American Political Science Review*, 101(3):591–604.

Lax, J. R. (2011). The new judicial politics of legal doctrine. *Annual Review of Political Science*, 14(1):131–157.

Lax, J. R. (2012). Political constraints on legal doctrine: How hierarchy shapes the law. *The Journal of Politics*, 74(3):765–781.

Lax, J. R. and Cameron, C. M. (2007). Bargaining and opinion assignment on the US Supreme Court. *Journal of Law, Economics, and Organization*, 23(2):276–302.

Leibniz Institute for the Social Sciences (2018). German General Social Survey: Studien-Nr. 4602, 4614 & 5270.

Llanos, M., Tibi Weber, C., Heyl, C., *et al.* (2015). Informal interference in the judiciary in new democracies: A comparison of six African and Latin American cases. *Democratization* 23(7):1236–1253.

Madison, J. (1961). The Federalist 51. In: B. Fletcher Wright (ed.), *The Federalist*, 355–359. Cambridge, Mass: Harvard University Press.

Mark, A., and Zilis, M. A. (2019). The conditional effectiveness of legislative threats: How court curbing alters the behavior of (some) Supreme Court Justices. *Political Research Quarterly*, 72(3):570–583.

Martinsen, D. S. (2011). Judicial policy-making and Europeanization: The proportionality of national control and administrative discretion. *Journal of European Public Policy*, 18(7):944–961.

Martinsen, D. S. (2015). *An Ever More Powerful Court? The Political Constraints of Legal Integration in the European Union*. Oxford: Oxford University Press.

Mayhew, D. (1974). *Congress: The Electoral connection*. New Haven, CT: Yale University Press.

McCarty, N. and Meirowitz, A. (2007). *Political Game Theory. An Introduction*. Cambridge, Mass: Cambridge University Press.

McCubbins, M. D., Noll, R., and Weingast, B. R. (1992). Positive Canons: The role of legislative bargains in statutory interpretation. *Georgetown Law Journal*, 80(June): 705–742.

Mishler, W. and Sheehan, R. S. (1993). The Supreme Court as a countermajoritarian institution? The impact of public opinion on Supreme Court decisions. *American Political Science Review*, 87(1):87–101.

Mondak, J. J. (1992). Institutional legitimacy, policy legitimacy, and the Supreme Court. *American Politics Quarterly*, 20(4):457–477.

Moraski, B. J. and Shipan, C. R. (1999). The politics of Supreme Court nominations: A theory of institutional constraints and choices. *American Journal of Political Science*, 43(4):1069–1095.

Moustafa, T. (2003). Law versus the State: The judicialization of politics in Egypt. *Law & Social Inquiry*, 28(4):883–930.

Moustafa, T. (2007). *The Struggle for Constitutional Power: Law, Politics, and Economic Development in Egypt*. New York: Cambridge University Press.

Moustafa, T. and Ginsburg, T. (eds) (2008). *Rule by Law: The Politics of Courts in Authoritarian Regimes*. Cambridge: Cambridge University Press.

North, D. C. and Weingast, B. R. (1989). Constitutions and commitment: The evolution of institutions governing public choice in seventeenth-century England. *Journal of Economic History*, 49(4):803–832.

Ovádek, M. (2021). Supranationalism, constrained? Locating the Court of Justice on the EU integration dimension. *European Union Politics*, 22(1):46–69.

Pavone, T. (2019). From Marx to Market: Lawyers, European Law, and the contentious transformation of the Port of Genoa. *Law and Society Review*, 53(3):851–888.

Pócza, K. (2018). *Constitutional Politics and the Judiciary: Decision-Making in Central and Eastern Europe*. London: Routledge.

Poole, K. T. (1998). Recovering a basic space from a set of issue scales. *American Journal of Political Science*, 42(3):954–993.

Ramseyer, M. J. (1994). The puzzling (in)dependence of courts: A comparative approach. *The Journal of Legal Studies*, 23(2):721–747.

Ramseyer, M. J. and Rasmusen, E. B. (2001). Why are Japanese judges so conservative in politically charged cases? *American Political Science Review*, 95(2):331–344.

Rasmusen, E. B. (1994). Judicial legitimacy as a repeated game. *Journal of Law, Economics, and Organization*, 10(1):63–83.

Riker, W. and Weingast, B. R. (1988). Constitutional regulation of legislative choice: The political consequences of judicial deference to legislatures. *Virginia Law Review*, 74: 373–401.

Rogers, J. R. (2001). Information and judicial review: A signaling game of legislative-judicial interaction. *American Journal of Political Science*, 45(1):84–99.

Rogers, J. R. and Vanberg, G. (2007). Resurrecting Lochner: A defense of unprincipled judicial activism. *Journal of Law, Economics, and Organization*, 23(2):442–468.

Rusteberg, B. (2017). Die Entscheidung des Bundesverfassungsgerichts zum Bundeskriminalamtsgesetz – Eine Zwischenbilanz des allgemeinen Sicherheitsrechts. *Kritische Vierteljahresschrift für Gesetzgebung und Rechtswissenschaft*, 100(1): 24–35.

Salzberger, E. M. (1993). A positive analysis of the doctrine of separation of powers, or: Why do we have an independent judiciary? *International Review of Law and Economics*, 13(4):349–379.

Schain, M. A. (2006). The extreme-right and immigration policy-making: Measuring direct and indirect effects. *West European Politics*, 29(2):270–289.

Schmidt, S. K. (2018). *The European Court of Justice and the Policy Process: The Shadow of Case Law*. Oxford: Oxford University Press.

Schwartz, H. (2000). *The Struggle for Constitutional Justice in Post-Communist Eastern Europe*. Chicago : Chicago University Press.

Segal, J. A. (1984). Predicting Supreme Court cases probabilistically: The search and seizure cases, 1962-1981. *American Political Science Review*, 78(4):891–900.

Segal, J. A. and Cover, A. D. (1989). Ideological values and the votes of U.S. Supreme Court justices. *American Political Science Review*, 83(2):557–565.

Segal, J. A. and Spaeth, H. J. (1993). *The Supreme Court and the Attitudinal Model.* Cambridge: Cambridge University Press.

Segal, J. A. and Spaeth, H. J. (2002). *The Supreme Court and the Attitudinal Model Revisited.* Cambridge: Cambridge University Press.

Segal, J. A., Westerland, C., and Lindquist, S. A. (2011). Congress, the Supreme Court, and judicial review: Testing a constitutional separation of powers model. *American Journal of Political Science*, 55(1):89–104.

Shapiro, M. and Stone Sweet, A. (1994). The new constitutional politics of Europe. *Comparative Political Studies*, 26(4):397–420.

Shipan, C. R. (2000). The legislative design of judicial review: A formal analysis. *Journal of Theoretical Politics*, 12(3):269–304.

Spoon, J. J. and Klüver, H. (2020). Responding to far right challengers: Does accommodation pay off? *Journal of European Public Policy*, 27(2):273–291.

Spriggs, J. F. and Hansford, T. G. (2001). Explaining the overruling of U.S. Supreme Court precedent. *Journal of Politics*, 63(4):1091–1111.

Stan Development Team (2016). rstanarm: Bayesian applied regression modeling via Stan.

Staton, J. K. (2006). Constitutional review and the selective promotion of case results. *American Journal of Political Science*, 50(1):98–112.

Staton, J. K. (2010). *Judicial Power and Strategic Communication in Mexico*. Cambridge: Cambridge University Press.

Staton, J. K., Reenock, C. M., and Holsinger, J. (2022). *Can Courts Be Bulwarks of Democracy?* Cambridge: Cambridge University Press.

Staton, J. K. and Vanberg, G. (2008). The value of vagueness: Delegation, defiance, and judicial opinions. *American Journal of Political Science*, 52(3):504–519.

Stephenson, M. C. (2003). When the devil turns. . . : The political foundations of independent judicial Review. *The Journal of Legal Studies*, 32(January):59–89.

Stone, A. (1989). In the shadow of the constitutional council: The 'Juridicisation' of the legislative process in France. *West European Politics*, 12(2):12–34.

Stone, A. (1992). *The Birth of Judicial Politics in France*. Oxford: Oxford University Press.

Stone, H. F. (1936). The common law in the United States. *Harvard Law Review*, 50(1):4–26.

Stone Sweet, A. (1999). Judicialization and the construction of governance. *Comparative Political Studies*, 32(2):147–184.

Stone Sweet, A. (2000a). Constitutional adjudication and parliamentary democracy. In *Governing with Judges: Constitutional Politics in Europe*. Oxford: Oxford University Press.

Stone Sweet, A. (2000b). *Governing with Judges: Constitutional Politics in Europe*. Oxford: Oxford University Press.

Stone Sweet, A. (2007). The politics of constitutional review in France and Europe. *International Journal of Constitutional Law*, 5(1):69–92.

Sunstein, C. R. (2007). If people would be outraged by their rulings, should judges care? *Stanford Law Review*, 60(1):155–212.

Tate, C. N. (1995). Why the expansion of judicial power? In: C. N. Tate and T. Vallinder (eds), *The Global Expansion of Judicial Power*, 27–38. New York: New York University Press.

Tate, C. N. and Vallinder, T. (eds) (1995). *The Global Expansion of Judicial Power*. New York: New York University Press.

Tiller, E. H., and Cross, F. B. (2006). WhatiIs legal doctrine? *Northwestern University Law Review*, 100(1):517–533.

Trochev, A. (2004). Less democracy, more courts: A puzzle of judicial review in Russia. *Law and Society Review*, 38(3):513–548.

Tsebelis, G. (2002). *Veto Players: How Political Institutions Work*. Princeton: Princeton University Press.

Ura, J. D. (2014). Backlash and legitimation: Macro political responses to Supreme Court decisions. *American Journal of Political Science*, 58(1):110–126.

Vallinder, T. (1995). When the courts go marching in. In: C. N. Tate and T. Vallinder (eds), *The Global Expansion of Judicial Power*, 13–26. New York: New York University Press.

van Spanje, J. (2010). Contagious parties: Anti-immigration parties and their impact on other parties' immigration stances in contemporary western europe. *Party Politics*, 16(5):563–586.

Vanberg, G. (1998). Abstract judicial review, legislative bargaining, and policy compromise. *Journal of Theoretical Politics*, 10(3):299–326.

Vanberg, G. (2001). Legislative-judicial relations: A game-theoretic approach to constitutional review. *American Journal of Political Science*, 45(2):346–361.

Vanberg, G. (2005). *The Politics of Constitutional Review in Germany*. Cambridge: Cambridge University Press.

Vanberg, G. (2008). Establishing and maintaining judicial independence. In: G. A. Caldeira, R. D. Kelemen, and K. E. Whittington (eds), *The Oxford Handbook of Law and Politics*. Oxford: Oxford University Press.

Vanberg, G. (2015). Constitutional courts in comparative perspective: A theoretical assessment. *Annual Review of Political Science*, 18:167–185.

Voigt, S., Ebeling, M., and Blume, L. (2007). Improving credibility by delegating judicial competence — the case of the Judicial Committee of the Privy Council. *Journal of Development Economics*, 82(2):348–373.

Volcansek, M. L. (2000). *Constitutional Politics in Italy: The Constitutional Court*. Basingstoke: Macmillan.

Waldron, J. (2006). The core of the case against judicial review. *The Yale Law Journal*, 115(6):1346–1406.

Ward, D. G. and Gabel, M. (2019). Judicial review timing and legislative posturing: Reconsidering the moral hazard problem. *Journal of Politics*, 81(2):681–685.

Wasserfallen, F. (2010). The judiciary as legislator? How the European Court of Justice shapes policy-making in the European Union. *Journal of European Public Policy*, 17(8):1128–1146.

Weingast, B. R. (1997). The political foundations of democracy and the rule of law. *The American Political Science Review*, 91(2):245–263.

Whittington, K. E. (2003). Legislative sanctions and the strategic environment of judicial review. *International Journal of Constitutional Law*, 1(3):446–474.

Whittington, K. E. (2005). 'Interpose Your Friendly Hand': Political supports for the exercise of judicial review by the United States Supreme Court. *American Political Science Review*, 99(4):1–14.

Whittington, K. E. (2007). *Political Foundations of Judicial Supremacy*. Princeton: Princeton University Press

Williams, C. J. and Hunger, S. (2022). How challenger party issue entrepreneurship and mainstream party strategies drive public issue salience: Evidence from radical-right parties and the issue of immigration. *European Political Science Review*, 14(4): 544–565.

Zink, J. R., Spriggs, J. F., and Scott, J. T. (2009). Courting the public: The influence of decision attributes on individuals' views of court opinions. *The Journal of Politics*, 71(3):909–925.

Zürn, M. and Joerges, C. (2005). *Law and Governance in Postnational Europe: Compliance beyond the Nation-State*. Cambridge: Cambridge University Press.

Index

abstract norm control, 50, 74
accommodation, 13
Act Amending Procedural Law concerning Asylum, Foreign Nationals and Citizenship, 77
Act Amending the Basic Law (Article 13), 111
Act Amending the Law on Political Parties and Other Acts, 75
Act Implementing the Residency and Asylum Directives of the European Union, 62, 70
Act on Amendments to the Basic Law (Article 16 and Article 18), 77
Act on Determining Standard Needs and Amending the Second and Twelfth Book of the Code of Social Law, 73
Act on Establishing a Federal Air Traffic Controlling Office, 72
Act on Parental Allowance and Parental Leave, 70
Act on Prevention by the Federal Criminal Police Office of Threats from International Terrorism, 5, 117
Act on the Amendment of the Federal Criminal Police Office Act, 131
Act on the Re-regulation of the Provision of Services to Asylum Seekers, 77
Act Reforming Inheritance and Valuation Taxation, 25
Alexander Hamilton, 2
Alternative für Deutschland, 13
amendment laws, 70
Angela Merkel, 59, 115
Argentine Supreme Court, 36, 139
asylum compromise, 77
asylum policy, 77
Asylum Seekers Benefits Act, 13
auto-limitation, 1, 32, 61, 141
Aviation Security Act, 72

Basic Law, 5, 49, 70
Burkhard Hirsch, 78, 112

case selection, 55, 59
case-space model, 29
CDU/CSU, 4, 54, 77, 109, 131
challenger parties, 13
compliance dilemma, 2, 6, 48, 56, 140
conciliation committee, 71, 119
concrete norm control, 50, 74
constitutional blackmail, 12
constitutional complaints, 50, 74, 99
Constitutional Court Database, 60, 70
constitutional review, 1, 7, 24, 48, 70, 110
costly signalling, 91, 104
countermajoritarian difficulty, 18
court curbing, 16, 39, 147
Court of Justice of the European Union, 20, 24, 52, 140
credible commitments, 8
cross-party proposals, 89

Die Linke, 13, 72, 117, 135
dissenting opinions, 126
Donald Trump, 3

Egypt, 43
elections, 58, 88, 95
electoral backlash, 55
executive order, 3

FDP, 5, 54, 66, 77, 111
Federal Constitutional Court Act, 51
Fight Against Organised Crime Act, 111
France, 13, 20, 51

Gerhard Schröder, 59, 82
Gerhart Baum, 112
government of judges, 6, 18
Greens, 30, 76, 82
Großer Lauschangriff, 109
Grundrechtssenat, 49

Hans Kelsen, 49
Hartz IV legislation, 30
Helmut Kohl, 58, 82
Herta Däubler-Gmelin, 5, 118

imminent risk, 114
infringement proceedings, 20, 114

insurance theory, 8
Italy, 20, 51

James Madison, 105, 147
judicial deference, 2, 91
judicial independence, 8, 17
judicialization, 146
Justice Anthony Kennedy, 4
Justice John Roberts, 4
Justice Sonia Sotomayor, 4

Kernbereich privater Lebensgestaltung, 5, 113
Korematsu v. United States, 4

legal precedent, 29, 110
legal rules, 29, 38, 144
legitimacy, 9, 32, 89, 139

Mexican Supreme Court, 139
mixed-methods, 48, 60

non-compliance, 6, 27, 44, 57, 84, 128

OECD, 11
organised crime, 111

Partij voor de Vrijheid, 13
Portugal, 51
preliminary reference procedure, 52, 145
principle of legal clarity and specificity, 122
principle of proportionality, 122
principle of purpose limitation, 123, 133
public support, 9, 19, 56, 98, 140

Rassemblement National, 13

Sabine Leutheusser-Schnarrenberger, 66, 111
South African Constitutional Court, 139
Spain, 51
SPD, 4, 30, 59, 82, 110, 119
Staatsrechtssenat, 49
state surveillance, 5, 109, 143
strategic defection, 17
supermajority requirements, 54
surveillance data, 109, 123

terrorism, 4, 66, 115

United States, 3, 54
U.S. Supreme Court, 4, 145

Varieties of Democracy, 11
virtue-signalling, 64